WORKSHOP ON RESEARCH METHODOLOGY

WORKSHOP ON RESEARCH METHODOLOGY

Dr. Sudhir Gupta

CENTRUM PRESS
NEW DELHI-110002 (INDIA)

CENTRUM PRESS
H.O.: 4360/4, Ansari Road, Daryaganj,
New Delhi-110002 (India)
Tel: 23278000, 23261597, 23255577, 23286875
B.O.: No. 1015, Ist Main Road, BSK IIIrd Stage,
IIIrd Phase, IIIrd Block, Bangalore-560085 (INDIA)
Tel: 080-41723429
Email: centrumpress@gmail.com
Visit us at: www.centrumpress.com

Workshop on Research Methodology

First Edition, 2011

ISBN 978-93-80921-15-0

PRINTED IN INDIA

Printed at Balaji Offset, Delhi.

Contents

Preface

The system of collecting data for research projects is known as research methodology. The data may be collected for either theoretical or practical research for example management research may be strategically conceptualized along with operational planning methods and change management. Some important factors in research methodology include validity of research data, Ethics and the reliability of measures most of your work is finished by the time you finish the analysis of your data. Formulating of research questions along with sampling weather probable or non-probable is followed by measurement that includes surveys and scaling. This is followed by research design, which may be either experimental or quasi-experimental. The last two stages are data analysis and finally writing the research paper, which is organised carefully into graphs and tables so that only important relevant data is shown.

This book is based upon my experiences as a research student, practitioner and teacher. The difficulties I faced in understanding research as a student, my discoveries about what was applicable and inapplicable in the field as a practitioner, and my development of the ability to communicate difficult concepts in simple language without sacrificing technicality and accuracy as a teacher have become the basis of this book.

Author

1

Concept of Research

INTRODUCTION

Research is the cornerstone of any science, including both the hard sciences such as chemistry or physics and the social sciences such as psychology, management, or education. It refers to the organized, structured, and purposeful attempt to gain knowledge about a suspected relationship.

Many argue that the structured attempt at gaining knowledge dates back to Aristotle and his identification of deductive reasoning.

Deductive reasoning refers to a structured approach utilizing an accepted premise, a related minor premise, and an obvious cease. This way of gaining knowledge has been called a syllogism, and by following downward from the general to the specific, knowledge can be gained about a particular relationship.

An example of an Aristotelian syllogism might be:

Major Premise:	All students attend school regularly
Minor Premise:	John is a student
Cease:	John attends school regularly

In the early 1600s, Francis Bacon identified a different approach to gaining knowledge. Rather than moving from the general to the specific, Bacon looked at the gathering of specific information in order to make general ceases. This type of reasoning is called inductive and unlike Aristotelian logic allows new major premises to be determined. Inductive reasoning has been adopted into the sciences as the preferred way to explore new relationships because it allows us to use accepted knowledge as a means to gain new knowledge.

For example:

Specific Premises:	John, Sally, Lenny and Sue attended class regularly
Specific Premises:	John, Sally, Lenny, and Sue received high grades
Cease:	Attending class regularly results in high grades

Researchers combine the powers of deductive and inductive reasoning into what is referred to now as the scientific method. It involves the determination of a major premise and then the analysis of the specific examples that would logically follow.

The results might look something like:

Major Premise:	**Attending classes regularly results in high grades**	
Class Attendance: (Suspected Cause)	Group 1:	John, Sally, Lenny and Sue attend classes regularly
	Group 2:	Heather, Lucinda, Ling, and Bob do not attend classes regularly
Grades: (Suspected Effect)	Group 1:	John, Sally Lenny, and Sue received A's and B's
	Group 2:	Heather, Lucinda, Ling, and Bob received C's and D's
Cease:	Attending class regularly results in higher grades when compared with not attending class regularly (the Major Premise or Hypothesis is therefore supported)	

Utilizing the scientific method for gaining new information and testing the validity of a major premise, John Dewey suggested a series of logical steps to follow when attempting to support a theory or hypothesis with actual data. In other words, he proposed using deductive reasoning to develop a theory followed by inductive reasoning to support it. These steps can be found in Table.

TableDewey's Scientific Method

1. Identify and define the problem
2. Determine the hypothesis or reason why the problem exists
3. Collect and analyse data
4. Formulate conclusions
5. Apply conclusion to the original hypothesis

The steps involved in the research process can vary depending on the type of research being done and the hypothesis being tested. The most stringent types of research, such as experimental methods, contain the most structured process.

Naturalistic observation, surveys, and other non-intrusive studies, are often less structured. A general process guide for doing research, especially laboratory research, can be found in Table.

Table.Steps Involved in the Research Process

1. Determine your theory or educated guess about a relationship. Involves identifying and defining a problem and reviewing the current literature.
2. Operationally define all variables to be involved in the research.
3. Develop hypothesis by plugging variables into original theory. A hypothesis is a testable theory with operationally defined variables.
4. Standardized the research methods by developing a research protocol to be used with every subject. Include in this step the methods for subject selection and assignment as well as how you will attempt to control for any extraneous variable.
5. Select subjects and assign to groups using the protaocol developed in step 4.
6. Test subjects using the protocol developed in step 4.
7. Analyse results.
8. Determine the significance of the results and how these results compare with other studies. Critique

your research and suggest needs for further research based on your findings.

9. Communicate results through journal publication, book, book chapter, repor, presentation, or any means that will benefit those to whom the reserarch applies.
10. Replicate, while part of the research process, this step is most often completed by a different researcher.

DETERMINING A THEORY

While you may see a theory as an absolute, such as the theory of gravity or the theory of relativity, it is actually a changing phenomenon, especially in the soft or social sciences. Theories are developed based on what is observed or experienced, often times in the real world. In other words, a theory may have no additional backing other than an educated guess or a hunch about a relationship. For example, while teaching a college course in research, we notice that non-traditional students tend to be more involved in class lectures and perform better on class exams than traditional students. Our theory, then, could be that older students are more dedicated to their education than younger students.

At this point, however, we have noticed only a trend within a single class that may or may not exist. We have developed a theory based on our observations and this theory, at least at this point, has no practical applications. Most theories are less concerned with application and more concerned with explanations. For example, we could assume, based on our observations, that older students have witnessed the importance of education through their work and interactions with others. With this explanation, we now have a theoretical cause and effect relationship: Students who have had prior experience in the workforce are more dedicated to their education than students who have not had this experience.

This point it is always wise to do a literature review on your topic and areas related to your topic. Results from this search will likely help you determine how to proceed with your research. If, for example, you find that several studies have already been completed on this topic with similar results, doing yet another experiment may add little to what is already known. If this is the case, you would need to rethink your ideas and perhaps replicate the previous research using a different type of subject or a different situation or you may choose to scrap the study all together.

DEFINING VARIABLES

Variables can be defined as any aspect of a theory that can vary or change as part of the interaction within the theory. In other words, variables are anything can effect or change the results of a study. Every study has variables as these are needed in order to understand differences.

In our theory, we have proposed that students exposed to the workforce take a more active role in their education than those who have no exposure. Looking at this theory, you might see that several obvious variables are at play, including 'prior work experience' and 'age of student.' However, other variables may also play a role in or influence what we observed. It is possible that older students have better social skills causing them to interact more in the classroom. They may have learned better studying skills, resulting in higher examination grades. They may feel awkward in a classroom of younger students or doubt their ability more and therefore try harder to succeed. All of these potential explanations or variables need to be addressed for the results of research to be valid.

Let's start with the variables that are directly related to the theory. First, the prior work experience is what we are saying has the effect on the classroom performance. We could say that work history is therefore the cause and classroom grades are the effect. In this example, our independent variable, the variable we start with is work experience. Our dependent variable or the variable we end up with is grades.

We could add additional variables to our list to create more complex research. If we also looked at the affect of study skills on grades, study skills would become a second independent variable. If we wanted to measure the length of time to graduation along with grades, this would become a second dependent variable. There is no limit to the number of variables that can be measured, although the more variables, the more complex the study and the more complex the statistical analysis.

The most powerful benefit of increasing our variables, however, is control. If we suspect something might impact our outcome, we need to either include it as a variable or hold it constant between all groups. If we find a variable that we did not include or hold constant to have an impact on our outcome, the study is said to be confounded. Variables that can confound our results, called confounding variables, are categorized into two groups: extraneous and intervening.

EXTRANEOUS VARIABLES

Extraneous variables can be defined as any variable other than the independent variable that could cause a change in the dependent variable. In our study we might realise that age could play a role in our outcome, as could family history, education of parents or partner, interest in the class topic, or even time of day, preference for the instructor's teaching style or personality. The list, unfortunately, could be quite long and must be dealt with in order to increase the probability of reaching valid and reliable results.

INTERVENING VARIABLES

Intervening variables, like extraneous variables, can alter the results of our research. These variables, however, are much more difficult to control for. Intervening variables include motivation, tiredness, boredom, and any other factor that arises during the course of research. For example, if one group becomes bored with their role in the research more so than the other group, the results may have less to do with our independent variable, and more to do with the boredom of our subjects.

DEVELOPING THE HYPOTHESIS

The hypothesis is directly related to a theory but contains

operationally defined variables and is in testable form. Hypotheses allow us to determine, through research, if our theory is correct. In other words, does prior work experience result in better grades? When doing research, we are typically looking for some type of difference or change between two or more groups. In our study, we are testing the difference between having work experience and not having work experience on college grades. Every study has two hypotheses; one stated as a difference between groups and one stated as no difference between groups.

When stated as a difference between groups, our hypothesis would be, "students with prior work experience earn higher grades than students without prior work experience." This is called our research or scientific hypothesis. Because most statistics test for no difference, however, we must also have a null hypothesis. The null hypothesis is always written with the assumption that the groups do not differ. In this study, our null hypothesis would state that, "students with work experience will not receive different grades than students with no work experience."

The null hypothesis is what we test through the use of statistics and is abbreviated H_0. Since we are testing the null, we can assume then that if the null is not true then some alternative to the null must be true. The research hypothesis stated earlier becomes our alternative, abbreviated H_1. In order to make research as specific as possible we typically look for one of two outcomes, either the null or the alternative hypothesis. To conclude that there is no difference between the two groups means we are accepting our null hypothesis. If we, however, show that the null is not true then we must reject it and therefore conclude that the alternative hypothesis must be true. While there may be a lot of gray area in the research itself, the results must always be stated in black and white.

STANDARDIZATION

Standardization refers to methods used in gathering and treating subjects for a specific study. In order to compare the results of one group to the results of a second group, we must assure that each group receives the same opportunities to succeed. Standardized tests, for instance, painstakingly assure that each student receives the same questions in the same order and is given the same amount of time, the same resources, and the same type of testing environment. Without standardization, we could never adequately compare groups.

For example, imagine that one group of students was given a particular test and allowed four hours to complete it in a quiet and well lit room. A second group was given the same test but only allowed 30 minutes to complete it while sitting in a busy school lunchroom full of laughing and talking children. If group 1 scored higher than group 2 could we truly say that they did better? The answer is obviously 'no.' To make sure we can compare results, we must make everything equal between the two or more groups. Only then could we say that group 1 performed better than group 2.

Standardization of the research methods is often a lengthy process. The same directions must be read to each student, the same questions must be given, and the same amount of time must be assured. All of these factors must be decided before the first subject can be tested. While standardization refers mainly to the testing situation itself, these principles of 'sameness' involve the selection of subjects as well.

SELECTING SUBJECTS

If we want to know if Billy performed better than Sally, or if boys scored higher than girls in our class, or even if Asian children receive higher grades in our school than Caucasian children, the selection of subjects is rather simple. When we are testing the entire population of possible subjects, we are adequately assured that no subject bias has occurred.

A population refers to the entire pool of possible subjects. In a classroom or other setting where the entire population is relatively small, testing all subjects may be simple. However, if we are attempting to understand or gain knowledge related to a large population, such as all third grade children, all depressed adults, or all retail employees, gathering and testing everyone would be relatively impossible. In this situation, we would need to gather a sample of the population, test this sample, and then make inferences aimed at the entire population of which they represent.

When determining which potential subjects from a large population to include in our study there are several approaches to choose from. Each of these sampling techniques have its own strengths and, of course, its own weaknesses. The idea behind adequate sampling, however, remains the same: to gather a sample of subjects that is representative of the greater population. The ideal research sample is therefore often referred to as a representative sample.

SIMPLE RANDOM SAMPLE

To assure that the sample of subjects taken from a known population truly represents the population, we could test every subject in the population and choose only those who fall around the mean of the entire population. This technique is usually pointless because doing so means we could just as easily have tested the entire population on our independent and dependent variables. Therefore in order to make sure all possible subjects have an equal opportunity to be chosen, simple random sampling is most often the selection method used.

To choose a random group of 10 students from a class of 30, for example, we could put everyone's name in a hat and use the first ten names drawn as our sample. In this method, subjects are chosen just as 'B6' is chosen in a game of BINGO. This technique can work well with a small population but can be time consuming and archaic when the population size is large. To choose 30 students from a class of 250 students would be easier utilizing technology and what is referred to as a random number table.

A random number table is a computer generated list of numbers placed in random order. Each of the 250 students would be randomly assigned a number between one and 250. Then the groups would be formed once again using a random number generator.

SYSTEMATIC SAMPLE

When a population is very large, assigning a number to each potential subject could also be tiresome and time consuming. A systematic sample is a random sample compiled in a systematic manner. If you had a list of all licensed teachers, for example, and wanted to mail a survey to 200 of them, systematic sampling might be the sampling method of choice. For this example, a page and a teacher number on that page are determined at random. This would represent the first subject and the starting point for choosing the remaining subjects.

A random number would be generated, for example 150. Then every 150th teacher would become a subject until you have selected enough for your study. If you complete the list before selecting enough subjects, you would continue back at the beginning of the list. Once the subjects are selected, the technique of random assignment can be used to assign subjects to particular groups.

STRATIFIED RANDOM SAMPLE

The use of a stratified sample refers to the breaking down of the population into specific subsets before choosing which ones will take part in the study. For example, if you are studying all third grade students in your state, you may want to make sure that every county in your state is represented in your study. If you used a simple random sampling technique, you could conceivably end up with many subjects from one county and no subjects from other counties. A stratified sample allows you to choose your subject pool randomly from a predetermined set of subsets. In this example, we may want to choose 10 subjects at random from each county within the state.

Other subsets can also be used, such as age, race, or socioeconomic background. If you wanted to make sure that there were an equal number of males and females, you could use sex as your subset and then randomly choose the same number of subjects from each subset. This type of sampling is useful when the population has some known differences that could result in different outcomes. For instance, if you already know that 80% of the students are male, you may want to select 40 male students and 10 female students so that your sample represents the breakdown of sex within the population.

CLUSTER SAMPLE

Cluster sampling could be considered a more specific type of stratified sample. When this technique is used, potential subsets of subjects are first randomly eliminated and then the remaining subsets are used to randomly select the sample of subjects to be used in the study. For example, if you are measuring the effect of prior work experience on college grades in a particular state, you may first make a list of all colleges in the state. Then you would randomly select a number of colleges to either include or eliminate in the selection process. Once you have a subset of colleges, you could use the same technique to randomly include or eliminate the specific classes. From the remaining classes, you would then randomly select a group of students with work experience and a group of students with no work experience to be placed in your two groups.

NON-PROBABILITY SAMPLE

Nonprobability refers to a group of subjects chosen based on their availability rather then their degree of representativeness of the population. Surveys are often done in this manner. Imagine going to the local mall to gather information about the buying habits of mall shoppers. Your subject pool does not represent all mall shoppers but rather those mall shoppers who happen to walk by your location on that day. The same would hold true for a survey over the phone or via mail. Those who respond to your questions or return the mailed survey do not necessarily represent the population at large. Instead, they represent the population who was home and was willing to respond to your questions or those who took the time to complete and return the survey.

While at first glance this method seems unprofessional, it allows for the gathering of information in a short amount of time. It is not considered standardized research and would be scrutinized if submitted to a professional journal, but it does have its place. If you've ever visited a website and seen a survey, you might have felt compelled to click on the results link. When watching a news programme you may have not changed channels because you are waiting for the results of a survey that will be reported at the end of the programme. We are highly interested in these 'informal' polls and using a nonprobability sample is a quick way to gather large amounts of information in a relatively short amount of time.

TESTING SUBJECTS

Once you determined your variables, applied the concept of standardization, and selected your subjects, you are almost ready to begin the testing process. The concept of testing refers to the application or analysis of your independent and dependent variables. If there is any manipulation of the subjects in your study, it occurs during this phase. Before testing any human subject, however, some type of consent form is necessary. Consent forms basically describe the study, how the results will be used, and any possible negative effects that may occur. They also give the subject the right to withdrawal from the study at any time without consequence. Your specific hypothesis does not need to be disclosed but each subject must be made aware of any general concerns and be able to ask questions before testing can begin..

If your hypothesis, for example, asked if there is a difference in effectiveness of different treatments for depression, you might assign your subjects to one of several different groups: cognitive therapy, dynamic therapy, humanistic therapy and possibly no therapy. Each subject would likely be tested prior to the study to determine a baseline for his or her level of depression and would then begin a predetermined and standardized treatment plan. Because you are standardizing your study, each subject should get identical treatment short o the independent variable. In other words, the only thing you want to be different between the groups is the type of therapy received.

The no therapy group would be considered a control group and may participate in some type of non-therapy related activity while the other subjects receive therapy. This group is used to determine if time plays a role in the decrease of depressive symptoms. Without a control group you couldn't say that any particular therapy was more helpful than no therapy because subjects may have improved merely because of some outside factor unrelated to treatment. These factors are called extraneous variables, and control groups, along with randomization, help to keep the impact of these variables to a minimum.

ANALYZING RESULTS

The specific analysis performed on the subjects depends on the type of subjects, the type of questions being asked, and the purpose of the research. When we gathered and tested all possible subjects from a known population we would use descriptive statistics to analyse our results. Descriptive statistics require the testing of everyone in the population and are used to describe the qualities of the population in numerical format. For example, we could say that the mean score on an IQ test for all third graders at Jefferson High School is 102. We could also state that there is no difference between the IQs of boys and girls within our subjects if the data support these ceases.

When we are using a sample of subjects smaller than the entire population, we must make some inferences using what we call inferential statistics. Like any inferences, we also assume a certain degree of error when making determinations about a population based on a sample of that population. Because of this, the results of inferential statistics are often stated within a predetermined level of confidence.

If we found that the mean of one group was 10 points higher than the mean of a second group in our work experience and college grades study, we could not assume that the population means are identical. We could, however, state that the means of the entire population are likely to differ by five to 15 points or that there is a 95% probability that the means of the entire population differs by ten points. In this sense, we are predicting the scores of the entire population based on the scores of our sample and stating them within a range or a predetermined level of confidence. This allows us to include the likely error that occurs whenever an inference is made.

DETERMINING SIGNIFICANCE

The term significance when related to research has a very specific role. Significance refers to the level of certainty in the results of a study. We can say that our subjects differed by an average of ten points with 100% certainty because we personally witnessed this difference. To say that the population will differ is another story. To do this, we must determine how valid our results are based on a statistical degree of error. If we find, through the use of inferential statistics, that the grades of those with and without work experience are different me must state the estimated error involved in this inference. While the standard acceptable error is 5%, it can be as high as 20% or as low as 0.1%.

The amount of error to be accepted in any study must be determined prior to beginning the study. In other words, if we want to be 95% confident in our results, we set the significance level at.05. If we want to be 99% confident, our significance level is set at.01. We can then state that there is a difference in the population means at the 95% significance level or at the 99% significance level if our statistics support this statement. If our statistics estimate that there is 10% error and we said we would accept only 5%, the results of our study would be stated as 'not significant.' When determining significance, we are saying that a difference exists within our acceptable level of error and we must therefore reject the null hypothesis. When results are found to be not significant, the only option available is to accept the null hypothesis.

COMMUNICATING RESULTS

Results of a study are disseminated in many forms. The highest level of communicating results is often in a peer-reviewed professional journal. Peer-reviewed refers to a group of professionals in a particular field who read all submissions and publish only those that meet the highest degree of scrutiny and applicability. When errors are found in the sampling of subjects, the statistical analysis, or the inferences made, the study will often be rejected or returned to the author for revisions. Published substances in peer-reviewed would likely be the best source for research when you begin looking into your theory.

Results of research studies are also disseminated through textbooks, book chapters, conferences, presentations, and newsletters. For example, a study comparing the average salary in a particular county might be published in the local newspaper or in a brochure for the chamber of commerce. Our study of non-traditional students and work experience might be summarized in a board meeting of the college's department of student retention or published in a trade journal such as the "Journal of Higher Education."

Some studies are never released, especially if the results do not add to the already available research. Other studies are meant only to provide direction for larger studies. Our study of college students may be used only to determine if a larger study is likely to result in important findings. If we get significant results then a larger study, including a broader subject pool, may then be conducted. These types of studies are often called pilot studies because the goal is not to gather knowledge about the population, but rather to guide further research in a particular area.

REPLICATION

Replication is the key to the support of any worthwhile theory. Replication involves the process of repeating a study using the same methods, different subjects, and different experimenters. It can also involve applying the theory to new situations in an attempt to determine the generalizability to different age groups, locations, races, or cultures. For example, our study of non-traditional students may be completed using students from another college or from another state. It may be changed slightly to add additional variables such as age, sex, or race to determine if these variables play any role in our results.

Replication, therefore, is important for a number of reasons, including:

- Assurance that results are valid and reliable;
- Determination of generalizability or the role of extraneous variables;
- Application of results to real world situations; and
- Inspiration of new research combining previous findings from related studies.

PUTTING IT ALL TOGETHER

We asked the question,'do college students with work experience earn better grades than those without work experience.' Knowing the steps involved in doing research and now having a basic understanding of the process, we could design our experiment and with fictional results could determine our ceases and how to report our findings to the world. To do this, lets start with our theory and progress through each of the ten steps.

DETERMINING A THEORY

Theories are developed through our interaction with our environment. For our particular theory, we observed that older college students tend to perform better on classroom tests than younger students.

As we attempt to explain why, we developed our theory that real world work experience creates a motivation in students that allows them to perform better than students without this motivation. Our theory, therefore, states that prior work experience will result in higher grades.

Defining Variables

Every experiment has an independent and a dependent variable. The independent variable is what we start with; it refers to the separation of our groups. In our case, we want to look at prior work experience so the presence or absence of this would constitute our experimental groups. We may place those students who have been in the work force for more than one year in group 1 and those with less than one year in group 2.

Our dependent variable is our outcome measure so in our case we are looking for a difference in class grades. To operationally define the variable grades, we might use the final course average as our outcome measure. If the independent and dependent variable(s) are difficult to determine, you can always complete the following statement to help narrow them down: The goal of this study is to determine what effect ________ (IV) has on ________ (DV). For us, the goal is to determine what effect one year or more of prior work experience has on course average.

DETERMINING HYPOTHESIS

When we plug our variables into our original theory we get our research hypothesis. Simply stated, Students with one or more years of prior work experience will receive higher final course averages than students with less than one year of prior work experience. Since statistical analysis often tests the null hypothesis or the idea that there is no difference between groups, our null hypothesis could be stated as: Final course averages of students with one or more years of prior work experience will not differ from final course averages of students with less than one year of prior work experience.

STANDARDIZATION

To make sure that each subject, no matter which group they belong to, receives the same treatment, we must standardize our research. While this may be difficult in the real world, our goal is to get as close as possible to the ideal.

Therefore, we may choose to gather subjects from a general psychology class since this is a class required of most students and will not be affected by college major. We may further decide to research only those students who have a specific instructor to keep the instruction between the two groups as similar as possible. Remember, our goal is to assure, at least as much as possible, that the only difference between the two groups is the independent variable.

SELECTING SUBJECTS

Because our population consists of all college students, it will be impossible to include everyone in the study. Therefore we need to apply some type of random selection. Since we want to use only those students who have the same instructor, we may ask all of this instructors students, prior to any teaching, how much work experience they have had.

Those who report a year or more become the potential subject pool for group 1 and those who have less than one year become the subject pool for group 2.

We could, at this point decide to include all of these subjects or to further reduce the subjects randomly. To reduce the subject pool we could assign each student in each group a random number and then choose, at random, a specific number of students to become subjects in our study. For the purpose of this example, as suggested, randomly choose 20 students in each group to participate in our study.

TESTING SUBJECTS

Since we are not applying any type of treatment to our subjects, this phase in the procession can be omitted. If we were determining if the teaching styles of different instructors played a role in grades, we would randomly assign each student to a teacher. In that case, teaching style would become an independent variable in our study.

ANALYZING RESULTS

Our original question asked if final averages would be different between our two groups. To determine this as suggested, look at the mean of each group. Therefore, as suggested, add up the averages of the 20 subjects in each group and divide each of these by 20.

If, after comparing the means of each group, we find that group 1 has a mean of 88 and group 2 has a mean of 82 then we can descriptively state that there is a six-point difference between the means of the two groups. Based on this statistic, we would then begin to show support for our alternative hypothesis and can progress to the next step.

DETERMINATION OF SIGNIFICANCE

Our goal was not to describe what their averages were, but rather to make inferences about what is likely happening in the entire population. We must therefore apply inferential statistics to our results to determine the significant or lack of significant findings. As suggested, set our confidence level at 95 per cent and then apply statistical analysis to our results to see if the difference of six points with a sample size of 40 is significant.

Imagine that we did find a significant difference. In this case we could say that with a 95% confidence level, students with one year of more work experience receive higher averages than those with less than one year of work experience. Since the null hypothesis, which stated that no difference exists between the two groups, was not correct, we must reject it. And by rejecting the null, we automatically accept our alternative hypothesis.

COMMUNICATING RESULTS.

When communicating the results of our study we need to do several things. We need to make a case for why we did this research, which is often based on our literature search. We then need to report the process we took in gathering our sample and applying the treatment. We can then report our results and argue that there is a difference between the two groups and that this difference is significant enough to infer it will be present in the entire population.

Finally, we must evaluate our research in terms of its strengths, weaknesses, applicability, and needs for further study. In terms of strengths, we might include the rigors of gathering subjects and the fact that we used a random sample of students.

We may argue that the statistical methods used were ideal for the study or that we considered the recommendations of previously completed studies in this area. Weaknesses might include the small sample size, the limited pool from which our sample was gathered, or the reliance on self-reported work experience.

To discuss applicability and needs for further studies we could suggest that more studies be completed that use a broader base of subjects or different instructors. We could recommend that other variables be investigated such as student age, type and location of college, family educational history, sex, race, or socioeconomic background.

We might even suggest that while our findings were significant they are not yet applicable until these other variables are investigated.

REPLICATION

The final step in any research is replication. This can be done by us but is most often completed by other researchers based on their own review of the literature and the recommendations made by previous researchers. If others compete a similar study, or look at different variables and continue to find the same results, our results become stronger. When ten other studies agree with ours, the chances are greatly improved that our results were accurate.

If ten other studies disagree with our findings then the validity of our study will be, and most certainly should be, called into question.

By replicating studies and using previously gained knowledge to search for new answers, our profession continues to move forward. After all, we used the ideas of other researchers to design our research, and future researchers may incorporate our findings to make recommendations in their research. The cycle is never ending and allows for perpetual seeking of new knowledge.

SCOPE OF RESEARCH

NATIONAL INNOVATIVE CAPACITY: MODELING, MEASURING AND COMPARING NATIONAL CAPACITIES

National innovative capacity is the ability of a country to produce and commercialise a flow of innovative technology over the long term.

It depends on:

- The strength of a nation's common infrastructure;
- The cluster-specific innovation environment.
- The quality of linkages.

This research strand aims at building innovation indexes and measuring various dimensions of national innovation capacities.

For instance:

- Strategic capacity: it deals with the ability to mobilise and concentrate resources under some centralised decision making processes to achieve a critical scientific or technological objective.
- Revolutionary capacities: it deals with the ability to shift resources out of areas of lower and into areas of higher productivity and greater yield. This is a capacity to manage transitions. The difficulty is that such a capacity involves various dimensions which can be conflicting.

DESIGNING EFFICIENT INCENTIVE SYSTEMS FOR INVENTION AND INNOVATION: INTELLECTUAL PROPERTY RIGHTS, PRIZES, PUBLIC SUBSIDIES

One central problem in the economics of knowledge is the design of incentive systems that both reward inventors/knowledge producers and encourage dissemination of their output. Several scholars have described the two regimes that allocate resources for the creation of new knowledge: one is the system of granting intellectual property rights, as exemplified by modern patent and copyright systems, the other is the open science regime, as often found in the realm of pure scientific research and sometimes in the realm of commercial technological innovation, often in infant industries.

A large range of issues have to be addressed to elucidate the problem of designing efficient incentive systems:

- What is the best solution in case of particular kind of new technologies?
- What is the nature of the tension that arises when the two systems come up against each other?

- How designing proper incentive systems to encourage research and innovation in areas of high social return and low private profitability?
- In what condition a prize-based reward system provides a more efficient solution than granting intellectual property rights?
- Is there an economic case for granting intellectual property rights in the domain of research tools, instruments, basic knowledge?

RESEARCH IN EPFL LABS: NEW ECONOMICS OF SCIENCE

CEMI will be at the forefront of the College to develop and undertake research in the field of "economics of science" with EPFL as the main case. In this perspective, several topics are obvious:

- Assessing the impact of organizational practice on the productivity of university technology transfer offices
- Measuring the social value of basic research and the local spillovers. Accounting for the effects associated with mobility
- Scale, scope and spillovers: the determinants of research productivity in several fields
- Exploring the role of patents in knowledge transfer from EPFL
- Exploring the effect of the patenting of research tools and biomedical innovation: transfer opportunities and social costs
- Access policy for large scale research instrument, data bases.

All these topics should give rise to research design in close collaboration with the other EPFL Schools in order to benefit from the great opportunity to be located in an Institute of Technology.

These projects will be designed in close collaboration with Jan-Anders Manson, vice-president for Innovation and Knowledge Transfer.

NEW R&D METHODS AND THE PRODUCTION OF RELIABLE KNOWLEDGE IN SECTORS WHICH LAGGED BEHIND

Unequal access to pertinent knowledge bases may well constitute an important condition underlying perceptible differences in the success with which different areas of endeavour are pursued within the same society, and the pace at which productivity advances in different sectors of the economy during a given historical epoch. Today, it remains astonishing to observe the contrast between fields of economic activity where improvements in practice are closely reflecting rapid advances in human knowledge - such as is the case for information technologies, transportation, and certain areas of medical care —and other areas where the state of knowledge appears to be far more constraining.

The fact is that knowledge is not being developed to the same degree in every sector. A major policy concern is to understand the factors at the origin of such uneven development, and to implement a proper strategy in order to fill the gap between sectors with fast knowledge accumulation processes and those in which these processes remain weak.

To summarise, rapid and effective creation of know-how is most likely to occur when the following conditions converge:

- Practice in the field needs to be well specified, sustainable, replicable, imitable;
- There needs to be ability to learn from experience and experiment;
- The ability to experiment offline, with less expense than that would be involved in online experimentation, and to gain reliable information relevant to online use, greatly facilitates progress.
- A strong body of "scientific" knowledge greatly facilitates effective offline experimentation, and also quick and reliable evaluation of varying practice online.

Part of the problem in sectors which are lagging behind deals with the limited ability to conduct experiments. The main research issue here is to analyse the impact of new experimental methods and design, which have the potential to profoundly transform the way reliable knowledge is produced in these sectors. For instance, one of the most significant developments in modern medicine has been the randomised controlled trial, the significance and use of which grew rapidly after its application to tuberculosis in the 1940s.

Today the RCT is widely treated as the evidential 'gold standard' for demonstrating 'what works' and what is medical 'best practice'. Education might be the next sector to be profoundly transformed through the application of RCTs. The growth of RCTs as an approach in educational research has been pushed forward by three important factors: computers, statistical techniques and demand for accountability in both practice and research. There is, therefore, a favourable context. The question is whether this new feature can change and transform the way knowledge is produced and distributed in a sector like education.

NEW MODELS OF INNOVATION: OPEN, DISTRIBUTED SYSTEMS AND THE ROLE OF USERS

This project involves the contribution of users in the innovation process not only in terms of sending market signals but also in terms of actively contributing to the modification of the product.

This project emphasizes, therefore, the functional source of innovation: while an innovation is considered a manufacturer's innovation when the developer expects to benefit by selling it, an innovation is a user innovation when the user expects to benefit by using it.

This research aims at understanding the capabilities and limitations of user innovation processes, which involve quite often an open and distributed system. Its advocates claim that user innovation, involving freely revealing, is an efficient means of producing socially desirable innovation and maximizing "spillovers," or knowledge transfer/ leakage. The generation of innovation by users may be a complement or it may compete with innovations produced by manufacturers.

In its role as a complement, user innovation may extend the diversity of products without endangering market positions of manufacturers and may help manufacturing firms to mitigate information asymmetry problems vis-à-vis future market needs. As a competitor, user innovation may offer products that better meet user needs.

The model involves two major deviations from the private investment model of innovation, which assumes that manufacturers innovate in products and processes to improve their competitive position and that returns to innovation result from excluding other manufacturers from adopting it. First, users of technologies, rather than manufacturers, are often the innovators. Second, user-innovators often freely reveal the proprietary knowledge they have developed at their private expense.

A host of empirical studies, mainly conducted by Eric von Hippel, his research group at MIT and his colleagues, show that user innovation is an important economic phenomenon. It constitutes the main source of knowledge in some sectors or an important contributor in others.

Deepening our understanding of the conditions leading to user innovation and of its economic impact is, therefore, a relevant issue:

- For a better assessment both of intangibles and intellectual capital at the firm level and of innovation capacities at the national level; and
- For a better understanding of some new organizational forms, such as user communities, which appear to be becoming more relevant in a knowledge society.

Thus our main research questions are the following:

- What are the different channels through which user innovations influence the economy and how should manufacturers adapt and respond to user innovations?
- What kinds of learning processes/ dynamic capabilities do user innovations enable across product/ technological generations?
- What kind of policy issues and challenges pertain to

user innovation? Given the fact that user innov-ations contribute significantly to productivity growth and national competitiveness, what kinds of policy should be devised to promote them.

OTHER ISSUES TO BE DEVELOPED

- *The economics of knowledge policy*: While it is relatively easy to provide a long list of policy recomme-ndations which are of some relevance in the context of the knowledge economy, it is far more difficult to develop the welfare economics of knowledge investment in order to build a framework for addressing policy issues.
- *Methodology for the optimal allocation of R&D funds to new technologies*: How does the R&D manager maximize the probability of developing a commercializable technology over a specific period.

LIMITATIONS OF RESEARCH

The limitations of the research are first addressed by discussing the purposes of the research, then discussing the limitations of the data management, data analysis, and the validity of the analysis.

PURPOSES OF RESEARCH

The "trustworthiness" of research depends on "What counts as knowledge?". The general purposes of research can include knowledge production, understanding, and prediction.

This study has focused on the first two purposes: production of applied knowledge and process knowledge, both of which are suitable for developmental research. Applied knowledge is context-specific, useful for the solution of practical problems, while process knowledge is usually specified in terms of models. A qualitative approach is called for in the study of context and contextual influences. A second purpose of research is promoting understa-nding of a process;

in this case, the instructional approach and the underlying phenomena, including participation and dialogue. A secondary aspect of understanding is a better understanding of what it requires in using the development cycle as a form of inquiry.

DATA MANAGEMENT

Data management involves the procedures used for a systematic, coherent process of data collection, storage and retrieval for the purpose of high quality, accessible data, the documentation of analysis, and retention of data. The design decisions, implementation, and evaluation of the instructional design course were documented in eight data sources: working logs, electronic mail, syllabi, conferences, draft ID projects, completed ID projects, course evaluations, and self-evaluations. These data sources, which were based on observations, interviews, or documents, were event-driven, meaning that they served our instructional needs to watch, ask, and examine.

These observations, interviews, and documents were in place prior to the conceptual framework of the study. As a result, the data sources were not as complete, tightly defined, or structured across the six cases if they had been researcher-driven. Some data sources, such as syllabi, course evaluations, and selfevaluations, evolved to suit the learning needs of the students.

However, because we had presented at research conferences, we had collected and stored data for each case, as well as conducted analysis with most of the data sources, although using different methodologies. These research efforts can be regarded as interim analyses in which we became familiar with procedures in recording observations and personal conferences, as well as retaining and analyzing documents. Over the six cases, we came to have a better understanding of the instructional setting, being sensitive to research opportunities and more systematic in our data collection ar management efforts, but also retaining instruction and responsiveness to learners as our top priority.

DATA ANALYSIS

Within-Case Analysis

Data displays, structured summaries, and charts allowed a condensed view of the data sources and revealed that some further analysis was needed, such as coding of structured summaries to reveal themes as well as to identify exceptions and differences.

Across-Case Analysis

A means to report the changes in design decisions, implementation, and evaluation of the model across the six Cases."Each case has a specific history-which we discard at our peril-but it is a history contained within the general principles that influence its development". This summary attempted to preserve the uniqueness of each case, yet also make comparisons along the developmental cycle. In an effort to extend external validity, what participants'"did, said, or designed," were examined in multiple settings.

The processes of participation and dialogue within participation were examined in six different, developmental configurations and can be viewed as a replication of the focus of the study. A set of generalizations on how the model was implemented, as well as conditions necessary for its use. The danger to this generalization is that"multiple cases will be analysed at high levels of inference, aggregating out the local webs of causality and ending with a smoothed set of generalizations that may not apply to any single case". The goal was to better understand the overall processes at work across the cases; in this case, teacher and student thinking, participation and dialogue, and teacher responsivity, represented within design decisions, class implementation, and model evaluation. We did not average, for example, course evaluation results, as one way to avoid misinterpretation and superficiality and to preserve case uniqueness.

Analytic Validity

In traditional instances of qualitative data collection and

analysis, the research"shifts between cycles of inductive data collection and analysis to deductive cycles of testing and verification".

In this study, sources of data were already in place prior to conceptualizing a conceptual study framework. However, in this study the details of the conceptual framework and the subsequent data analysis of the six cases cycled back and forth to realise more appropriate matches of methodology and method to existing data sources and research objectives. The analytic cycle for this study could be better described as one which moved between conceptual framework, case analysis, and being clear as to the purpose of the study. Although being clear as to the purpose of the study is preferable before constructing a methodology, such purposes are not always clear based on the complexity of processes to be studies, amount of data, and personal involvement over time.

Potential shortcomings in this research that are sources for bias include the large amount of data which may have led to missing important information or overweighting some findings due to focusing on a particular and large set of data. Personal involvement with the course also increases the possibility that our recorded observations in working logs highlighted particular incidents while ignoring others. On the other hand, the working log recorded observations or design decisions that would have been lost to our collective memories over the five years of involvement with the course. Personal involvement as a co-instructor also implied a danger in being selective and overconfident with some data. Another shortcoming was not checking descriptions with each case of students and additional peer review outside of the co-instructor.

To address these shortcomings, we used multiple data sources for triangulation to achieve an agreement of one data source with another. Multiple sources of data, such as working logs, email, and syllabi, also provided different strengths and complemented each other. Syllabi compactly recorded design decisions, while working logs and email documented our thinking that influenced these design decisions. The data sources were a mix of student-generated and instructor-generated data. A significant amount of time and effort was spent in carefully assembling the data reduction notebooks, which included data displays of structured summaries and charts.

The effort was made towards a goal of being able to track in the documents the reasoning behind descriptions and summary and the generalizations made about the model.

During the analysis of these data sources we looked for contrasts, comparisons, and exemplars and reported these during the data reduction so as not to filter out outliers and extreme instances. For example, in the ID project analysis we added a column to record any unique features of the project that might not be addressed by the completeness, consistency, and coherency criteria. Replication of the conceptual framework across multiple cases helped to provide evidence that what was described in one Case was based upon the details of the instructional approach and uniqueness of the setting and participants.

We attempted to remain"descriptive" and to report what decisions were made for the ID course, what occurred during the implementation of the reflexive approach, and systematically report the evaluation of the model in terms of student performance on ID projects, their perceptions of their learning and the course and data informing our responsivity to learner needs. Another means of addressing verification of findings and ceases was an"auditing" by the dissertation chair who was also co-instructor in the cases under study. Through periodic reviews of methodology and analysis, numerous inconsistencies in design decisions, for example, were identified and prompted for clarification. Feedback also prompted me to clarify procedures used to analyse the different data sources. This feedback, although one of the responsibilities of a doctoral chairperson, is another aspect of the reflexive stance that we had used on previous research: the need to assume regular, ongoing, and self-conscious documentation of our teaching. The working logs also served as a"reflexivity journal" to record these efforts.

TYPES OF RESEARCH

Research can be classified by purpose or by method. If we categorise it by purpose, it would fall into two major categories: Basic Research and Applied Research, while in case of method, it would be deductive research and inductive research.

BASIC RESEARCH

Also called Pure or fundamental Research, it is undertaken for increase in knowledge. There is no direct benefit as it is a research for the sake of research.

It is conducted to satisfy any curiosity such as:

- What makes things happen,
- Why society changes and
- Why social relations are in a certain way.

In fact, it is the source of most new theories, principles and ideas. Basic research rarely helps anyone directly. It only stimulates new ways of thinking. The main motivation is to *expand man's knowledge.* There is absolutely no commercial value to the discoveries resulting from such research.

However, in the long run, it forms the basis of applied research or development commercial products. If basic work is done first, then applied spin-offs often eventually result from this research.

As Dr. George Smoot of LBNL says, "People cannot foresee the future well enough to predict what's going to develop from basic research. If we only did "applied research", we would still be making better spears."

To sum up, basic research is purely theoretical to increase our understanding of certain phenomena or behaviour but does not seek to solve any existing problem.

APPLIED RESEARCH

It is use of basic research or past theories, knowledge and methods for solving an existing problem. It deals with practical problems. It is opposed to pure research which is not problem-oriented but for the increase in knowledge which may or may not be used in future.

In the present world situation, more emphasis is being given to applied research to solve problems arising out of overpopulation and scarcity of natural resources. Applied research should not be treated the same as Researchand Development which is involved in developing products demanded by the existing clients.

Applied Research, on the other hand, focuses on uncovering what needs are not being met and use that information in designing products or services that would create their own demand. Thus, applied research brings in new customers and also provides better products and services to the existing customers. In old days, the mobile phone was expensive, bulky and had a short range. Applied Research foresaw that this product would have a limited market and stressed on cost-cutting, reduced weight and long-distance communication. Such measures caused a heavy demand.

METHODS OR APPROACHES

In research, ceases are based two methods known as the *deduction* and *induction*. Both are widely used in research projects. This helps the researchers to understand, explain, or predict business phenomena. Deduction follows an approach which is "top-down" or "from general to specific." On the other hand, induction is "bottom-up" in nature or from specific to general. In deduction, we start from a theory and try to prove it right with the help of available information. In induction, we observe some happening, deduct a pattern and draw cease.

Example of Deduction

- All men are mortal.
- Socrates is a man
- Socrates is mortal

Example of Induction

- This ice is cold.
- All ice is cold.

Take another example: 3 + 5 = 8 and eight is an even number.

Therefore, an odd number added to another odd number will result in an even number.

Example of Both Deduction And Induction

- You push the light switch and find no light
- You ask the question, Why no light?
- You infer a cease to answer the question and explain the fact that the bulb is burned out.
- You use this hypothesis to conclude that the light will not go on when we push the switch. We know from experience that burned-out bulb will not light.

DEDUCTIVE METHOD

Like Sherlock Holmes, the starting point is a given situation and moving to a specific cease. All relevant information is assembled, studies to solve the mystery. Aristotle, a Greek philosopher, described deduction as "drawing ceases by applying rules or principles; logically moving from a general rule or principle to a specific solution". It is the process of reaching a cease that is guaranteed to follow, if the evidence provided is true and the reasoning used to reach the cease is correct.

An investigator is distracted with the noise and thinks that "noise adversely affects mental problem solving." It can be turned into a research question like "would it be more conducive to solve mental puzzle when there is no noise."

In order to test it, two puzzles are given to the same group, one in noise-less conditions and other in a blaring noise. If the results of test conducted under noisy-enironment are poor it can be deduced or concluded that controlling the aversive noise is helpful in solving mental puzzles. Someone may say "why research, it is apparent?" It is logical to say it but it had been previously proved and awareness has been created of the noise pollution. In fact, noise can be measure in term of decibel (dB) and by research, it has been established how much noise is tolerable under what conditions. Zero dB describes perfect silence while 140 dB would reflect a gunshot.

In deductive method, the premises provide a guarantee of the true cease.

Consider the following example:

- There are 32 books on the top-shelf of the book case,
- There are 12 books on the lower-shelf of the book case.
- There are no books anywhere on the bookcase

It can be concluded there are 44 books in the bookcase.

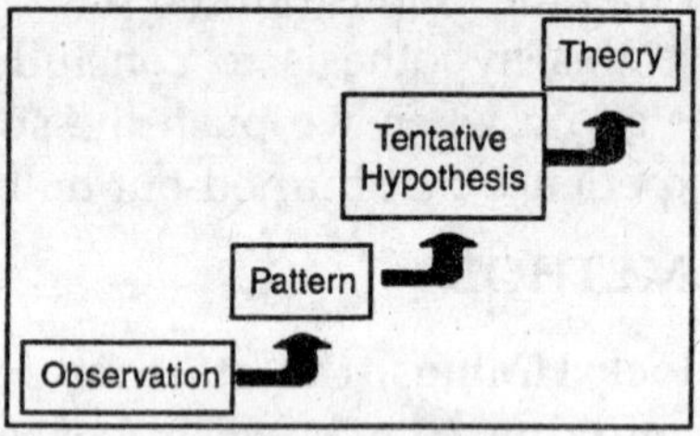

Fig. Inductive Approach

INDUCTIVE METHOD

Also known as Inductive reasoning or logic, this methods involves moving from a specific situation to a general cease This is a way of "theory-building", whereby "specific facts are used to create a theory that explains relationships between the facts and allows prediction of future knowledge". This method is more open-ended and exploratory. This does not give 100% guarantee of truth but probability of being true.

Here is an example:

- Socrates was Greek.
- Most Greeks eat fish.
- Socrates ate fish.

While the premises were true, it is possible that cease was false. Maybe Socrates was allergic to fish, for example. It can be said that inductive approach is weaker than deductive approach as there is possibility of arriving at false cease. However, it is not entirely true.

2

Objectives of Research

There are 5 general objectives that research—in general and more specifically about processes—may attempt to achieve.

They are:

1. Description
2. Explanation
3. Forecasting
4. Control
5. Modelling

These objectives are not completely independent from each other, for the explanation of a phenomenon relies in part on its description, its forecast requires a detailed explanation, and so on.

But researchers may concentrate on one or the other aspect. Most important, the objective pursued will affect the tools and techniques employed for the analyses.

The two most frequent objectives are description and explanation. Description is most often an exploratory phase undertaken using graphical representations and statistical measures that are not inferential, while explanation involves precise hypotheses to be confronted and employs inferential statistical tests.

Modelling is the latest, broadest objective Bossel Bossel1994]. It requires that the descriptive and explanatory phases brought sufficient information and knowledge about the system, so to build a model that synthetically gathers the various variables in a coherent and parsimonious way.

DESCRIPTION

One major thrust of current research concerns implicit mathematical models. Depending on the area of application, such systems are called differential algebraic equations, singular systems, descriptor systems, semi-state equations, constrained systems, or differential equations on a manifold. Usually the term DAE refers to systems of ordinary differential equations $F(x', x, t)=0$ with the Jacobian of F with respect to x′ being singular. Many physical systems are most naturally and easily first modeled as an implicit system.

This is often the case with computer generated models. A goal of our research is to be able to carry out analysis and simulation from the original implicit description thus reducing the time between formulation and numerical results. An implicit formulation also allows one to consider more complex phenomena and to explore different designs or parametre values from one model. We are interested in mathematical theory, numerical analysis and design of algorithms, and application.

Control applications are of special interest. This research currently includes both numerical approaches to optimal control problems and also problems in failure detection and failure identification

Among the topics being investigated are:

- The mathematical analysis of nonlinear DAEs.
- All aspects of the development and analysis of numerical algorithms, especially for higher index, fully implicit nonlinear DAEs. Of particular interest is the development of algorithms which can be included in design and simulation packages both for simulation and for model diagnostics. These algorithms are both to increase the robustness of the software and to assist users.
- Control theory, especially for implicitly modeled systems.
- The incorporation of DAE integrators into nonlinear control algorithms. One example is the design of observers for complex nonlinear systems. Another is

using the DAE integrator to numerically compute a stabilizing nonlinear feedback.

- Simulation of physical systems including how to exploit problem structure. In the past, particular attention has been given to constrained mechanical systems and nonlinear circuits. The results are also of interest in areas such as chemical process control but to date that classes of applications has not been carefully considered by our group.
- Numerical algorithms for various questions in nonlinear control. Of particular interest has been prescribed path control and optimal control.
- Failure detection and failure identification. In particular, we have been investigating the use of auxiliary signals to be used either when controller action masks the onset of system deterioration or when there has been a failure of the monitoring system itself but it is still necessary to continue operations. There are currently several collaborations in progress with groups at other institutions. All of these collaborations have several different aspects not all of which are given here.
- INRIA-Rocquencourt and INRIA Renes. This collaboration has considered a variety of control problems including stabilization and observer design. Currently we are studying of some issues in failure detection and fault isolation. There is also an ongoing consideration of simulation and computer aided design some of which is implemented in SciLAB. In particular, we have been involved in the extension of the integrators in Scicos to handle implicit blocks.
- Boeing's Mathematical and Engineering Analysis Division. This project includes the optimization and simulation of large complex DAE modeled systems with applications to manufacturing. In particular, we are investigating direct transcription methods which are using in Boeings Sparse Optimal Control Software (SOCS).

NAVSEA. This project concerns failure detection and failure identification problems on Systems of interest to the US Navy. It has both aspects of technology transfer and fundamental research since it involves an extension of some techniques originally developed for linear systems to nonlinear systems.

EXPLANATION

An explanation is a set of statements constructed to describe a set of facts which clarifies the causes, context, and consequences of those facts.

This description may establish rules or laws, and may clarify the existing ones in relation to any objects, or phenomena examined. The components of an explanation can be implicit, and be interwoven with one another.

An explanation is often underpinned by an understanding that is represented by different media such as music, text, and graphics. Thus, an explanation is subjected to interpretation, and discussion. In scientific research, explanation is one of the purposes of research, e.g., exploration and description. Explanation is a way to uncover new knowledge, and to report relationships among different aspects of studied phenomena.

EXPLANATIONS AND ARGUMENTS

While arguments attempt to show that something is, will be, or should be the case, explanations try to show why or how something is or will be. If Fred and Joe address the issue of whether or not Fred's cat has fleas, Joe may state: "Fred, your cat has fleas.

Observe the cat is scratching right now." Joe has made an argument that the cat has fleas. However, if Fred and Joe agree on the fact that the cat has fleas, they may further question why this is so and put forth an explanation: "The reason the cat has fleas is that the weather has been damp." The difference is that the attempt is not to settle whether or not some claim is true, it is to show why it is true.

In this sense, arguments aim to contribute knowledge, whereas explanations aim to contribute understanding.

Arguments and explanations largely resemble each other in rhetorical use. This is the cause of much difficulty in thinking critically about claims.

There are several reasons for this difficulty:

- People often are not themselves clear on whether they are arguing for or explaining something.
- The same types of words and phrases are used in presenting explanations and arguments.
- The terms 'explain' or 'explanation,' et cetera are frequently used in arguments.
- Explanations are often used within arguments and presented so as to serve as arguments.

EXPLANATIONS AND JUSTIFICATION

Justification is the reason why someone properly holds a belief, the explanation as to why the belief is a true one, or an account of how one knows what one knows. In much the same way arguments and explanations may be confused with each other, so too may explanations and justifications. Statements which are justifications of some action take the form of arguments. For example attempts to justify a theft usually explain the motives.

It is important to be aware when an explanation is not a justification. A criminal profiler may offer an explanation of a suspect's behaviour. Such statements may help us understand why the person committed the crime, however an uncritical listener may believe the speaker is trying to gain sympathy for the person and his or her actions. It does not follow that a person proposing an explanation has any sympathy for the views or actions being explained. This is an important distinction because we need to be able to understand and explain terrible events and behaviour in attempting to discourage it.

TYPES OF EXPLANATIONS

There are many and varied events, objects, and facts which require explanation. So too, there are many different types of explanation. Among the various types of explanation are

Deductive-nomological, Functional, Historical, Psychological, Reductive, Teleological, Methodological explanations.

FORECASTING

Most people view the world as consisting of a large number of alternatives. Futures research evolved as a way of examining the alternative futures and identifying the most probable. Forecasting is designed to help decision making and planning in the present.

Forecasts empower people because their use implies that we can modify variables now to alter the future. A prediction is an invitation to introduce change into a system.

There are several assumptions about forecasting:

- There is no way to state what the future will be with complete certainty. Regardless of the methods that we use there will always be an element of uncertainty until the forecast horizon has come to pass.
- There will always be blind spots in forecasts. We cannot, for example, forecast completely new technologies for which there are no existing paradigms.
- Providing forecasts to policy-makers will help them formulate social policy. The new social policy, in turn, will affect the future, thus changing the accuracy of the forecast.

Many scholars have proposed a variety of ways to categorize forecasting methodologies. The following classification is a modification of the schema developed by Gordon over two decades ago:

GENIUS FORECASTING

This method is based on a combination of intuition, insight, and luck. Psychics and crystal ball readers are the most extreme case of genius forecasting. Their forecasts are based exclusively on intuition. Science fiction writers have sometimes described new technologies with uncanny accuracy.

There are many examples where men and women have been remarkable successful at predicting the future. There are also many examples of wrong forecasts. The weakness in genius forecasting is that its impossible to recognize a good forecast until the forecast has come to pass.

Some psychic individuals are capable of producing consistently accurate forecasts. Mainstream science generally ignores this fact because the implications are simply to difficult to accept. Our current understanding of reality is not adequate to explain this phenomena.

TREND EXTRAPOLATION

These methods examine trends and cycles in historical data, and then use mathematical techniques to extrapolate to the future. The assumption of all these techniques is that the forces responsible for creating the past, will continue to operate in the future. This is often a valid assumption when forecasting short term horizons, but it falls short when creating medium and long term forecasts. The further out we attempt to forecast, the less certain we become of the forecast.

The stability of the environment is the key factor in determining whether trend extrapolation is an appropriate forecasting model. The concept of"developmental inertia" embodies the idea that some items are more easily changed than others. Clothing styles is an example of an area that contains little inertia. It is difficult to produce reliable mathematical forecasts for clothing. Energy consumption, on the other hand, contains substantial inertia and mathematical techniques work well. The developmental inertia of new industries or new technology cannot be determined because there is not yet a history of data to draw from.

There are many mathematical models for forecasting trends and cycles. Choosing an appropriate model for a particular forecasting application depends on the historical data. The study of the historical data is called exploratory data analysis. Its purpose is to identify the trends and cycles in the data so that appropriate model can be chosen.

The most common mathematical models involve various forms of weighted smoothing methods. Another type of model is known as decomposition. This technique mathematically separates the historical data into trend, seasonal and random components. A process known as a"turning point analysis" is used to produce forecasts. ARIMA models such as adaptive filtering and Box-Jenkins analysis constitute a third class of mathematical model, while simple linear regression and curve fitting is a fourth.

The common feature of these mathematical models is that historical data is the only criteria for producing a forecast. One might think then, that if two people use the same model on the same data that the forecasts will also be the same, but this is not necessarily the case. Mathematical models involve smoothing constants, coefficients and other parametres that must decided by the forecaster. To a large degree, the choice of these parametres determines the forecast.

It is vogue today to diminish the value of mathematical extrapolation. Makridakis correctly points out that judgmental forecasting is superior to mathematical models, however, there are many forecasting applications where computer generated forecasts are more feasible. For example, large manufacturing companies often forecast inventory levels for thousands of items each month. It would simply not be feasible to use judgmental forecasting in this kind of application.

CONSENSUS METHODS

Forecasting complex systems often involves seeking expert opinions from more than one person. Each is an expert in his own discipline, and it is through the synthesis of these opinions that a final forecast is obtained.

One method of arriving at a consensus forecast would be to put all the experts in a room and let them"argue it out". This method falls short because the situation is often controlled by those individuals that have the best group interaction and persuasion skills.

A better method is known as the Delphi technique. This method seeks to rectify the problems of face-to-face confrontation in the group, so the responses and respondents remain anonymous. The classical technique proceeds in well-defined sequence. In the first round, the participants are asked to write their predictions. Their responses are collated and a copy is given to each of the participants. The participants are asked to comment on extreme views and to defend or modify their original opinion based on what the other participants have written. Again, the answers are collated and fed back to the participants. In the final round, participants are asked to reassess their original opinion in view of those presented by other participants.

The Delphi method general produces a rapid narrowing of opinions. It provides more accurate forecasts than group discussions. Furthermore, a face-to-face discussion following the application of the Delphi method generally degrades accuracy.

SIMULATION METHODS

Simulation methods involve using analogs to model complex systems. These analogs can take on several forms. A mechanical analog might be a wind tunnel for modeling aircraft performance. An equation to predict an economic measure would be a mathematical analog. A metaphorical analog could involve using the growth of a bacteria colony to describe human population growth. Game analogs are used where the interactions of the players are symbolic of social interactions.

Mathematical analogs are of particular importance to futures research. They have been extremely successful in many forecasting applications, especially in the physical sciences. In the social sciences however, their accuracy is somewhat diminished. The extraordinary complexity of social systems makes it difficult to include all the relevant factors in any model.

Clarke reminds us of a potential danger in our reliance on mathematical models. As he points out, these techniques often begin with an initial set of assumptions, and if these are incorrect, then the forecasts will reflect and amplify these errors.

One of the most common mathematical analogs in societal growth is the S-curve. The model is based on the concept of the logistic or normal probability distribution. All processes experience exponential growth and reach an upper asymptopic limit. Modis has hypothesized that chaos like states exist at the beginning and end of the S-curve. The disadvantage of this S-curve model is that it is difficult to know at any point in time where you currently are on the curve, or how close you are to the asymtopic limit. The advantage of the model is that it forces planners to take a long-term look at the future.

Another common mathematical analog involves the use of multivariate statistical techniques. These techniques are used to model complex systems involving relationships between two or more variables. Multiple regression analysis is the most common technique. Unlike trend extrapolation models, which only look at the history of the variable being forecast, multiple regression models look at the relationship between the variable being forecast and two or more other variables.

Multiple regression is the mathematical analog of a systems approach, and it has become the primary forecasting tool of economists and social scientists. The object of multiple regression is to be able to understand how a group of variables affect another variable.

The multiple regression problem of collinearity mirrors the practical problems of a systems approach. Paradoxically, strong correlations between predictor variables create unstable forecasts, where a slight change in one variable can have dramatic impact on another variable. In a multiple regression approach, as the relationships between the components of the system increase, our ability to predict any given component decreases.

Gaming analogs are also important to futures research. Gaming involves the creation of an artificial environment or situation. Players are asked to performance out an assigned role. The"role" is essentially a set of rules that is used during interactions with other players. While gaming has not yet been proven as a forecasting technique, it does serve two important functions. First, by the performance of designing the game, researchers learn to define the parametres of the system they are studying. Second, it teaches researchers about the relationships between the components of the system.

CROSS-IMPACT MATRIX METHOD

Relationships often exist between events and developments that are not revealed by univariate forecasting techniques.

The cross-impact matrix method recognizes that the occurrence of an event can, in turn, effect the likelihoods of other events. Probabilities are assigned to reflect the likelihood of an event in the presence and absence of other events. The resultant inter-correlational structure can be used to examine the relationships of the components to each other, and within the overall system. The advantage of this technique is that it forces forecasters and policy-makers to look at the relationships between system components, rather than viewing any variable as working independently of the others.

SCENARIO

The scenario is a narrative forecast that describes a potential course of events. Like the cross-impact matrix method, it recognizes the interrelationships of system components. The scenario describes the impact on the other components and the system as a whole. It is a "script" for defining the particulars of an uncertain future.

Scenarios consider events such as new technology, population shifts, and changing consumer preferences. Scenarios are written as long-term predictions of the future. A most likely scenario is usually written, along with at least one optimistic and one pessimistic scenario. The primary purpose of a scenario is to provoke thinking of decision makers who can then posture themselves for the fulfillment of the scenario(s).

The three scenarios force decision makers to ask:

1. Can we survive the pessimistic scenario,
2. Are we happy with the most likely scenario, and
3. Are we ready to take advantage of the optimistic scenario?

DECISION TREES

Decision trees originally evolved as graphical devices to help emphasize the structural relationships between alternative choices. These trees were originally presented as a series of yes/no choices. As our understanding of feedback loops improved, decision trees became more complex. Their structure became the foundation of computer flow charts.

Computer technology has made it possible create very complex decision trees consisting of many subsystems and feedback loops. Decisions are no longer limited to dichotomies; they now involve assigning probabilities to the likelihood of any particular path.

Decision theory is based on the concept that an expected value of a discrete variable can be calculated as the average value for that variable. The expected value is especially useful for decision makers because it represents the most likely value based on the probabilities of the distribution function. The application of Bayes' theorem enables the modification of initial probability estimates, so the decision tree becomes refined as new evidence is introduced.

Utility theory is often used in conjunction with decision theory to improve the decision making process. It recognizes that dollar amounts are not the only consideration in the decision process. Other factors, such as risk, are also considered.

COMBINING FORECASTS

It seems clear that no forecasting technique is appropriate for all situations. There is substantial evidence to demonstrate that combining individual forecasts produces gains in forecasting accuracy. There is also evidence that adding quantitative forecasts to qualitative forecasts reduces accuracy. Research has not yet revealed the conditions or methods for the optimal combinations of forecasts.

Judgmental forecasting usually involves combining forecasts from more than one source. Informed forecasting begins with a set of key assumptions and then uses a combination of historical data and expert opinions. Involved forecasting seeks the opinions of all those directly affected by the forecast. These techniques generally produce higher quality forecasts than can be attained from a single source.

Combining forecasts provides us with a way to compensate for deficiencies in a forecasting technique. By selecting complementary methods, the shortcomings of one technique can be offset by the advantages of another.

DIFFICULTIES IN FORECASTING TECHNOLOGY

Clarke describes our inability to forecast technological futures as a failure of nerve. When a major technological breakthrough does occur, it takes conviction and courage to accept the implications of the finding. Even when the truth is starring us in the face, we often have difficulty accepting its implications.

Clark refers to this resistance to change as cowardice, however, it may be much deeper. Cognitive dissonance theory in psychology has helped us understand that resistance to change is a natural human characteristic. It is extremely difficult to venture beyond our latitudes of acceptance in forecasting new technologies. Clarke states that knowledge can sometimes clog the wheels of imagination. He embodied this belief in his self-proclaimed law:

"When a distinguished but elderly scientist states that something is possible, he is almost certainly right. When he states that something is impossible, he is very probably wrong."

Nearly all futurists describe the past as unchangeable, consisting as a collection of knowable facts. We generally perceive the existence of only one past. When two people give conflicting stories of the past, we tend to believe that one of them must be lying or mistaken.

This widely accepted view of the past might not be correct. Historians often interject their own beliefs and biases when they write about the past. Facts become distorted and altered over time. It may be that past is a reflection of our current conceptual reference. In the most extreme viewpoint, the concept of time itself comes into question.

The future, on the other hand, is filled will uncertainty. Facts give way to opinions. As de Jouvenel points out, the facts of the past provide the raw materials from which the mind makes estimates of the future. All forecasts are opinions of the future. The performance of making a forecast is the expression of an opinion. The future, as described by de Jouvenel, consists of a range of possible future phenomena or events. These futuribles are those things that might happen.

DEFINING A USEFUL FORECAST

Science fiction novelist Frederik Pohl has suggested that the "only time a forecast has any real utility is when it is not totally reliable". He proposes a thought experiment where a Gypsy fortune teller predicts that as suggested, be run over and killed when we leave the tea room. If we know that the Gypsy's predictions are one hundred per cent accurate, then Pohl states that the fortune is useless, because we would be unable to alter the forecast. In other words, predictions only become useful when they are not completely reliable.

The apparent paradox created by Pohl's thought experiment is only a function of the particular situation.

The paradox exists only when:

- We want the future to be different than the prediction, and
- When we believe that there is no way for us to adapt to or affect the forthcoming changes.

Pohl's thought experiment actually doesn't even meet that criteria, since one could present a convincing argument that it is more desirable to spend the rest of our lives confined to the comfort of a tea room than to leave and meet certain death. Obviously, our new life would be difficult to accept and adapt to, but it could be done. Prisoners do it all the time.

A forecast can be one hundred per cent accurate and still be useful. For example, suppose our Gypsy had told us that after leaving her tea room we would safely return home. Again, since we know that her forecasts are completely accurate, we would receive emotional comfort from her predictions. In a more tangible example, suppose the prediction is that our manufacturing company will receive twice as many orders for widgets as we had anticipated. Since the forecast is one hundred per cent accurate, we would be wise to order more raw materials and increase our production staff to meet the coming demand.

Pohl is wrong. The goal of forecasting is to be as accurate as possible. In the case of business demand forecasting, it is naive to suggest that an accurate forecast is useless. On the contrary, a more accurate forecast enables us to plan the use our resources in a more ecological fashion. We can minimize waste by adapting to our expectations of the future.

It is sometimes useful in thought experiments to look at the situation from the opposite perspective. Suppose we know that our Gypsy is always wrong in her predictions. Her accuracy is guaranteed to be zero. Note that this is different than random forecasts, where she might hit the mark once in a while. The Gypsy sighs with relief and says that there is no fatal accident in store for us today. Pohl's reasoning, this should provide the most useful forecast because it has the least accuracy. It's obvious, though, that this fortune is as useless as the one where she is completely accurate. Leaving the Gypsy's tea-room is not something we would want to do.

If we view accuracy as a continuum, it may be that the antonym of accuracy is randomness. In this case, Pohl's theory would suggest that random forecasts are more useful than accurate forecasts. In demand forecasting, the degree of over- and under-utilization of our resources is proportional to the difference between the observed and predicted values. Random forecasts are entirely unacceptable for this type of application.

Pohl's thought experiment is very important because it forces us to look at the theoretical foundations of forecasting. First, Pohl's experiment may not be valid because it violates a basic assumption of forecasting. Second, the usefulness of a forecast does not always seem to be related to its accuracy. Both extremes can produce useful or useless forecasts.

The usefulness of a forecast is not something that lends itself readily to quantification along any specific dimension.

It involves complex relationships between many things, including the type of information being forecast, our confidence in the accuracy of the forecast, the magnitude of our dissatisfaction with the forecast, and the versatility of ways that we can adapt to or modify the forecast. In other words, the usefulness of a forecast is an application sensitive construct. Each forecasting situation must be evaluated individually regarding its usefulness.

One of the first rules of doing research is to consider how the results will be used. It is important to consider who the readers of the final report will be during the initial planning stages of a project. It is wasteful to expend resources on research that has little or no use. The same rule applies to forecasting. We must strive to develop forecasts that are of maximum usefulness to planners. This means that each situation must be evaluated individually as to the methodology and type of forecasts that are most appropriate to the particular application.

DO FORECASTS CREATE THE FUTURE

A paradox exists in preparing a forecast. If a forecast results in an adaptive change, then the accuracy of the forecast might be modified by that change. Suppose the forecast is that our business will experience a ten per cent drop in sales next month. We adapt by increasing our promotion effort to compensate for the predicted loss. This action, in turn, could affect our sales, thus changing the accuracy of the original forecast.

Many futurists have expressed the idea that the way we contemplate the future is an expression of our desire to create that future. Physicist Dennis Gabor, discoverer of holography, claimed that the future is invented, not predicted. The implication is that the future is an expression of our present thoughts. The idea that we create our own reality is not a new concept. It is easy to imagine how thoughts might translate into actions that affect the future.

Biblical records speak of faith as the force that could move mountains. Recent research in quantum mechanics suggests that this may be more than just a philosophical concept. At a quantum level, matter itself might simply be a manifestation of thought. Electrons and other subatomic particles seem to exist only when physicists are looking for them, otherwise, they exist only as energy.

An incredible discovery was made at the University of Paris in 1982. A team of researchers lead by Alain Aspect found that under certain conditions, electrons could instantaneously communicate with each other across long distances. The results of this experiment have been confirmed by many other researchers, although the implications are exceedingly hard to accept.

Three explanations are possible:

1 Information can be transferred at speeds exceeding the speed of light,
2 The passage of time is an illusion,
3 The distance between the electrons is an illusion. All three explanations rock our perception of reality.

David Bohm has explained Aspect's experiment by hypothesizing a holographic universe in which reality is essentially a projection of some deeper dimension that we are not able to comprehend. Instantaneous communication is possible because the distance between the particles is an illusion. Neurophysiologist Karl Pribram has also theorized about the holographic nature of reality. His theory is based on a study of the way that the brain recalls memory patterns, but the implications are the same. Reality is a phantasm.

If reality is an illusion, then the future is also an illusion.

The phenomena of being able to see the future is known as precognition. Most people believe that they can predict the future. Fortune-tellers, however, believe they can view the future. There is a major difference. We predict the future based on knowledge, intuition and logic. Precognitive persons claim to "see" the future. Knowledge and logic are not involved.

Throughout history, there have been many reports of gifted psychics with precognitive powers. Through some unknown mechanism, these people are able predict things that will happen in the future. If we admit that even a single person in history has possessed this capability, then we must accept the fact that our concept of reality needs dramatic alteration. Time itself may not exist as we currently perceive it. Forecasting may be a method of creating illusions.

Forecasting can, and often does, contribute to the creation of the future, but it is clear that other factors are also operating. A holographic theory would stress the interconnectedness of all elements in the system. At some level, everything contributes to the creation of the future. The degree to which a forecast can shape the future has yet to be determined experimentally and experientially.

Sometimes forecasts become part of a creative process, and sometimes they don't. When two people make mutually exclusive forecasts, both of them cannot be true. At least one forecast is wrong. Does one person's forecast create the future, and the other does not? The mechanisms involved in the construction of the future are not well understood on an individual or social level.

Modis believes that the media provides the mechanism by which social forecasts take on a creative context. In this theory, extensive media coverage acts as a resonating cavity for public opinion, and creates a "cultural epidemic" that modifies social behaviour.

Dublin points out that the "future has become so integral to the fabric of modern consciousness that few people feel compelled to question it...". Because of the power of a prediction to affect the future, he goes on to state that prophesy is usually a self-interest quest for power.

THE ETHICS OF FORECASTING

Are predictions of the future a form of propaganda, designed to evoke a particular set of behaviours? Dublin states that the desire for control is implicit in all forecasts. Decisions made today are based on forecasts, which may or may not come to pass. The forecast is a way to control today's decisions.

Dublin is correct. The purpose of forecasting is to control the present. In fact, one of the assumptions of forecasting is that the forecasts will be used by policy-makers to make decisions. It is therefore important to discuss the ethics of forecasting. Since forecasts can and often do take on a creative role, what right do we have to make forecasts that involve other peoples futures?

Nearly everyone would agree that we have the right to create our own future. Goal setting is a form of personal forecasting. It is one way to organize and invent our personal future.

Each person has the right to create their own future. On the other hand, a social forecast might alter the course of an entire society.

Such power can only be accompanied by equivalent responsibility. There are no clear rules involving the ethics of forecasting. In Future Shock, Toffler discussed the importance of value impact forecasting, the idea that social forecasting must involve physical, cultural and societal values. It is doubtful that forecasters can leave their own personal biases out of the forecasting process. Even the most mathematically rigorous techniques involve judgmental inputs that can dramatically alter the forecast.

Many futurists have pointed out our obligation to create socially desirable futures. Unfortunately, a socially desirable future for one person might be another person's nightmare. For example, modern ecological theory says that we should think of our planet in terms of sustainable futures.

The finite supply of natural resources forces us to reconsider the desirability of unlimited growth. An optimistic forecast is that we achieve and maintain an ecologically balanced future.

That same forecast, the idea of zero growth, is a catastrophic nightmare for the corporate and financial institutions of the free world. Our Keynesian system of profit depends on continual growth for the well-being of individuals, groups, and institutions.

Desirable futures is a subjective concept. It can only be understood relative to other information. The ethics of forecasting certainly involves the obligation to create desirable futures for the person(s) that might be affected by the forecast.

If a goal of forecasting is to create desirable futures, then the forecaster must ask the ethical question of"desirable for whom?".

To embrace the idea of liberty is to recognize that each person has the right to create their own future. Forecasters can promote libertarian beliefs by empowering people that might be affected by the forecast. Involving these people in the forecasting process, gives them the power to become co-creators in their futures.

CONTROL

In research, control subjects or control procedures permit comparison with experimental results. The first controlled clinical research was probably done in 1875 by the British naval surgeon James Lind who, on board the HMS Salisbury, gave sailors with scurvy either oranges or lemons or cider or vinegar or nutmeg and after just six days discovered that the citrus-consuming sailors had recovered from scurvy, until then the scourge of extended sea voyages, while the sailors who had been given the other treatments remained uncured.

Where does an ordinary citizen encounter control? Control is experienced in processing of telephone calls, in car steering, in modern forms of information and control of motorways, in stabilization control of air planes, in orbit control of satellites for hand held phones and tv channels, etc. Almost all engineering products operate properly only because control is used to safeguard their proper operation and to optimize their performance. In the last two decades motivating control problems have arisen in control of high-performance communication networks, of motorway traffic, in air traffic control, of chemical plants, and in finance and insurance to name only a few areas. Control and system theory are highly relevant to the functioning of the Western industrialized societies.

At about half of the ERCIM institutes research in this research area is carried out in designated research groups while at other institutes control is sometimes integrated in research of computer science.

PROBLEMS OF CONTROL AND SYSTEM THEORY

What is control? Engineering systems require command signals such that controlled variables remain at a specified setpoint say. This function is called control. Control is also the name for a research area in which the design of controllers is studied at the engineering level and in which synthesis of controllers is studied at a theoretical level. System theory is the research area in which study is made of mathematical models for control and signal processing. Besides engineering, mathematics and computer science are the main academic disciplines used in control and system theory.

A system is a mathematical model of an engineering phenomenon that involves an input signal, an output signal, and a state function. The input can be commanded by a controller. The output refers to that part of the state function that can be observed and as such is available to the controller. At any time the current state and the current input value determine the dynamics of the state and the current output value. Systems are usually classified just as to the spaces involved and to the equations that specify the dynamics. Thus there are linear, bilinear, polynomial, and stochastic systems depending on the character of the transition map.

Control is based on the principle of feedback. In the closed-loop system the output of the system is used by the controller to determine the input to the system. The control problem for a system is then to synthesize a controller such that the closed-loop system meets the control objectives. General control objectives include: stability of the state function, optimization of performance, robustness with respect to noise signals and poorly modeled dynamics, and avoidance of unsafe states. The engineering constraint of a controller that can be implemented with finite memory is essential. Control and signal processing require mathematical models in the form of a system with finite memory. Consider a map from input signals to output signals. A realization is a system in a prespecified class such that the associated map from inputs to outputs associated with the system equals a considered map.

The realization problem is to establish conditions for the existence of a realization. Furthermore, it also includes the classification of all such realizations. The system identification problem for a pair of observed input-output signals is to determine a system such that the input-output signals approximate the specified input-output signals.

CURRENT AND RECENT RESEARCH

There is a large body of literature on control of linear systems. In the last decades much attention has been given to robust control of linear systems. Currently there is attention for control of systems with saturations and with space constraints such as linear systems for artificial neural nets. Motivated by coding theory, linear systems on groups are receiving renewed interests. Primarily motivated by mechanics, control of nonlinear systems has developed within a differential geometric framework. Other engineering areas lead to bilinear systems and to polynomial systems. Control of stochastic systems has led to a body of results for filtering and stochastic control. Optimal stochastic control with an exponential type cost function has led to results on robust control and to interpretations of large deviations. Problems of detection and failure diagnosis for stochastic systems and for discrete event systems motivated by engineering problems have led to theory and algorithms that are applied in wide ranging fields.

Realization theory has started with the work of R.E. Kalman for linear finite-dimensional systems. Since then it has been generalized to other classes of systems and from input-output maps to input-output trajectories. The behavioural approach to realization theory concerns the distinction of observed signals into input and output signals. Stochastic realization theory has been developed for Gaussian systems and finite-stochastic systems. For system identification of linear systems and of Gaussian systems there is a well developed theory for single-input-single-output systems. For multi-input-multi-output systems algorithms based on stochastic realization theory and on the singular value decomposition of numerical linear algebra are quite effective. The approximation problem of system identification takes inspiration from stochastic complexity theory which in turn is based on Kolmogorov complexity. Adaptive control of linear and Gaussian systems is well developed for single-input/single-output systems but there remain difficult conceptual problems for the multi-input/multi-output case. The interaction of control, state estimation, and parametre estimation needs more fundamental thinking.

Motivated by the use of computers for control, there has been developed a control and system theory for discrete-event systems. Modeling formalisms used include automata, Petri nets, process algebras, and linear systems over the (max,+)-algebra. This research benefits from interaction with theoretical computer science. Results concern control synthesis, hierarchical control, and failure diagnosis. Applications have been made in control of communication networks, manufacturing, chemical process control, road traffic, and air traffic control. Research for the class of hybrid systems is primarily motivated by the use of computers for control of engineering systems. The interaction between the discrete and the continuous dynamics is in some models so tight that these must be treated jointly.

MODELING

Computer-based modeling environments offer real potential for breakthroughs in science learning. Computer models help students visualize scientific concepts that are not observable in real life. For example, students can use a model of atoms and a temperature sensor to visualize and better understand the connection between temperature and the motion of atoms.

Research by the Concord Consortium and others has demonstrated that guided exploration of models can strengthen student understanding of fundamental concepts in math and science. However, more research is needed to demonstrate the effectiveness of this approach in reaching all learners.

In December 1999 the Molecular Workbench project began developing and testing professional grade molecular models adapted for the classroom; an extension project, CCATоms, funded initial development of modeling chemical reactions and 3D biology. Molecular Logic extended the modeling to high school biology, and Molecular Literacy to biotechnology and nanotechnology students in community colleges. In November 2001 with our partner organizations the Concord Consortium launched Modeling Across the Curriculum, a longitudinal study that will measure the educational impact of model-based technologies in high school science classes.

To guide student exploration of models, we have developed a hypermodel architecture that can flexibly scaffold learning and assess student progress. We are currently producing model-based activities for genetics, and atomic and molecular systems. In our research project Dataand Models we are investigating middle school students' conceptual understandings of heat and temperature through hands-on experimentation and model-based visualizations.

With our partners at the University of California at Berkeley, we are developing model-based curricula for teaching plate tectonics. With only a few simple modeling tools, students can visualize hidden processes inside the earth, which helps them better understand geological phenomena such as earthquakes, volcanoes, continental drift, and mountain formation.

3

Research Process

AN OVERVIEW

We understand the world by asking questions and searching for answers. Our construction of reality depends on the nature of our inquiry.

Until the sixteenth century, human inquiry was primarily based on introspection. The way to know things was to turn inward and use logic to seek the truth. This paradigm had endured for a millennium and was a well-established conceptual framework for understanding the world. The seeker of knowledge was an integral part of the inquiry process.

A profound change occurred during the sixteenth and seventeenth centuries. Copernicus, Kepler, Galileo, Descartes, Bacon, Newton, and Locke presented new ways of examining nature. Our method of understanding the world came to rely on measurement and quantification. Mathematics replaced introspection as the key to supreme truths. The Scientific Revolution was born.

Objectivity became a critical component of the new scientific method. The investigator was an observer, rather than a participant in the inquiry process. A mechanistic view of the universe evolved. We believed that we could understand the whole by performing an examination of the individual parts. Experimentation and deduction became the tools of the scholar. For two hundred years, the new paradigm slowly evolved to become part of the reality framework of society. The Age of Enlightenment had arrived.

Scientific research methodology was very successful at explaining natural phenomena. It provided a systematic way of knowing. Western philosophers embraced this new structure of inquiry. Eastern philosophy continued to stress the importance of the one seeking knowledge. By the beginning of the twentieth century, a complete schism had occurred. Western and Eastern philosophies were mutually exclusive and incompatible.

Then something remarkable happened. Einstein's proposed that the observer was not separate from the phenomena being studied. Indeed, his theory of relativity actually stressed the role of the observer. Quantum mechanics carried this a step further and stated that the performance of observation could change the thing being observed. The researcher was not simply an observer, but in fact, was an integral part of the process. In physics, Western and Eastern philosophies have met.

This idea has not been incorporated into the standard social science research model, and today's social science community see themselves as objective observers of the phenomena being studied. However, "it is an established principle of measurement that instruments react with the things they measure." The concept of instrument reactivity states that an instrument itself can disturb the thing being measured.

DEFINITION AND PROBLEM RECOGNITION

All research begins with a question. Intellectual curiosity is often the foundation for scholarly inquiry. Some questions are not testable. The classic philosophical example is to ask, "How many angels can dance on the head of a pin?" While the question might elicit profound and thoughtful revelations, it clearly cannot be tested with an empirical experiment. Prior to Descartes, this is precisely the kind of question that would engage the minds of learned men. Their answers came from within. The modern scientific method precludes asking questions that cannot be empirically tested. If the angels cannot be observed or detected, the question is considered inappropriate for scholarly research. A paradigm is maintained as much by the process of formulating questions as it is by the answers to those questions. By excluding certain types of questions, we limit the scope of our thinking. It is interesting to note, however, that modern physicists have began to ask the same kinds of questions posed by the Eastern philosophers. "Does a tree falling in the forest make a sound if nobody is there to hear it?" This seemingly trivial question is at the heart of the observer/observed dichotomy. In fact, quantum mechanics predicts that this kind of question cannot be answered with complete certainty. It is the beginning of a new paradigm.

Defining the goals and objectives of a research project is one of the most important steps in the research process. Clearly stated goals keep a research project focused. The process of goal definition usually begins by writing down the broad and general goals of the study. As the process continues, the goals become more clearly defined and the research issues are narrowed.

Exploratory research goes hand-in-hand with the goal clarification process. The literature review is especially important because it obviates the need to reinvent the wheel for every new research question. More importantly, it gives researchers the opportunity to build on each others work.

The research question itself can be stated as a hypothesis. A hypothesis is simply the investigator's belief about a problem. Typically, a researcher formulates an opinion during the literature review process. The process of reviewing other scholar's work often clarifies the theoretical issues associated with the research question. It also can help to elucidate the significance of the issues to the research community.

The hypothesis is converted into a null hypothesis in order to make it testable. "The only way to test a hypothesis is to eliminate alternatives of the hypothesis." Statistical techniques will enable us to reject a null hypothesis, but they do not provide us with a way to accept a hypothesis. Therefore, all hypothesis testing is indirect.

CREATING A RESEARCH DESIGN

DESIGN AND THE PURPOSE OF THE RESEARCH

Your research *design* is your plan for providing a sound, and, if possible, conclusive answer to your research question. Designs vary greatly, depending on the research question being addressed and the methods of data collection the investigator chooses to use. Creating a design starts with the purpose of the research.

Most research is done for one of three purposes. The most common purpose is to *describe* some set of variables or relationships among them as accurately as possible. Other purposes of research are to *explore* a topic to learn more about it or to *explain* why certain social patterns or relationships occur as they do.

Some studies combine more than one purpose. For example, while the Sudan Fertility Study was designed primarily as a descriptive investigation, we showed how data from this study were analysed to explain why future fertility rates may decline in northern Sudan. Nevertheless, as suggested, describe each approach separately to show how each purpose affects design decisions. Exploratory research generally requires less rigorous design decisions; so as suggested, start with it.

Exploratory Research

Exploratory research, as the name suggests, is a way of gaining some initial information about a problem or topic. You may be interested in a certain problem, but don't have enough information to write a clear research question. Perhaps you are not sure what the critical variables are or what methods of data collection may work best. Before beginning an investigation, you might decide to explore the problem by doing some informal interviews or by living for a short time with the group you want to study. These techniques are often used in exploratory research.

Example. Julia and Ridha explored experiences of Kuwaiti women during the Iraqi invasion and following occupation of Kuwait in 1990. Twenty women who played various roles, including active opposition to the Iraqi invaders, told of their experiences before, during, and after the invasion. The women reported that they actively sought their own self-development and liberation, but once the conflict ended, their choices and rights tended to become restricted again by traditional male prerogatives.

Exploratory studies, however, seldom provide satisfactory answers to research questions. One reason is that most exploratory studies are based on samples too small to permit generalizing the results to a larger population. This is certainly true of the study of Kuwaiti women. But exploratory studies can provide valuable, even critical, information for designing larger scale descriptive or explanatory studies.

Descriptive Research

Descriptive research is more specific and focused than exploratory research. The researcher starts with a well defined problem or research question and a clearly defined plan for collecting and analyzing data. Descriptive research is intended to produce clear, well-founded answers to some question or specific, factual information. Surveys are frequently used in descriptive research.

Example. Fattah conducted interviews, using a questionnaire, with 200 randomly selected farm families in Iraq. The questionnaire contained over 200 items about husband-wife decision-making related to the operation of the farm, financial matters, social life, entertainment, training of children, and childcare. She also obtained information on whether the families had a "modern" or "traditional" view of things. These data provided a detailed description of the degree to which wives participated in decision-making with their husbands. Fattah concluded that factors associated with modernism will continue to increase and will enhance the position of women in rural Iraq, which, today, remains male dominated.

Explanatory Research

Explanatory research goes beyond exploratory or descriptive research by trying to find the reasons why certain relationships occur. It seeks to provide explanations for what has been observed. Explanations are based on interpretation of findings in terms of broader concepts and accepted theory.

Example. Using extensive interviews and observation, Dei developed an explanation for how Ghanian villagers survived prolonged drought and related hardships. He found they got through hard times by shifting from farm production for a market economy to shared production with other villagers for household consumption.

A strong sense of community solidarity developed and allowed the villages to survive with what they could produce together. The explanation for their survival was the successful return to earlier farming methods.

Regardless of the purpose of your research, you will also need to decide on a technique for data collection. There are two contrasting yet complimentary techniques - quantitative and qualitative means of collecting data.

QUANTITATIVE AND QUALITATIVE DATA

Many fields of science, particularly the physical sciences, report observations in terms of numbers. Observations reported in numbers are referred to as quantitative data. Social scientists obtain and analyse quantitative data, as you have seen with various studies we have cited. Social scientists also obtain and analyse data in qualitative form. These are observations recorded in words - descriptions of what persons said or did, how they interacted with one another, or what a researcher observed by watching their behaviour. Each technique is useful; each also has certain strengths and weaknesses; each also presents a different set of design decisions.

Some researchers draw a sharp distinction between quantitative and qualitative research. A different view is presented in Types of Data. This discussion shows how quantitative data is based in part on qualitative judgments and that qualitative data can also be described and analysed numerically.

Quantitative Research

A quantitative approach requires a well-developed research design.

Quantitative research is usually based on:

- Careful and precise specification of the question to be answered;
- Identification, definition, and measurement of the key variables;
- Selection and specification of one or more methods of collecting data;
- Development of a sampling plan; and
- Numerical analysis of the data, including use of appropriate statistical tests.

Numbers used in quantitative studies may be as simple as counting the number of"Yes" versus"No" responses to some question. More complex forms of measurement, however, are generally used. The descriptive research by Fattah, for example, used a quantitative design. The many decision-making variables were defined and measures were developed for each. These measures, in the form of questions, were then combined in a questionnaire that was used in interviewing a random sample of farm families.

Quantitative data has important strengths. Using numerical measures provides more precise descriptions of variables. In addition, quantitative research permits use of larger samples. Also, quantitative data can be combined and analysed using various statistical techniques. You are certainly familiar with averages and percentages as ways of summarizing data.

Most of this site focuses on planning and conducting quantitative research and analyzing data based on quantitative variables.

Qualitative Research

Qualitative research, in contrast to quantitative research, seeks to dig deeper into the reasons for behaviour we observe. Generally, researchers doing qualitative research start with a broad idea of what they are looking for. In qualitative studies, researchers often combine informal interviews, in the form of long conversations with people, with systematic observation of their daily activities.

Data are derived continuously from what the persons in the group being studied do and say, how they say they feel about things, and the reasons they give the researcher for what they do. The researcher accumulates a large amount of data, generally in the form of long sets of notes and written descriptions of what was observed. As data are recorded, the researcher tries to interpret what the data mean and to develop an explanation for what has been observed. In this sense, analysis of data proceeds with data collection. Qualitative research is generally a much more flexible process, allowing researcher to take advantage of new lines of inquiry as they develop.

The research studies cited earlier by Julia and Ridha and by Dei were based on qualitative research methods. Research by ElSayed and Ahmed on the "Socio-Cultural Aspect of Kala-azar among the Masalit and Hansa Tribes" further emphasizes use of qualitative techniques.

The authors used small group discussions with villagers, personal interviews with patients, and direct observation of health and sanitation practices in the villages. They found that lack of knowledge about the disease is the main reason for its spread.

Combining Quantitative and Qualitative Techniques

Researchers frequently use both quantitative and qualitative techniques in the same investigation. In this way, researchers benefit from the strengths of each approach and minimize their respective limitations. Altareb, for example, investigated attitudes towards Muslims held by undergraduate students at an American university. He began by conducting focus groups, a qualitative technique, to get an initial understanding of students' attitudes. After this exploratory phase, he developed a quantitative measure of attitudes for the main part of the investigation.

Davidson also combined qualitative and quantitative methods in his investigation of ways families in the Nuba Mountains of the Sudan were adapting to rapidly changing socio-economic conditions in their area. He began by interviewing village elders and then conducted a survey to identify the characteristics of each of the 12 villages in his study area. Following the survey, he carried out in-depth interviews with selected households. This combination of methods provided a rich mix of quantitative data for describing adaptive techniques used by villagers and detailed and qualitative data for understanding how they were adapting to changes.

UNIT OF ANALYSIS

In designing research you also have to decide on what basis you will analyse the data you will collect. This requires a decision about the part *of analysis* for the study. Units of analysis may consist of individuals, groups, organizations, geographical places, or other entities. Generally the way you state your research question indicates which part will be used as the basis of analyzing the data.

It is easy to confuse part of analysis with the entities you collect data from. Frequently, they are the same. In the Sudan Fertility Survey, for example, the data were collected from women and the data were analysed in terms of the same women.

In this case, the decision was clear. In another study, a researcher might interview factory managers to get information to compare the efficiency of different sized factories. In this case, the part of analysis is factories, not managers because the purpose of the research is to compare factories and managers happened to be the source of data. If you have any doubt, think about the question you are trying to answer. How do the data have to be organized to answer the question?

Individuals as the Part of Analysis

When the purpose of research is to say something about individuals, they become the part of analysis. Individuals are the most frequent part of analysis. They may be any age, either gender, or become the units of analysis because they have a common characteristic. Primary, intermediate and secondary students were the units of analysis in a trend study by Badri and Burchinal.

Many studies are based on collecting data from university students, who then become the part of analysis. Cook, for example, investigated the attitudes of Egyptian university students towards Islam and higher education; Had-Elzein and Ahmed obtained data on perceptions and vision of peace from Sudanese university students.

Married women were the part of analysis in the Sudan Fertility Survey. Mageed, Sulima and Kawther collected data about attitudes towards female genital mutilation from adult men and women. Agricultural technical workers were the part of analysis in a study of worker satisfaction in Kenya. Muneer selected farmers, who became the part of analysis, in his study of the role of cooperatives in western Sudan. Khalafalla selected policy-makers as her sample who also became her part of analysis.

Groups as the Part of Analysis

Research is often conducted by collecting and analyzing data for groups of people. When the purpose is to describe two or more persons as a unit, these groups become the part of analysis. Households, consisting of various numbers of persons, often are used as the part of analysis. Examples include the research by Julia and Ridha on Iraqi farm families and research by Davidson on changes in household life in the Nuba Mountains. Households were the part of analysis in an extensive study of year-long spending patterns among farm families in Sierra Leon. The sample used by Grotberg and Badri consisted of intact families with a child not older than five and one-half years. The mother-child pairs in these families became the part of analysis in this study. Other units of analysis at the group level include friendship groups, clubs, social groups, and groups of street children.

Organizations as the Part of Analysis

Research often is directed at learning about organizations, such as businesses, firms, ministries of government, universities, political parties, religious bodies, or military units. Although data about each organization may be obtained by interviewing members of an organization, the data would be used to describe and compare features of each organization. For example, Gimbel and associates studied job satisfaction in community-based organizations.

They collected data from employees but analysed their data in terms of characteristics of the organizations. Mohamed analysed operations in a sample of 150 government divisions in the United Arab Emirates.

In a study of safety programmes, Vredenburgh collected data about practices in 62 hospitals. These are only a few of the many management studies based on organizations as the part of analysis.

Geographical Places as the Part of Analysis

Places, such as where people live, can also become the focus of study and therefore be used as the part of analysis. Fishing villages in Uganda were the part of analysis in a socio-economic investigation by Namara. Cities, provinces, and rural versus urban areas are used as the part of analysis in most reports issued by international organizations. Countries frequently are used as the part of analysis. Bulluck compared the extent to which developing countries meet the social needs of citizens. Countries were also used in comparing infant mortality rates throughout sub-Saharan Africa. Wang examined the extent to which women's reproductive rights were protected in 101 countries.

Other Units of Analysis

Although most social research is based on the kinds of units of analysis just mentioned, other things may be selected for analysis. These include the contents of newspapers and magazines; rural development projects; and folk tales.

Table. Summarizes Frequently used Units of Analysis.

1. *Individuals*: By far the most frequently used
2. *Groups*: Husband-wife pairs, social groups
3. Organizations—businesses, offices, factories, government ministries
4. Classrooms, schools, university student bodies or groups
5. *Geographical areas*: Villages, communities, cities, regions of a country, entire countries
6. *Mass media materials*: Newspapers, magazines, television shows

Deciding on the Part of Analysis

Most likely the part of analysis you will use in a study will be clear from the way you defined your problem. If you have any doubts about the part you should use, you will need to resolve this confusion before going on. Otherwise, you may not analyse your data properly and your entire study could be jeopardized. Ask yourself what part you will base your analysis on. This is, as the term implies, your part of analysis. Also, in the process of analyzing your data, you may shift from one part to another.

In the study by Gimbel and associates mentioned under organizations as the part of analysis, the authors used organizations as the part of analysis. However, since they collected data from employees, they could have undertaken other analyses as well. For example, they might have become interested in the level of morale among employees and the length of time each worked for one of the organizations. In this case, they would have shifted to employees as the part of analysis. Our point is simple: just be sure of your part of analysis and that you have data appropriate to that unit.

Collecting Data at the Lowest Possible Part

Also, remember an important rule: Regardless of what you

are studying, always obtain data in terms of the lowest part of analysis possible. There is a simple reason for this. You can usually combine data collected at a lower level into a higher level for analysis, but it won't work the other way around. For example, if you intended to analyse data about the production of things by households, collect data about the production activities for each member of the household. Then you can combine the data from each household member for analysis at the level of the entire household. This way you can still do other analyses at the level of members of the household, such as what wives and daughters produced in contrast to husbands and sons, as well as for the entire household. But if you asked only for production of the household as a whole, you would not be able to describe production by separate members of the household.

Design Alternatives

Designing research is a creative process. Designs can be put together in a number of ways. By describing some of the more frequently used designs, we hope you will get an idea of the various kinds of research questions you can ask and designs you can use in answering them.

To start, designs can be developed for:

- Describing variables as they currently exist;
- For describing changes that have occurred; and
- For describing changes as they occur.

Cross-sectional Designs

Surveys are designed to describe some set of variables as they exist at the time of data collection. Data are collected from a sample over a relatively short period of time. The design used for a survey is also called a *cross-sectional* design because the sample is carefully selected to represent the cross section of some population. Either quantitative or qualitative techniques can be used to collect survey data, although, in general, quantitative techniques are used. The frequently cited Sudan Fertility Survey was based on a survey or cross-sectional design.

The survey design can be expanded to include more than one sample, as suggested, show shortly as part of the discussion of seeking differences between groups with respect to some variable.

SAMPLING

It is incumbent on the researcher to clearly define the target population. There are no strict rules to follow, and the researcher must rely on logic and judgment. The population is defined in keeping with the objectives of the study. Sometimes, the entire population will be sufficiently small, and the researcher can include the entire population in the study. This type of research is called a census study because data is gathered on every member of the population.

Usually, the population is too large for the researcher to attempt to survey all of its members. A small, but carefully chosen sample can be used to represent the population. The sample reflects the characteristics of the population from which it is drawn.

Sampling methods are classified as either probability or nonprobability. In probability samples, each member of the population has a known probability of being selected. Probability methods include random sampling, systematic sampling, and stratified sampling. In nonprobability sampling, members are selected from the population in some nonrandom manner.

These include convenience sampling, judgment sampling, quota sampling, and snowball sampling. The other common form of nonprobability sampling occurs by accident when the researcher inadvertently introduces nonrandomness into the sample selection process. The advantage of probability sampling is that sampling error can be calculated. Sampling error is the degree to which a sample might differ from the population. When inferring to the population, results are reported plus or minus the sampling error.

In nonprobability sampling, the degree to which the sample differs from the population remains unknown:

- *Random sampling*: Is the purest form of probability

sampling. Each member of the population has an equal chance of being selected. When there are very large populations, it is often difficult or impossible to identify every member of the population, so the pool of available subjects becomes biased. Random sampling is frequently used to select a specified number of records from a computer file.

- *Systematic sampling*: Is often used instead of random sampling. It is also called an Nth name selection technique. After the required sample size has been calculated, every Nth record is selected from a list of population members. As long as the list does not contain any hidden order, this sampling method is as good as the random sampling method. Its only advantage over the random sampling technique is simplicity.
- *Stratified sampling*: Is commonly used probability method that is superior to random sampling because it reduces sampling error. A stratum is a subset of the population that share at least one common characteristic. The researcher first identifies the relevant stratums and their actual representation in the population. Random sampling is then used to select subjects for each stratum until the number of subjects in that stratum is proportional to its frequency in the population.
- *Convenience sampling*: Is used in exploratory research where the researcher is interested in getting an inexpensive approximation of the truth. As the name implies, the sample is selected because they are convenient. This nonprobability method is often used during preliminary research efforts to get a gross estimate of the results, without incurring the cost or time required to select a random sample.
- *Judgment sampling*: Is a common nonprobability method. The researcher selects the sample based on judgment. This is usually and extension of convenience sampling. For example, a researcher may

decide to draw the entire sample from one "representative" city, even though the population includes all cities. When using this method, the researcher must be confident that the chosen sample is truly representative of the entire population.

- *Quota sampling*: Is the nonprobability equivalent of stratified sampling. Like stratified sampling, the researcher first identifies the stratums and their proportions as they are represented in the population. Then convenience or judgment sampling is used to select the required number of subjects from each stratum. This differs from stratified sampling, where the stratums are filled by random sampling.
- *Snowball sampling*: Is a special nonprobability method used when the desired sample characteristic is rare. It may be extremely difficult or cost prohibitive to locate respondents in these situations. Snowball sampling relies on referrals from initial subjects to generate additional subjects. While this technique can dramatically lower search costs, it comes at the expense of introducing bias because the technique itself reduces the likelihood that the sample will represent a good cross section from the population.

DATA COLLECTION

Data collection is a term used to describe a process of preparing and collecting data - for example as part of a process improvement or similar project. The purpose of data collection is to obtain information to keep on record, to make decisions about important issues, to pass information on to others. Primarily, data is collected to provide information regarding a specific topic.

Data collection usually takes place early on in an improvement project, and is often formalised through a data collection plan which often contains the following activity.

- *Pre collection activity*: Agree goals, target data, definitions, methods
- *Collection*: Data collection

- *Present Findings*: Usually involves some form of sorting analysis and/or presentation.

Prior to any data collection, pre-collection activity is one of the most crucial steps in the process. It is often discovered too late that the value of their interview information is discounted as a consequence of poor sampling of both questions and informants and poor elicitation techniques. After pre-collection activity is fully completed, data collection in the field, whether by interviewing or other methods, can be carried out in a structured, systematic and scientific way.

A formal data collection process is necessary as it ensures that data gathered is both defined and accurate and that subsequent decisions based on arguments embodied in the findings are valid. The process provides both a baseline from which to measure from and in certain cases a target on what to improve.

Types of data collection:

- 1-By mail questionnaires
- 2-By personal interview.

Other main types of collection include census, sample survey, and administrative by-product and each with their respective advantages and disadvantages. A census refers to data collection about everyone or everything in a group or population and has advantages, such as accuracy and detail and disadvantages, such as cost and time. A sample survey is a data collection method that includes only part of the total population and has advantages, such as cost and time and disadvantages, such as accuracy and detail. Administrative by-product data is collected as a byproduct of an organization's day-to-day operations and has advantages, such as accuracy, time simplicity and disadvantages, such as no flexibility and lack of control.

DATA ANALYSIS

Data analysis is a practice in which raw data is ordered and organized so that useful information can be extracted from it. The process of organizing and thinking about data is key to understanding what the data does and does not contain. There are a variety of ways in which people can approach data analysis, and it is notoriously easy to manipulate data during the analysis phase to push certain ceases or agendas. For this reason, it is important to pay attention when data analysis is presented, and to think critic

Raw data can take a variety of forms, including measurements, survey responses, and observations. In its raw form, this information can be incredibly useful, but also overwhelming. Over the course of the data analysis process, the raw data is ordered in a way which will be useful. For example, survey results may be tallied, so that people can see at a glance how many people answered the survey, and how people responded to specific questions.

In the course of organizing the data, trends often emerge, and these trends can be highlighted in the writeup of the data to ensure that readers take note. In a casual survey of ice cream preferences, for example, more women than men might express a fondness for chocolate, and this could be a point of interest for the researcher. Modeling the data with the use of mathematics and other tools can sometimes exaggerate such points of interest in the data, making them easier for the researcher to see.

Charts, graphs, and textual writeups of data are all forms of data analysis. These methods are designed to refine and distill the data so that readers can glean interesting information without needing to sort through all of the data on their own. Summarizing data is often critical to supporting arguments made with that data, as is presenting the data in a clear and understandable way.

When people encounter summarized data and ceases, they should view them critically. Asking where the data is from is important, as is asking about the sampling method used to collect the data, and the size of the sample. If the source of the data appears to have a conflict of interest with the type of data being gathered, this can call the results into question. Likewise, data gathered from a small sample or a sample which is not truly random may be of questionable utility. Reputable researchers will always provide information about the data gathering techniques used, the source of funding, and the point of the data collection in the beginning of the analysis so that readers can think about this information while they review the analysis.

VALIDITY AND RELIABILITY

Validity refers to the accuracy or truthfulness of a measurement. Are we measuring what we think we are? "Validity itself is a simple concept, but the determination of the validity of a measure is elusive".

Face validity is based solely on the judgment of the researcher. Each question is scrutinized and modified until the researcher is satisfied that it is an accurate measure of the desired construct. The determination of face validity is based on the subjective opinion of the researcher.

Content validity is similar to face validity in that it relies on the judgment of the researcher. However, where face validity only evaluates the individual items on an instrument, content validity goes further in that it attempts to determine if an instrument provides adequate coverage of a topic. Expert opinions, literature searches, and pretest open-ended questions help to establish content validity.

Criterion-related validity can be either predictive or concurrent. When a dependent/independent relationship has been established between two or more variables, criterion-related validity can be assessed. A mathematical model is developed to be able to predict the dependent variable from the independent variable(s). Predictive validity refers to the ability of an independent variable to predict a future value of the dependent variable. Concurrent validity is concerned with the relationship between two or more variables at the same point in time.

Construct validity refers to the theoretical foundations underlying a particular scale or measurement. It looks at the underlying theories or constructs that explain a phenomena. This is also quite subjective and depends heavily on the understanding, opinions, and biases of the researcher. Reliability is synonymous with repeatability. A measurement that yields consistent results over time is said to be reliable. When a measurement is prone to random error, it lacks reliability.

The reliability of an instrument places an upper limit on its validity. A measurement that lacks reliability will necessarily be invalid. There are three basic methods to test reliability: test-retest, equivalent form, and internal consistency.

A test-retest measure of reliability can be obtained by administering the same instrument to the same group of people at two different points in time. The degree to which both administrations are in agreement is a measure of the reliability of the instrument. This technique for assessing reliability suffers two possible drawbacks. First, a person may have changed between the first and second measurement. Second, the initial administration of an instrument might in itself induce a person to answer differently on the second administration.

The second method of determining reliability is called the equivalent-form technique. The researcher creates two different instruments designed to measure identical constructs. The degree of correlation between the instruments is a measure of equivalent-form reliability. The difficulty in using this method is that it may be very difficult to create a totally equivalent instrument.

The most popular methods of estimating reliability use measures of internal consistency. When an instrument includes a series of questions designed to examine the same construct, the questions can be arbitrarily split into two groups. The correlation between the two subsets of questions is called the split-half reliability. The problem is that this measure of reliability changes depending on how the questions are split. A better statistic, known as Chronbach's alpha, is based on the mean interitem correlation for all possible variable pairs. It provides a conservative estimate of reliability, and generally represents "the lower bound to the reliability of an unweighted scale of items". For dichotomous nominal data, the KR-20 is used instead of Chronbach's alpha.

VARIABILITY AND ERROR

Most research is an attempt to understand and explain variability. When a measurement lacks variability, no statistical tests can be performed. Variability refers to the dispersion of scores. Ideally, when a researcher finds differences between respondents, they are due to true difference on the variable being measured. However, the combination of systematic and random errors can dilute the accuracy of a measurement. Systematic error is introduced through a constant bias in a measurement. It can usually be traced to a fault in the sampling procedure or in the design of a questionnaire. Random error does not occur in any consistent pattern, and it is not controllable by the researcher.

Scientific research involves the formulation and testing of one or more hypotheses. A hypothesis cannot be proved directly, so a null hypothesis is established to give the researcher an indirect method of testing a theory. Sampling is necessary when the population is too large, or when the researcher is unable to investigate all members of the target group. Random and systematic sampling are the best methods because they guarantee that each member of the population will have an known non-zero chance of being selected. The mathematical reliability of a measurement, or group of measurements, can be calculated, however, validity can only be implied by the data, and it is not directly verifiable. Social science research is generally an attempt to explain or understand the variability in a group of people

HYPOTHESIS TESTING

Questions like the ones fall into a domain called *hypothesis testing*. Hypothesis testing is a way of systematically quantifying how certain you are of the result of a statistical experiment. In the coin example the "experiment" was flipping the coin 100 times. There are two questions you can ask. One, assuming the coin was fair, how likely is it that you'd observe the results we did? Two, what is the likelihood that the coin is fair given the results you observed? Of course, an experiment can be much more complex than coin flipping. Any situation where you're taking a random sample of a population and measuring something about it is an experiment, and for our purposes this includes A/B testing.

Let's focus on the coin flip example understand the basics.

THE NULL HYPOTHESIS

The most common type of hypothesis testing involves a *null hypothesis*. The null hypothesis, denoted H_0, is a statement about the world which can plausibly account for the data you observe. Don't read anything into the fact that it's called the "null" hypothesis — it's just the hypothesis we're trying to test. For example, "the coin is fair" is an example of a null hypothesis, as is "the coin is biased." The important part is that the null hypothesis be able to be expressed in simple, mathematical terms. We'll see how to express these statements mathematically in just a bit.

The main goal of hypothesis testing is to tell us whether we have enough evidence to reject the null hypothesis. In our case we want to know whether the coin is biased or not, so our null hypothesis should be "the coin is fair." If we get enough evidence that contradicts this hypothesis, say, by flipping it 100 times and having it come up heads only once, then we can safely reject it.

All of this is perfectly quantifiable, of course. What constitutes "enough" and "safely" are all a matter of statistics.

THE STATISTICS, INTUITIVELY

So, we have a coin. Our null hypothesis is that this coin is fair. We flip it 100 times and it comes up heads 51 times. Do we know whether the coin is biased or not?

Our gut might say the coin is fair, or at least probably fair, but we can't say for sure. The expected number of heads is 50 and 51 is quite close. But what if we flipped the coin 100,000 times and it came up heads 51,000 times? We see 51% heads both times, but in the second instance the coin is more likely to be biased. Lack of evidence to the contrary is not evidence that the null hypothesis is true. Rather, it means that we don't have sufficient evidence to conclude that the null hypothesis is false. The coin might actually have a 51% bias towards heads, after all. If instead we saw 1 head for 100 flips that would be another story. Intuitively we know that the chance of seeing this if the null hypothesis were true is so small that we would be comfortable rejecting the null hypothesis and declaring the coin to be biased.

THE COIN FLIP

Formally the flip of a coin can be represented by a Bernoulli trial. A Bernoulli trial is a random variable X such that,

$$\Pr(X=1)=1-\Pr(X=0)=1-q=p$$

That is, X takes on the value 1 with probability *p*, and 0 with probability *1 – p*. Now, let's say we have 100 coin flips. Let X_i represent the ith coin flip. Then the random variable,

$$Y=\sum_{i=1}^{100} X_i$$

represents the run of 100 coin flips.

THE STATISTICS, MATHEMATICALLY

Say you have a set of observations O and a null hypothesis H_0. In the coin example we were trying to calculate,

$$P(O \setminus H_0)$$

i.e., the probability that we observed what we did given the null hypothesis. If that probability is sufficiently small we're confident concluding the null hypothesis is false. We can use whatever level of confidence we want before rejecting the null hypothesis, but most people choose 90%, 95%, or 99%. For example if we choose a 95% confidence level we reject the null hypothesis if,

$$P(O \setminus H_0) \le 1-0.95=0.05$$

The Central Limit Theorem is the main piece of math here. Briefly, the Central Limit Theorem says that the sum of any number of re-averaged identically distributed random variables approximates a normal distribution.

Remember our random variables from before? If we let,

$$p=\frac{Y}{N}$$

then p is the proportion of heads in our sample of 100 coin flips. In our case, it is equal to 0.51, or 51%. But by the central limit theorem we also know that p approximates a normal distribution. This means we can estimate the standard deviation of p as,

$$\sigma = \sqrt{\frac{p(1-p)}{N}}$$

WRAPPING IT UP

The coin is fair. Mathematically we're saying

$$H_0 : p_0 = 0.05$$

Here's the normal curve:

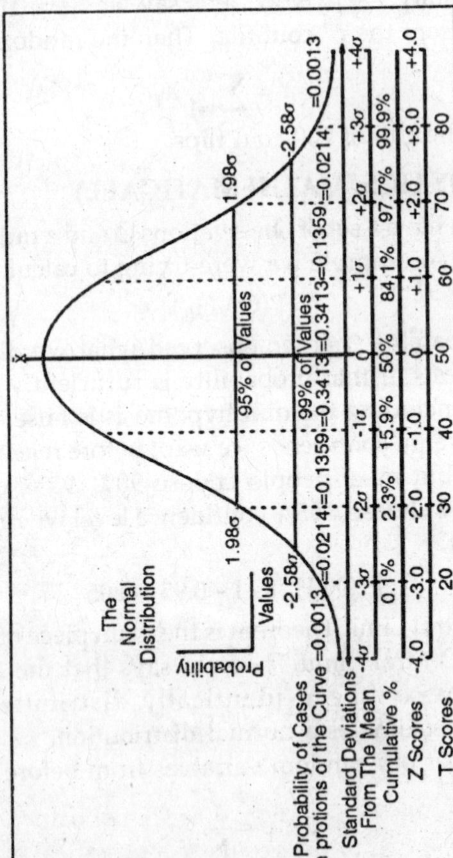

A 95% level of confidence means we reject the null hypothesis if *p* falls outside 95% of the area of the normal curve. Looking at that chart we see that this corresponds to approximately 1.98 standard deviations.

The so-called "z-score" tells us how many standard deviations away from the mean our sample is, and it's calculated as,

$$z = \frac{p - 0.50}{\sqrt{\frac{0.50(1-0.50)}{N}}}$$

The numerator is "p – 0.50" because our null hypothesis is that p = 0.50. This measures how far the sample mean, p, diverges from the expect mean of a fair coin, 0.50.

THE DATA

Let's say we flipped three coins 100 times each and got the following data.

Table. Data for 100 Flips of a Coin

Coin	Flips	Pct. Heads	Z-score
Coin 1	100	51%	0.20
Coin 2	100	60%	2.04
Coin 3	100	75%	5.77

Using a 95% confidence level we'd conclude that Coin 2 and Coin 3 are biased using the techniques we've developed so far. Coin 2 is 2.04 standard deviations from the mean and Coin 3 is 5.77 standard deviations.

When your test statistic meets the 95% confidence threshold we call it *statistically significant.*

This means there's only a 5% chance of observing what you did assuming the null hypothesis was true. Phrased another way, there's only a 5% chance that your observation is due to random variation.

RECAP

Hypothesis testing is a way of systematically quantifying how certain you are of the result of a statistical experiment.

You start by forming a null hypothesis, e.g., "this coin is fair," and then calculate the likelihood that your observations are due to pure chance rather than a real difference in the population.

The confidence interval is the level at which you reject the null hypothesis. If there is a 95% chance that there's a real difference in your observations, given the null hypothesis, then you are confident in rejecting it. This also means there is a 5% chance you're wrong and the difference is due to random fluctuations.

The null hypothesis can be any mathematical statement and the test you use depends on both the underlying data and your null hypothesis. In our coin flipping example the underlying data approximated a normal distribution and we wanted to test whether the observed proportion of heads was different enough to be significant. In this case we were measuring the *sample mean*.

We can measure anything, though: the sample variance, correlation, etc. Different tests needs to be used to determine whether these are statistically significant.

4

Research Design

EXPERIMENTAL QUASI-EXPERIMENTAL DESIGN

The design of any experiment is of utmost importance because it has the power to be the most rigid type of research. The design, however, is always dependent on feasibility. The best approach is to control for as many confounding variables as possible in order to eliminate or reduce errors in the assumptions that will be made. It is also extremely desirable that any threats to internal or external validity be neutralized. In the perfect world, all research would do this and the results of research would be accurate and powerful. In the real world, however, this is rarely the case. We are often dealing with human subjects, which in itself confounds any study. We are also dealing with the restraints of time and situation, often resulting in less than perfect conditions in which to gather information.

There are three basic experimental designs, each containing subsets with specific strengths and weaknesses.

These three basic designs include:

1. Pre-experimental design;
2. Quasi-experimental design; and
3. True experimental design.

PRE-EXPERIMENTAL DESIGN

Pre-experimental designs are so named because they follow basic experimental steps but fail to include a control group. In other words, a single group is often studied but no comparison between an equivalent non-treatment group is made. Examples include the following:

The One-Shot Case Study

In this arrangement, subjects are presented with some type of treatment, such as a semester of college work experience, and then the outcome measure is applied, such as college grades. Like all experimental designs, the goal is to determine if the treatment had any effect on the outcome. Without a comparison group, it is impossible to determine if the outcome scores are any higher than they would have been without the treatment. And, without any pre-test scores, it is impossible to determine if any change within the group itself has taken place.

One Group Pretest Posttest Study

A benefit of this design over the previously discussed design is the inclusion of a pretest to determine baseline scores. To use this design in our study of college performance, we could compare college grades prior to gaining the work experience to the grades after completing a semester of work experience. We can now at least state whether a change in the outcome or dependent variable has taken place. What we cannot say is if this change would have occurred even without the application of the treatment or independent variable. It is possible that mere maturation caused the change in grades and not the work experience itself.

The Static Group Comparison Study

This design attempts to make up for the lack of a control group but falls short in relation to showing if a change has occurred. In the static group comparison study, two groups are chosen, one of which receives the treatment and the other does not. A posttest score is then determined to measure the difference, after treatment, between the two groups. As you can see, this study does not include any pre-testing and therefore any difference between the two groups prior to the study are unknown.

One Shot Case Study

X O_2

One Group Pretest Posttest Study

O_1 X O_2

Static Group Comparison Study

X O2
  O2

Key:
X = Treatment
O_1= Pretest
O_2= Posttest
R = Randomization

Fig. Diagrams of Pre-Experimental Designs

QUASI-EXPERIMENTAL DESIGN

Quasi designs fair better than pre-experimental studies in that they employ a means to compare groups. They fall short, however on one very important aspect of the experiment: randomization.

Pretest Posttest Nonequivalent Group

With this design, both a control group and an experimental group is compared, however, the groups are chosen and assigned out of convenience rather than through randomization. This might be the method of choice for our study on work experience as it would be difficult to choose students in a college setting at random and place them in specific groups and classes. We might ask students to participate in a one-semester work experience programme. We would then measure all of the students' grades prior to the start of the programme and then again after the programme. Those students who participated would be our treatment group; those who did not would be our control group.

Time Series Designs

Tim series designs refer to the pretesting and posttesting of one group of subjects at different intervals. The purpose might be to determine long term effect of treatment and therefore the number of pre- and posttests can vary from one each to many. Sometimes there is an interruption between tests in order to assess the strength of treatment over an extended time period. When such a design is employed, the posttest is referred to as follow-up.

Nonequivalent Before-After Design

This design is used when we want to compare two groups that are likely to be different even before the study begins. In other words, if we want to see how a new treatment affects people with different psychological disorders, the disorders themselves would create two or more nonequivalent groups. Once again, the number of pretests and posttests can vary from one each to many. The obvious concern with all of the quasi-experimental designs results from the method of choosing subjects to participate in the experiment. While we could compare grades and determine if there was a difference between the two groups before and after the study, we could not state that this difference is related to the work experience itself or some other confounding variable. It is certainly possible that those who volunteered for the study were inherently different in terms of motivation from those who did not participate. Whenever subjects are chosen for groups based on convenience rather than randomization, the reason for inclusion in the study itself confounds our results.

Pretest Posttest Nonequivalent Groups

$O_1 \quad X \quad O_2$

$O_1 \quad X \quad O_2$

Time Series Designs

$O_1 \quad O_1 X \quad O_2$

Nonequivalent Before-After Design

$O_1 \quad O_1 \quad X \quad O_2 \quad O_2$

$O_1 \quad O_1 \quad X \quad O_2 \quad O_2$

Key:
X = Treatment
O_1 = Pretest
O_2 = Posttest
R = Randomization

Fig. Diagrams of Quasi Experimental Designs

TRUE EXPERIMENTAL DESIGN

True experimental design makes up for the shortcomings of the two designs previously discussed. They employ both a control group and a means to measure the change that occurs in both groups. In this sense, we attempt to control for all confounding variables, or at least consider their impact, while attempting to determine if the treatment is what truly caused the change. The true experiment is often thought of as the only research method that can adequately measure the cause and effect relationship.

Posttest Equivalent Groups Study

Randomization and the comparison of both a control and an experimental group are utilized in this type of study. Each group, chosen and assigned at random is presented with either the treatment or some type of control. Posttests are then given to each subject to determine if a difference between the two groups exists. While this is approaching the best method, it falls short in its lack of a pretest measure. It is difficult to determine if the difference apparent at the end of the study is an actual change from the possible difference at the beginning of the study. In other words, randomization does well to mix subjects but it does not completely assure us that this mix is truly creating an equivalency between the two groups.

Pretest Posttest Equivalent Groups Study

Of those discussed, this method is the most effective in terms of demonstrating cause and effect but it is also the most difficult to perform. The pretest posttest equivalent groups design provides for both a control group and a measure of change but also adds a pretest to assess any differences between the groups prior to the study taking place.

To apply this design to our work experience study, we would select students from the college at random and then place the chosen students into one of two groups using random assignment.

We would then measure the previous semester's grades for each group to get a mean grade point average. The treatment, or work experience would be applied to one group and a control would be applied to the other.

It is important that the two groups be treated in a similar manner to control for variables such as socialization, so we may allow our control group to participate in some activity such as a softball league while the other group is participating in the work experience programme.

At the end of the semester, the experiment would end and the next semester's grades would be gathered and compared. If we found that the change in grades for the experimental group was significantly different than the change in the grades of our control group, we could reasonably argue that one semester of work experience compared to one semester of non-work related activity results in a significant difference in grades.

Posttest Equivalent Group

R X O_2

R X O_2

Pretest Posttest Equivalent Group

R O_1 X O_2

R O_1 X O_2

Key:

X = Treatment

O_1 = Pretest

O_2 = Posttest

R = Randomization

Fig. Diagrams of True Experimental Designs

NOW WE CAN SAY

The experiment, especially the true experimental design is often the measure of choice when attempting to determine a cause and effect relationship. Utilizing randomization and the pre-testing and post-testing of both an experimental group and a control group allows us to control for more confounding variables than any other research method. These confounding variables, when not addressed, can often result in inaccurate findings.

Controlling for confounding variables is important in research and especially important in the experimental designs.

This process helps us assure valid results both internally and externally. The threats to internal validity, those that apply to the experimental situation itself, and external validity, those relating to the generalizability of our results to the real world are also issues of great concern to researchers. As the saying goes: garbage in, garbage out. If we start with a flawed design as suggested, end up with flawed results.

As the degree of control for each of the designs discussed increases, the difficulty in performing the research also increases. Feasibility is always an issue and even when the most stringent control is used, the mere fact that the subjects have agreed to participate in the experiment may have a negative effect on the study's generalizability. Are volunteer subjects truly representative of the population at large? As you can see, there are varying degrees of experimental research, but there is no perfect experiment that controls for all possible variables and assures us of 100% generalizability.

CORRELATIONAL DESIGNS

Alternative Explanatory Variables:

- A developmental psychologist has noticed that children with bigger feet tend to have greater vocabularies than children with smaller feet?
- This is an example of a simple correlational design. Can you think of a powerful alternative explanation?

TYPES OF DATA AND CORRELATIONAL DESIGNS

- Varieties of data
  - Direct
    - i. Self report of personality/attitudes/values
    - ii. Peer/supervisor/subordinate ratings of performance
    - iii. Ability scales
  - Indirect
    - i. Implicit measures
    - ii. Unobtrusive measures
- Historical, archival

THEORY AND THEORY TESTING I: THEORY

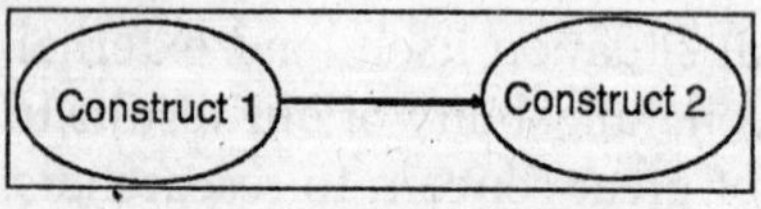

THEORY AND THEORY TESTING II: EXPERIMENTAL MANIPULATION

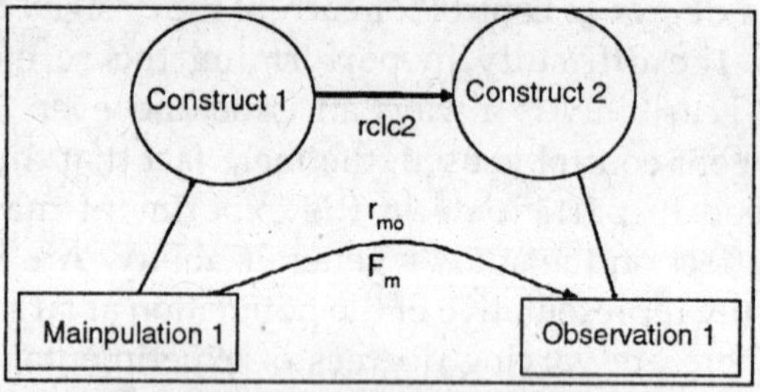

THEORY AND THEORY TESTING III: CORRELATIONAL INFERENCE

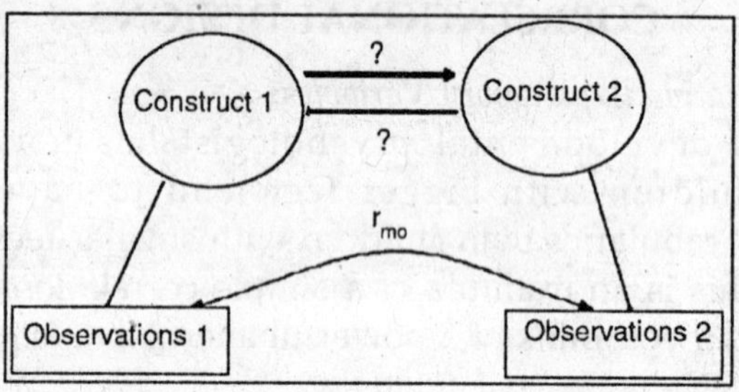

THEORY AND THEORY TESTING IV: CORRELATIONAL INFERENCE

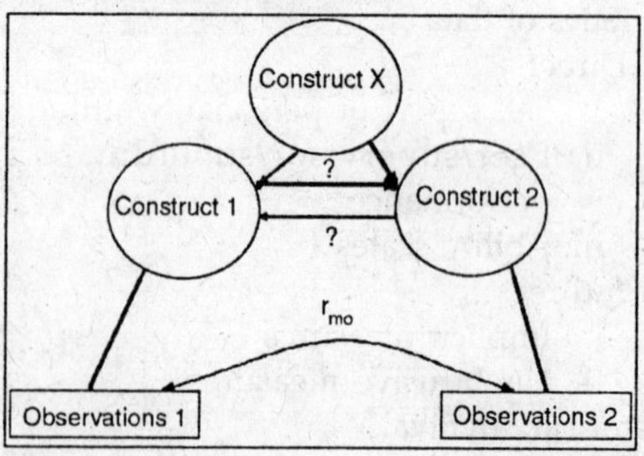

THEORY AND THEORY TESTING V: ALTERNATIVE EXPLANATIONS

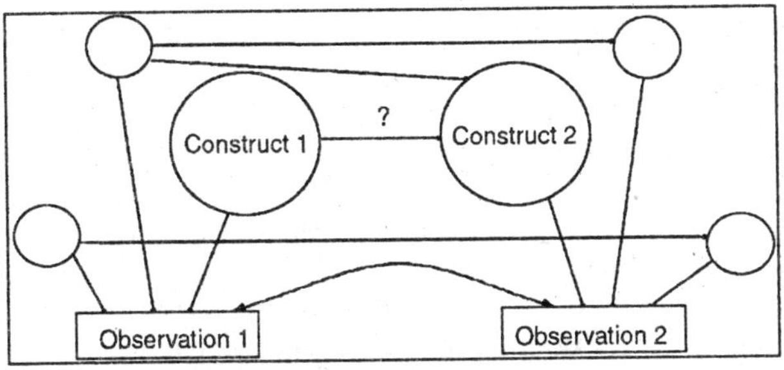

THEORY AND THEORY TESTING VI: ELIMINATE ALTERNATIVE EXPLANATIONS

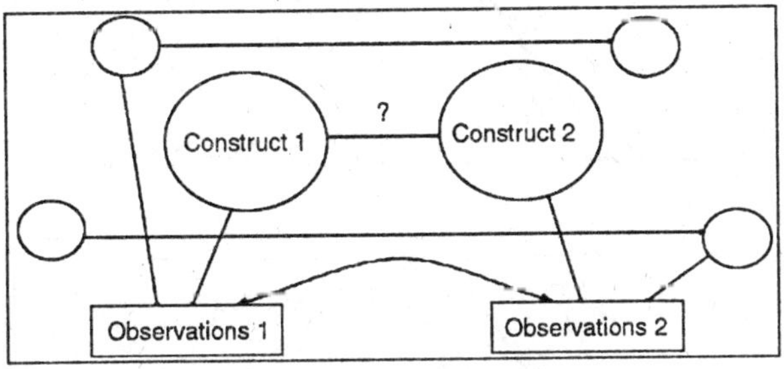

STEPS IN CORRELATIONAL INFERENCE

- Estimate the reliability of the variables
  - Magnitude of correlation is influenced by the reliability of the correlation
  - Varieties of reliability
- Estimate the construct validity of the measures
  - Convergent, Discriminant, Incremental validity
- Consider alternative explananatory variables

CLASSIC RELIABILITY THEORY: HOW WELL DO WE MEASURE WHAT EVER WE ARE MEASURING

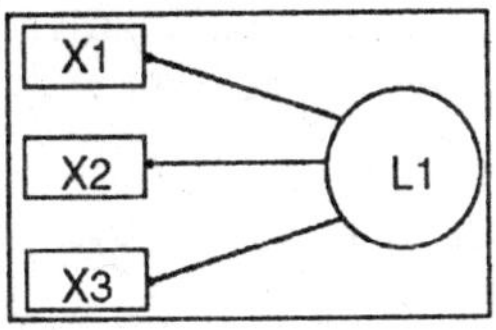

Classic Reliability Theory

How well do we measure what ever we are measuring and what is the relationships between latent variables.

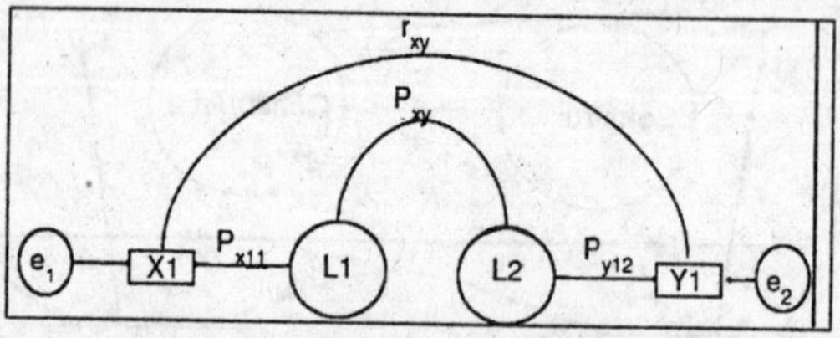

Fig. Observed= True + Error

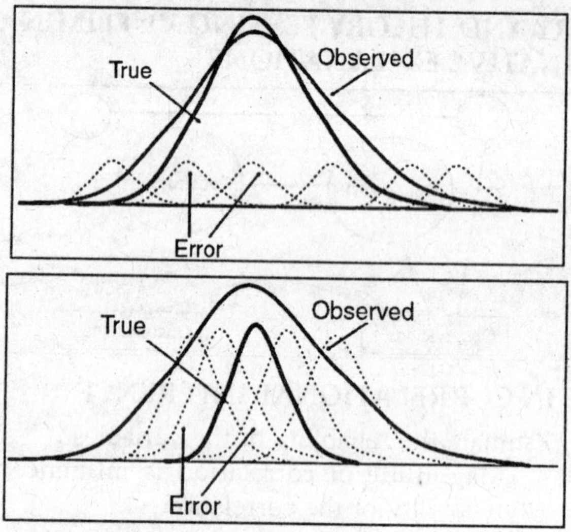

RELIABILITY OF MEASUREMENT

(How well does an observation reflect the construct)

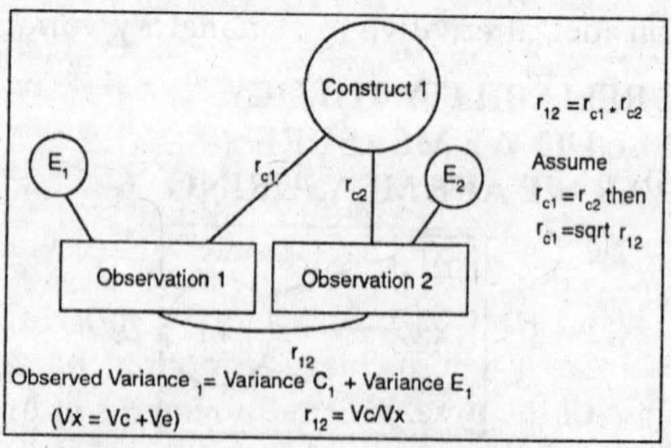

(How well does an observation reflect the construct)

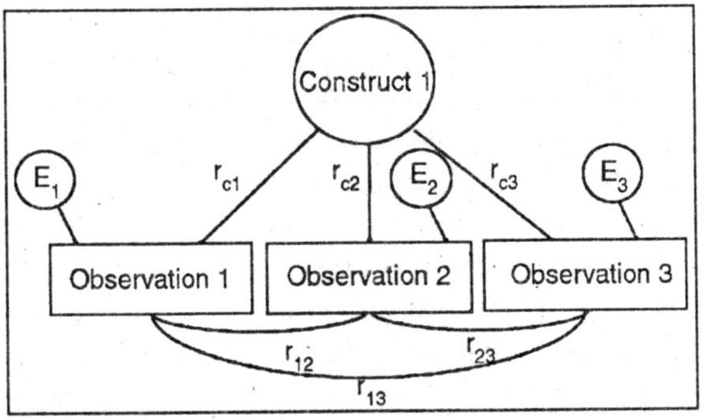

DOMAIN SAMPLING THEORY

Consider a domain (D) of k items relevant to a construct.. Let Di represent the number of items in D which the subject can pass given all D items. Call this the domain score for subject I. What is the correlation of scores on an item j with the domain scores?

THE NATURE OF CORRELATION

Correlational research studies almost always use the correlation coefficient to indicate the degree of relationship bwtween two variaables. The correlation coefficient is a number ranging from 1 through 0 to –1. It is tempting to think of a correlation coefficient as indicating the proportaion of sameness between the two variables.

But this is not true: A correlation of.90 does not mean that the two variables are 90% the same. In fact, the proportion of common variance for a correlation of.90 is.81 or 81%. The proportion of commmon variance is the square of the correlation coefficient. If we have a correlation of.50 between two variables the proportion of common variance is only.25 or 25% (.50 x.50 =.2500). We could say that the two variables demonstrate 25% sameness but 75% (100 – 25) differentness.

ACTION RESEARCH DESIGN

Action Research (AR) represents a growing field of educational research whose chief identifying characteristic is the recognition of the pragmatic requirements of educational practitioners for organized reflective inquiry into classroom instruction. AR is an process designed to empower all participants in the educational process (students, instructors and other parties) with the means to improve the practices conducted within the educational experience. All participants were knowing, active members of the research process.

Action research has been described as an informal, qualitative, formative, subjective, interpretive, reflective and experiential model of inquiry in which all individuals involved in the study are knowing and contributing participants. Action research has the primary intent of providing a framework for qualitative investigations by teachers and researchers in complex working classroom situations. *Some of the most widely accepted definitions of Action Research include following*:

- *Action Research*: Aims to contribute both to the practical concerns of people in an immediate problematic situation and to the goals of social science by joint collaboration within a mutually acceptable ethical framework.
- Action Research is a form of self-reflective enquiry undertaken by participants in social (including educational) situations in order to improve the rationality and justice of
  - Their own social or educational practices,
  - Their understanding of these practices, and
  - The situations in which the practices are carried out. It is most rationally empowering when undertaken by participants collabor-atively... sometimes in cooperation with outsiders.
- *Action Research*: Is the systematic study of attempts to improve educational practise by groups of participants by means of their own practical actions and by means of their own reflection upon the effects of those actions.

The action research framework is most appropriate for participants who recognize the existence of shortcomings in their educational activities and who would like to adopt some initial stance in regard to the problem, formulate a plan, carry out an intervention, evaluate the outcomes and develop further strategies in an iterative fashion. In short, action research is characterized by those constraints and strengths given a research methodology intended to be a workable technique for working classroom teachers.

ACTION RESEARCH DESIGN

The essentials of action research design are considered by Elliott as per the following characteristic cycle:

- Initially an exploratory stance is adopted, where an understanding of a problem is developed and plans are made for some form of interventionary strategy.
- Then the intervention is carried out.
- During and around the time of the intervention, pertinent observations are collected in various forms.
- The new interventional strategies are carried out, and the cyclic process repeats, continuing until a sufficient understanding of the problem is achieved.

The protocol is iterative or cyclical in nature and is intended to foster deeper understanding of a given situation, starting with conceptualizing and particularizing the problem and moving through several interventions and evaluations. A representation of an AR protocol by Kemmis is provided in Figure.

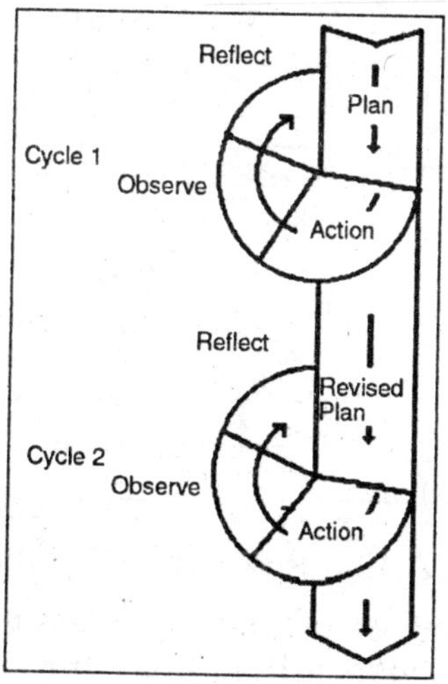

Fig. Action Research Protocol after Kemmis

Figure clearly displays the iterative nature of AR along with the major steps of planning, action, observation and reflection before revising the plan. This may be thought of as similar in nature to the numerical computing technique known as successive approximation - the idea is to close in upon a final goal or outcome by repeated iterations.

Later protocols reflect changes in the goal as determined via experience during the reflections of earlier iterations of AR. For instance, Figure reflects the evolution of the general idea or main topic of interest throughout the process.

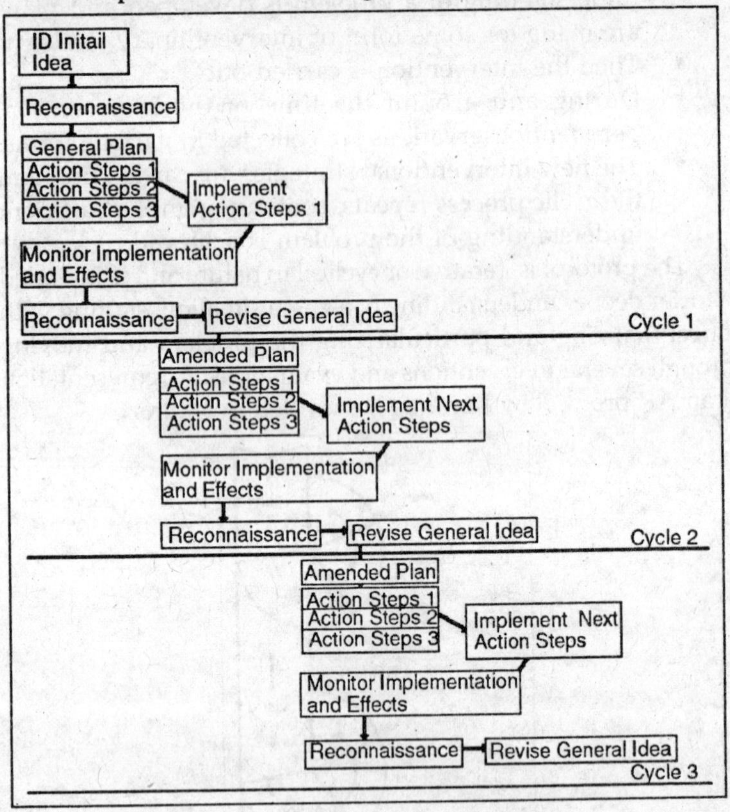

Fig. Action Research after Elliott

Elliott's model emphasizes constant evolution and redefinition of the original goal through a series of reconnaissances recurring every cycle. The reconnaissance necessarily includes some degree of analysis. This design permits much greater flexibility, and seeks to "*...recapture some of the 'messiness' which the Kemmis version tends to gloss [over]* ". Ebbutt further emphasizes the evolution of the overall plan through a spiral analogy.

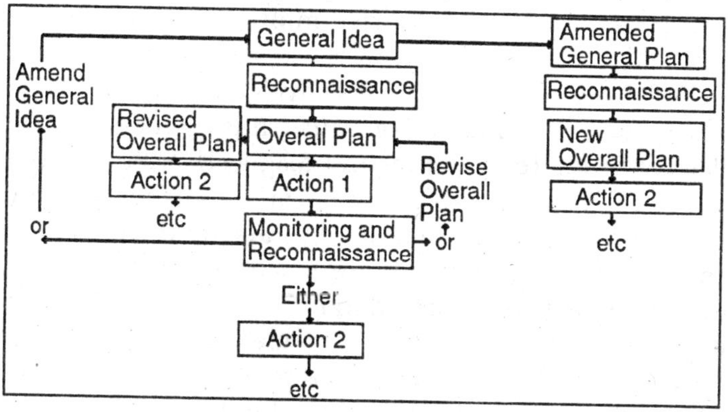

Fig. Action Research Protocol after Ebbutt

THE ROLE OF COMMUNICATION

Another distinguishing characteristic of Action Research is the degree of empowerment given to all participants. Involvement is of a knowing nature, with no hidden controls or preemption of direction by the researcher. All participants negotiate meaning from the data and contribute to the selection of interventionary strategies, including the university researchers, the teachers and the students.

THE ROLE OF REFLECTION

Another distinguishing characteristic of action research is the degree of empowerment given to all participants. Involvement is of a knowing nature, with no hidden controls or preemption of direction by the researcher. All participants including the university researchers, the teachers and the students negotiate meaning from the data and contribute to the selection of interventionary strategies.

Elliott considers the need for communication between all participants to be of paramount importance:

Since action research looks at a problem from the point of view of those involved it can only be validated in unconstrained dialogue with them....Since action research involves unconstrained dialogue between"researcher" (whether he be an outsider or teacher/researcher) and the participants, there must be free information flow between them.

Perhaps the key component involved in action research is the notion of praxis. Action research is intended to be the reflective counterpart of practical diagnosis. Schon describes the use of reflection to generate models from a body of previous knowledge. These models are used to re-frame a problem; then experiments are performed to bring about outcomes which are subjected to further analysis. This model (called reflection-in-action) frames means and ends interdependently and recognizes that there is little or no separation of research from practice, little or no separation of knowing and doing. Schon's model of reflection-in-action compliments the iterative and investigative natures of action research.

CASE STUDY RESEARCH DESIGN

The case study research design have evolved over the past few years as a useful tool for investigating trends and specific situations in many scientific disciplines, especially social science, psychology, anthropology and ecology. This method of study is especially useful for trying to test theoretical models by using them in real world situations. For example, if an anthropologist were to live amongst a remote tribe, whilst their observations might produce no quantitative data, they are still useful to science.

WHAT IS A CASE STUDY?

Basically, a case study is an in depth study of a particular situation rather than a sweeping statistical survey. It is a method used to narrow down a very broad field of research into one easily researchable topic. Whilst it will not answer a question completely, it will give some indications and allow further elaboration and hypothesis creation on a subject. The case study research design is also useful for testing whether scientific theories and models actually work in the real world. You may come out with a great computer model for describing how the ecosystem of a rock pool works but it is only by trying it out on a real life pool that you can see if it is a realistic simulation.

For psychologists, anthropologists and social scientists they have been regarded as a valid method of research for many years. Scientists are sometimes guilty of becoming bogged down in the general picture and it is sometimes important to understand specific cases and ensure a more holistic approach to research.

THE ARGUMENT FOR AND AGAINST THE CASE STUDY RESEARCH DESIGN

Some argue that because a case study is such a narrow field that its results cannot be extrapolated to fit an entire question and that they show only one narrow example. On the other hand, it is argued that a case study provides more realistic responses than a purely statistical survey. The truth probably lies between the two and it is probably best to try and synergize the two approaches. It is valid to conduct case studies but they should be tied in with more general statistical processes. For example, a statistical survey might show how much time people spend talking on mobile phones, but it is case studies of a narrow group that will determine why this is so. The other main thing to remember during case studies is their flexibility.

Whilst a pure scientist is trying to prove or disprove a hypothesis, a case study might introduce new and unexpected results during its course, and lead to research taking new directions. The argument between case study and statistical method also appears to be one of scale. Whilst many 'physical' scientists avoid case studies, for psychology, anthropology and ecology they are an essential tool. It is important to ensure that you realise that a case study cannot be generalized to fit a whole population or ecosystem. Finally, one peripheral point is that, when informing others of your results, case studies make more interesting topics than purely statistical surveys, something that has been realised by teachers and magazine editors for many years. The general public has little interest in pages of statistical calculations but some well placed case studies can have a strong impact.

HOW TO DESIGN AND CONDUCT A CASE STUDY

The advantage of the case study research design is that you can focus on specific and interesting cases. This may be an attempt to test a theory with a typical case or it can be a specific topic that is of interest. Research should be thorough and note taking should be meticulous and systematic. The first foundation of the case study is the subject and relevance. In a case study, you are deliberately trying to isolate a small study group, one individual case or one particular population.

For example, statistical analysis may have shown that birthrates in African countries are increasing. A case study on one or two specific countries becomes a powerful and focused tool for determining the social and economic pressures driving this.

In the design of a case study, it is important to plan and design how you are going to address the study and make sure that all collected data is relevant. Unlike a scientific report, there is no strict set of rules so the most important part is making sure that the study is focused and concise; otherwise you will end up having to wade through a lot of irrelevant information.

It is best if you make yourself a short list of 4 or 5 bullet points that you are going to try and address during the study. If you make sure that all research refers back to these then you will not be far wrong. With a case study, even more than a questionnaire or survey, it is important to be passive in your research. You are much more of an observer than an experimenter and you must remember that, even in a multi-subject case, each case must be treated individually and then cross case ceases can be drawn.

HOW TO ANALYSE THE RESULTS

Analyzing results for a case study tends to be more opinion based than statistical methods. The usual idea is to try and collate your data into a manageable from and construct a narrative around it.

Use examples in your narrative whilst keeping things concise and interesting. It is useful to show some numerical data but remember that you are only trying to judge trends and not analyse every last piece of data. Constantly refer back to your bullet points so that you do not lose focus.

It is always a good idea to assume that a person reading your research may not possess a lot of knowledge of the subject so try to write accordingly.

In addition, unlike a scientific study which deals with facts, a case study is based on opinion and is very much designed to provoke reasoned debate. There really is no right or wrong answer in a case study.

5

Data

DATA COLLECTION

Data collection is a term used to describe a process of preparing and collecting data - for example as part of a process improvement or similar project. The purpose of data collection is to obtain information to keep on record, to make decisions about important issues, to pass information on to others. Primarily, data is collected to provide information regarding a specific topic.

Data collection usually takes place early on in an improvement project, and is often formalised through a data collection plan which often contains the following activity:

- *Pre collection activity*: Agree goals, target data, definitions, methods
- *Collection*: Data collection
- *Present Findings*: Usually involves some form of sorting analysis and/or presentation.

Prior to any data collection, pre-collection activity is one of the most crucial steps in the process. It is often discovered too late that the value of their interview information is discounted as a consequence of poor sampling of both questions and informants and poor elicitation techniques. After pre-collection activity is fully completed, data collection in the field, whether by interviewing or other methods, can be carried out in a structured, systematic and scientific way.

A formal data collection process is necessary as it ensures that data gathered is both defined and accurate and that subsequent decisions based on arguments embodied in the findings are valid. The process provides both a baseline from which to measure from and in certain cases a target on what to improve.

Types of data collection:

- 1-By mail questionnaires
- 2-By personal interview.

Other main types of collection include census, sample survey, and administrative by-product and each with their respective advantages and disadvantages. A census refers to data collection about everyone or everything in a group or population and has advantages, such as accuracy and detail and disadvantages, such as cost and time. A sample survey is a data collection method that includes only part of the total population and has advantages, such as cost and time and disadvantages, such as accuracy and detail. Administrative by-product data is collected as a byproduct of an organization's day-to-day operations and has advantages, such as accuracy, time simplicity and disadvantages, such as no flexibility and lack of control.

STUDY DESIGN

EFFECT SIZE

In statistics, an effect size is a measure of the strength of the relationship between two variables in a statistical population, or a sample-based estimate of that quantity. An effect size calculated from data is a descriptive statistic that conveys the estimated magnitude of a relationship without making any statement about whether the apparent relationship in the data reflects a true relationship in the population. In that way, effect sizes complement inferential statistics such as p-values. Among other uses, effect size measures play an important role in meta-analysis studies that summarize findings from a specific area of research, and in statistical power analyses.

The concept of effect size appears already in everyday language. For example, a weight loss programme may boast that it leads to an average weight loss of 30 pounds. In this case, 30 pounds is an indicator of the claimed effect size. Another example is that a tutoring programme may claim that it raises school performance by one letter grade. This grade increase is the claimed effect size of the programme. These are both examples of "absolute effect sizes," meaning that they convey the average difference between two groups without any discussion of the variability within the groups. For example, if the weight loss programme results in an average loss of 30 pounds, we do not know if every participant loses exactly 30 pounds, or if half the participants lose 60 pounds and half the participants lose no weight at all.

Reporting effect sizes is considered good practice when presenting empirical research findings in many fields. Effect sizes are particularly prominent in social and medical research. Relative and absolute measures of effect size convey different information, and can be used complementarily.

Types

Pearson r Correlation

Pearson's correlation, often denoted r and introduced by Karl Pearson, is widely used as an effect size when paired quantitative data are available; for instance if one were studying the relationship between birth weight and longevity. The correlation coefficient can also be used when the data are binary. Pearson's r can vary in magnitude from –1 to 1, with –1 indicating a perfect negative linear relation, 1 indicating a perfect positive linear relation, and 0 indicating no linear relation between two variables. Cohen gives the following guidelines for the social sciences: small effect size, r = 0.1 – 0.23; medium, r = 0.24 – 0.36; large, r = 0.37 or larger.

A related effect size is the coefficient of determination. In the case of paired data, this is a measure of the proportion of variance shared by the two variables, and varies from 0 to 1. An r^2 of 0.21 means that 21% of the variance of either variable is shared with the other variable. The r^2 is positive, so does not convey the polarity of the relationship between the two variables.

Effect Sizes Based on Means

A effect size θ based on means usually considers the standardized mean difference between two populations:

$$\theta = \frac{\mu_1 - \mu_2}{\sigma}$$

where μ_1 is the mean for one population, μ_2 is the mean for the other population, and σ is a standard deviation based on either or both populations.

In the practical setting the population values are typically not known and must be estimated from sample statistics. The several versions of effect sizes based on means differ with respect to which statistics are used.

This form for the effect size resembles the computation for a t-test statistic, with the critical difference that the t-test statistic includes a factor of $\sqrt{n}$. This means that for a given effect size, the significance level increases with the sample size. Unlike the t-test statistic, the effect size aims to estimate a population parametre, so is not affected by the sample size.

Cohen's d

Cohen's d is defined as the difference between two means divided by a standard deviation for the data

$$d = \frac{\bar{x}_1 - \bar{x}_2}{s},$$

What precisely the standard deviation s is was not originally made explicit by Jacob Cohen because he defined it as "the standard deviation of either population Other authors make the computation of the standard deviation more explicit with the following definition for a pooled standard deviation

$$s = \sqrt{\frac{(n_1 - 1)s_1^2 + (n_2 - 1)s_2^2}{n_1 + n_2}},$$

with $\bar{x}_k$ and s_k as the mean and standard deviation for group k, for k = 1, 2.

$$s_1^2 = \frac{1}{n_1 - 1}\sum_{i=1}^{n1}(x_{1,i} - \bar{x}_1)^2$$

This definition of "Cohen's d" is termed the maximum likelihood estimator by Hedges and Olkin, and it is related to Hedges' g by a scaling:

$$g = \sqrt{\frac{n_1 + n_2 - 2}{n_1 + n_2}}$$

Glass's Δ

In 1976 Gene V. Glass proposed an estimator of the effect size that uses only the standard deviation of the second group :

$$\Delta = \frac{\overline{x}_1 - \overline{x}_2}{s_2}$$

The second group may be regarded as a control group, and Glass argued that if several treatments were compared to the control group it would be better to use just the standard deviation computed from the control group, so that effect sizes would not differ under equal means and different variances.

Under an assumption of equal population variances a pooled estimate for ó is more precise.

Hedges' g

Hedges' g, suggested by Larry Hedges in 1981, is like the other measures based on a standardized difference

$$g = \frac{\overline{x}_1 - \overline{x}_2}{s^*}$$

but its pooled standard deviation s^* is computed slightly differently from Cohen's d

$$s^* = \sqrt{\frac{(n_1 - 1)s_1^2 + (n_2 - 1)s_2^2}{n_1 + n_2 - 2}}$$

As an estimator for the population effect size θ it is biased. However, this bias can be corrected for by multiplication with a factor

$$g^* = J(n_1 + n_2 - 2)g \approx \left(1 - \frac{3}{4(n_1 + n_2) - 9}\right)g$$

Hedges and Olkin refer to this unbiased estimator g^* as

d, but it is not the same as Cohen's d. The exact form for the correction factor J involves the gamma function

$$J(a) = \frac{\Gamma(a/2)}{\sqrt{a/2}\,\Gamma((a-1)/2)}.$$

Distribution of Effect Sizes Based on Means

Provided that the data is Gaussian distributed a scaled Hedges' g,

$$\sqrt{(n_1 n_2/(n_1+n_2)}\,g,$$

follows a noncentral t-distribution with the noncentrality parametre

$$\sqrt{(n_1 n_2/(n_1+n_2)}\,\theta$$

and $n_1 + n_2$ 2 degrees of freedom. Likewise, the scaled Glass' Δ is distributed with $n_2 - 1$ degrees of freedom.

From the distribution it is possible to compute the expectation and variance of the effect sizes.

In some cases large sample approximations for the variance are used. One suggestion for the variance of Hedges' unbiased estimator is

$$\hat{\sigma}^2(g^*) = \frac{n_1+n_2}{n_1 n_2} + \frac{(g^*)^2}{2(n_1+n_2)}.$$

Cohen's f^2

Cohen's f^2 is an appropriate effect size measure to use in the context of an F-test for ANOVA or multiple regression. The f^2 effect size measure for multiple regression is defined as:

$$f^2 = \frac{R^2}{1-R^2}$$

where R^2 is the squared multiple correlation.

The f^2 effect size measure for hierarchical multiple regression is defined as:

$$f^2 = \frac{R^2{}_{AB} - R^2 A}{1-R^2{}_{AB}}$$

where R^2_A is the variance accounted for by a set of one or more independent variables A, and R^2_{AB} is the combined variance accounted for by A and another set of one or more independent variables B.

By convention, f^2_A effect sizes of 0.02, 0.15, and 0.35 are termed small, medium, and large, respectively.

Cohen's $\hat{f}$ can also be found for factorial analysis of variance working backwards using:

$$\hat{f}_{effect} = \sqrt{(df_{effect} / N)(F_{effect} - 1)}.$$

In a balanced design of ANOVA, the corresponding population parametre of f^2 is,

$$\frac{SS(\mu_1, \mu_2, \cdots \mu k)}{K \times \sigma^2},$$

wherein μ_j denotes the population mean within the jth group of the total K groups, and ó the equivalent population standard deviations within each groups. SS is the sum of squares manipulation in ANOVA.

φ, Cramér's φ, or Cramér's V

The odds ratio is another useful effect size. It is appropriate when both variables are binary. For example, consider a study on spelling. In a control group, two students pass the class for every one who fails, so the odds of passing are two to one.

In the treatment group, six students pass for every one who fails, so the odds of passing are six to one. The effect size can be computed by noting that the odds of passing in the treatment group are three times higher than in the control group. Therefore, the odds ratio is 3. However, odds ratio statistics are on a different scale to Cohen's d. So, this '3' is not comparable to a Cohen's d of 3.

Relative Risk

The relative risk also called risk ratio, is simply the risk of an event relative to some independent variable. This measure of effect size differs from the odds ratio in that it compares probabilities instead of odds, but asymptotically approaches the latter for small probabilities. Using the example, the probabilities for those in the control group and treatment group passing is 2/3 and 6/7, respectively.

The effect size can be computed, but using the probabitities instead. Therefore, the relative risk is 1.28. Since rather large probabilities of passing were used, there is a large difference between relative risk and odds ratio. Had failure been used as the event, the difference between the two measures of effect size would not be so great.

While both measures are useful, they have different statistical uses. In medical research, for example, the odds ratio is favoured for case-control studies and retrospective studies. Relative risk is used in randomized controlled trials and cohort studies.

It is also worth noting that one cannot automatically predict the other, though with small probabilities one can be considered a fairly good estimate of the other.

Confidence Interval and Relation to Noncentral Parametres

Confidence interval of unstandardized effect size like difference of means can be found in common statistics textbooks and software, while confidence intervals of standardized effect size, especially Cohen's,

$$\tilde{d} := \frac{\mu_1 - \mu_2}{\sigma}$$

and

$$\tilde{f}^2 := \frac{SS(\mu_1, \mu_2, \cdots \mu_K}{K.\sigma},$$

rely on the calculation of confidence intervals of noncentral parametres. A common approach to construct confidence interval of ncp is to find the critical ncp values to fit the observed statistic to tail quantiles $\alpha/2$ and $(1 - \alpha/2)$. SAS and R-package MBESS provide functions for critical ncp. An online calculator based on R and MediaWiki provides interactive interface, which requires no coding and welcomes copy-left collaboration.

T test for Mean Difference of Single Group or Two Related Groups

In case of single group, $M(\mu)$ denotes the sample (population) mean of single group, and SD (σ) denotes the sample (population) standard deviation. N is the sample size of the group.

T test is used for the hypothesis on the difference between mean and a baseline $\mu_{baseline}$. Usually, $\mu_{baseline}$ is zero, while not necessary. In case of two related groups, the single group is constructed by difference in each pair of samples, while SD (σ) denotes the sample (population) standard deviation of differences rather than within original two groups.

$$t := \frac{M}{SD/\sqrt{N}} = \frac{\sqrt{N}\frac{M-\mu}{\sigma} + \sqrt{N}\frac{\mu-\mu_{baseline}}{\sigma}}{\frac{SD}{\sigma}}$$

$$ncp = \sqrt{N}\frac{\mu-\mu_{baseline}}{\sigma}$$

and Cohen's

$$d := \frac{M-\mu_{baseline}}{SD}$$

is the point estimate of,

$$\frac{\mu-\mu_{baseline}}{\sigma}.$$

So,

$$\tilde{d} = \frac{ncp}{\sqrt{N}}.$$

T test for Mean Difference Between Two Independent Groups

n_1 or n_2 is sample size within the respective group.

$$t := \frac{M_1 - M_2}{SD_{within} / \sqrt{\frac{n_1 n_2}{n_1 + n_2}}},$$

wherein,

$$SD_{within} := \sqrt{\frac{SS_{within}}{df_{within}}} = \sqrt{\frac{(n_1-1)SD_1^2+(n_2-1)SD_2^2}{n_1+n_2-2}}.$$

$$ncp = \sqrt{\frac{n_1 n_2}{n_1+n_2}}\frac{\mu_1-\mu_2}{\sigma}$$

and Cohen's

$$d := \frac{M_1-M_2}{SD_{within}} \text{ is the point estimate of } \frac{\mu_1-\mu_2}{\sigma}.$$

So,

$$\tilde{d} = \frac{ncp}{\sqrt{\frac{n_1 n_2}{n_1+n_2}}}.$$

One-way Anova Test for Mean Difference Across Multiple Independent Groups

One-way ANOVA test applies noncentral F distribution. While with a given population standard deviation ó, the same test question applies noncentral chi-square distribution.

$$F := \frac{\frac{SS_{between}}{\sigma^2}/df_{between}}{\frac{SS_{within}}{\sigma^2}/df_{within}}$$

For each j–th sample within i–th group $X_{i,j}$, denote,

$$M_i(X_{i,j}) := \frac{\sum_{w=1}^{n_i} X_{i,w}}{}; \mu_i(X_{i,j}) := \mu_i.$$

While,

$$SSbetween/\sigma^2$$

$$= \frac{SS(M_i(X_{i,j}); i=1,2,\cdots,K, j=1,2,\cdots,n_i}{\sigma^2}$$

$$= SS\left(\frac{M_i(X_{i,j}-\mu_i)}{\sigma} + \frac{\mu_i}{\sigma}; i=1,2,\cdots,K, j=1,2,\cdots,n_i\right)$$

$$\sim X^2\left(df = K-1, ncp = SS\left(\frac{\mu_i(X_{i,j})}{\sigma}; i=1,2,\cdots,K, j=1,2,\cdots,n_i\right)\right)$$

So, both ncp(s) of F and ÷² equate,

$$SS(\mu_i(X_{i;j})/\sigma; i=1,2,\cdots,K, j=1,2,\cdots,n_i).$$

In case of $n := n_1 = n_2 \cdots = n_K$ for K independent groups of same size, the total sample size is N:= n·K.,

$$\text{Cohens}\tilde{f}^2 := \frac{SS(\mu_1,\mu_2,\cdots\mu_K)}{K.\sigma^2} =$$

$$\frac{SS(\mu_i(X_{i,j})/\sigma; i=1,2,\cdots K, j=1,2,\cdots n_i)}{n.K} =$$

$$\frac{ncp}{n.K} = \frac{ncp}{N}.$$

T-test of pair of independent groups is a special case of one-way ANOVA. Note that noncentral parametre ncp_F of F is not comparable to the noncentral parametre ncp_t of the corresponding t. Actually, $ncp_F = ncp_t^2$, and

$$\tilde{f} = \left|\frac{d}{2}\right|$$

in the case.

"Small", "Medium", "Large"

Some fields using effect sizes apply words such as "small", "medium" and "large" to the size of the effect. Whether an effect size should be interpreted small, medium, or big depends on its substantial context and its operational definition. Cohen's conventional criteria small, medium, or big are near ubiquitous across many fields. Power analysis or sample size planning requires an assumed population parametre of effect sizes. Many researchers adopt Cohen's standards as default alternative hypotheses. Russell Lenth criticized them as T-shirt effect sizes

This is an elaborate way to arrive at the same sample size that has been used in past social science studies of large, medium, and small size (respectively). The method uses a standardized effect size as the goal. Think about it: for a "medium" effect size, you'll choose the same n regardless of the accuracy or reliability of your instrument, or the narrowness or diversity of your subjects. Clearly, important considerations are being ignored here. "Medium" is definitely not the message!

For Cohen's d an effect size of 0.2 to 0.3 might be a "small" effect, around 0.5 a "medium" effect and 0.8 to infinity, a "large" effect.

Cohen's text anticipates Lenth's concerns: "The terms 'small,' 'medium,' and 'large' are relative, not only to each other, but to the area of behavioural science or even more particularly to the specific content and research method being employed in any given investigation....In the face of this relativity, there is a certain risk inherent in offering conventional operational definitions for these terms for use in power analysis in as diverse a field of inquiry as behavioural science. This risk is nevertheless accepted in the belief that more is to be gained than lost by supplying a common conventional frame of reference which is recommended for use only when no better basis for estimating the ES index is available."

The last two decades have seen the widespread use of these conventional operational definitions as standard practice in the calculation of sample sizes despite the fact that Cohen was clear that the small-medium-large categories were not to be used by serious researchers, except perhaps in the context of research with entirely novel variables.

STANDARD ERROR

The standard error of a method of measurement or estimation is the standard deviation of the sampling distribution associated with the estimation method. The term may also be used to refer to an estimate of that standard deviation, derived from a particular sample used to compute the estimate. For example, the sample mean is the usual estimator of a population mean. However, different samples drawn from that same population would in general have different values of the sample mean. The standard error of the mean is the standard deviation of those sample means over all possible samples drawn from the population. Secondly, the standard error of the mean can refer to an estimate of that standard deviation, computed from the sample of data being analysed at the time.

The term standard error is derived from the fact that, as long as the estimator is unbiased, the standard deviation of the error is the same as the standard deviation of the estimates themselves; this is true since the standard deviation of the difference between the random variable and its expected value is equal to the standard deviation of a random variable itself.

In many practical applications, the true value of the standard deviation is usually unknown. As a result, the term standard error is often used to refer to an estimate of this unknown quantity.

In such cases it is important to be clear about what has been done and to attempt to take proper account of the fact that the standard error is only an estimate. Unfortunately, this is not often possible and it may then be better to use an approach that avoids using a standard error, for example by using maximum likelihood or a more formal approach to deriving confidence intervals.

One well-known case where a proper allowance can be made arises where the Student's t-distribution is used to provide a confidence interval for an estimated mean or difference of means.

In other cases, the standard error may usefully be used to provide an indication of the size of the uncertainty, but its formal or semi-formal use to provide confidence intervals or tests should be avoided unless the sample size is at least moderately large. Here "large enough" would depend on the particular quantities being analysed.

Standard Error of the Mean

The standard error of the mean is the standard deviation of the sample mean estimate of a population mean. SEM is usually estimated by the sample estimate of the population standard deviation divided by the square root of the sample size:

$$SE_{\bar{x}} = \frac{s}{\sqrt{n}}$$

where,

s is the sample standard deviation, and

n is the size of the sample.

This estimate may be compared with the formula for the true standard deviation of the mean:

$$SD_{\bar{x}} = \frac{\sigma}{\sqrt{n}}$$

where,

σ is the standard deviation of the population.

- *Note* 1: Standard error may also be defined as the standard deviation of the residual error term.
- *Note* 2: Both the standard error and the standard deviation of small samples tend to systematically underestimate the population standard error and deviations: the standard error of the mean is a biased estimator of the population standard error. With n = 2 the underestimate is about 25%, but for n = 6 the underestimate is only 5%. Gurland and Tripathi provide a correction and equation for this effect. Sokal and Rohlf give an equation of the correction factor for small samples of n < 20.
- *A practical result*: Decreasing the uncertainty in your mean value estimate by a factor of two requires that you acquire four times as many observations in your sample. Worse, decreasing standard error by a factor of ten requires a hundred times as many observations.

Assumptions and Usage

If the data are assumed to be normally distributed, quantiles of the normal distribution and the sample mean and standard error can be used to calculate approximate confidence intervals for the mean. The following expressions can be used to calculate the upper and lower 95% confidence limits, where $\bar{x}$ is equal to the sample mean, S_E is equal to the standard error for the sample mean, and 1.96 is the.975 quantile of the normal distribution:

$$\text{Upper 95\% Limit} = \overline{x} + (S_E.1.96),$$

$$\text{Lower 95\% Limit} = \overline{x} - (S_E.1.96),$$

In particular, the standard error of a sample statistic is the estimated standard deviation of the error in the process by which it was generated. In other words, it is the standard deviation of the sampling distribution of the sample statistic. The notation for standard error can be any one of SE, SEM or S_E.

Standard errors provide simple measures of uncertainty in a value and are often used because:

- If the standard error of several individual quantities is known then the standard error of some function of the quantities can be easily calculated in many cases;
- Where the probability distribution of the value is known, it can be used to calculate a good approximation to an exact confidence interval; and
- Where the probability distribution is unknown, relationships like Chebyshev's or the Vysochanskiï-Petunin inequality can be used to calculate a conservative confidence interval
- As the sample size tends to infinity the central limit theorem guarantees that the sampling distribution of the mean is asymptotically normal.

Correction for Finite Population

The formula given for the standard error assumes that the sample size is much smaller than the population size, so that the population can be considered to be effectively infinite in size. When the sampling fraction is large the estimate of the error must be corrected using a "finite population correction"

$$FPC = \sqrt{\frac{N-n}{N-1}}$$

to account for the added precision gained by sampling close to a larger percentage of the population. The effect of the FPC is that the error becomes zero when the sample size n is equal to the population size N.

Correction for Correlation in the Sample

If values of the measured quantity A are not statistically independent but have been obtained from known locations in parametre space x, an unbiased estimate of error in the mean may be obtained by multiplying the standard error by the factor f:

$$f = \sqrt{\frac{1+(n-1)\rho}{1-\rho}}$$

where the sample bias coefficient ñ is the average of the autocorrelation-coefficient $ñ_{ij}$ value for all sample point pairs.

Relative Standard Error

The relative standard error is simply the standard error divided by the mean and expressed as a percentage. For example, consider two surveys of household income that both result in a sample mean of $50,000. If one survey has a standard error of $10,000 and the other has a standard error of $5,000, then the relative standard errors are 20% and 10% respectively. Intuitively, the survey with the lower standard error would seem to be more reliable since there is less dispersion around the mean. In fact, data organizations often set reliability standards that their data must meet before publication. For example, the U.S. National Centre for Health Statistics typically does not report an estimate if the relative standard error exceeds 30%.

STATISTICAL POWER

The power of a statistical test is the probability that the test will reject a false null hypothesis. As power increases, the chances of a Type II error decrease. The probability of a Type II error is referred to as the false negative rate (β). Therefore power is equal to $1 - \beta$.

Power analysis can be used to calculate the minimum sample size required to accept the outcome of a statistical test with a particular level of confidence. It can also be used to calculate the minimum effect size that is likely to be detected in a study using a given sample size. In addition, the concept of power is used to make comparisons between different statistical tests: for example, between a parametric and a nonparametric test of the same hypothesis.

Statistical tests use data from samples to assess, or make inferences about, a population. In the concrete setting of a two-sample comparison, the goal is to assess whether the mean values of some attribute obtained for individuals in two sub-populations differ. For example, to test the null hypothesis that the mean scores of men and women on a test do not differ, samples of men and women are drawn, the test is administered to them, and the mean score of one group is compared to that of the other group using a statistical test such as the two-sample Z-test. The power of the test is the probability that the test will find a statistically significant difference between men and women, as a function of the size of the true difference between those two populations. Note that power is the probability of finding a difference that does exist, as opposed to the likelihood of declaring a difference that does not exist.

Factors Influencing Power

Statistical power may depend on a number of factors.

Some of these factors may be particular to a specific testing situation, but at a minimum, power nearly always depends on the following two factors:

1. The statistical significance criterion used in the test
2. The magnitude of the effect of interest in the population

A significance criterion is a statement of how unlikely a result must be, if the null hypothesis is true, to be considered significant. The most commonly used criteria are probabilities of 0.05 (5%, 1 in 20), 0.01 (1%, 1 in 100), and 0.001 (0.1%, 1 in 1000). If the criterion is 0.05, the probability of obtaining the observed effect when the null hypothesis is true must be less than 0.05, and so on. One easy way to increase the power of a test is to carry out a less conservative test by using a larger significance criterion. This increases the chance of obtaining a statistically significant result when the null hypothesis is false, that is, reduces the risk of a Type II error. But it also increases the risk of obtaining a statistically significant result when the null hypothesis is true; that is, it increases the risk of a Type I error.

The magnitude of the effect of interest in the population can be quantified in terms of an effect size, where there is greater power to detect larger effects. An effect size can be a direct estimate of the quantity of interest, or it can be a standardized measure that also accounts for the variability in the population. For example, in an analysis comparing outcomes in a treated and control population, the difference of outcome means Y – X would be a direct measure of the effect size, whereas (Y – X)/σ where σ is the common standard deviation of the outcomes in the treated and control groups, would be a standardized effcct size. If constructed appropriatcly, a standardized effect size, along with the sample size, will completely determine the power. An unstandardized effect size will rarely be sufficient to determine the power, as it does not contain information about the variability in the measurements.

The precision with which thc data are measured often influences the power. Power can often be improved by reducing the measurement error in the data. A related concept is to improve the"reliability" of the measure being assessed.

The design of an experiment or observational study often influences the power. For example, in a two-sample testing situation with a given total sample size n, it is optimal to have equal numbers of observations from the two populations being compared. In regression analysis and Analysis of Variance, there is an extensive theory, and practical strategies, for improving the power based on optimally setting the values of the independent variables in the model.

Interpretation

Although there are no formal standards for power, most researchers assess the power of their tests using 0.80 as a standard for adequacy.

There are times when the recommendations of power analysis regarding sample size will be inadequate. Power analysis is appropriate when the concern is with the correct rejection, or not, of a null hypothesis. In many contexts, the issue is less about determining if there is or is not a difference but rather with getting a more refined estimate of the population effect size. For example, if we were expecting a population correlation between intelligence and job performance of around.50, a sample size of 20 will give us approximately 80% power (alpha =.05, two-tail) to reject the null hypothesis of zero correlation. However, in doing this study we are probably more interested in knowing whether the correlation is.30 or.60 or.50. In this context we would need a much larger sample size in order to reduce the confidence interval of our estimate to a range that is acceptable for our purposes. Techniques similar to those employed in a traditional power analysis can be used to determine the sample size required for the width of a confidence interval to be less than a given value.

Many statistical analyses involve the estimation of several unknown quantities. In simple cases, all but one of these quantities is a "nuisance parametre." In this setting, the only relevant power pertains to the single quantity that will undergo formal statistical inference. In some settings, particularly if the goals are more "exploratory," there may be a number of quantities of interest in the analysis. For example, in a multiple regression analysis we may include several covariates of potential interest. In situations such as this where several hypotheses are under consideration, it is common that the powers associated with the different hypotheses differ. For instance, in multiple regression analysis, the power for detecting an effect of a given size is related to the variance of the covariate. Since different covariates will have different variances, their powers will differ as well.

Any statistical analysis involving multiple hypotheses is subject to inflation of the type I error rate if appropriate measures are not taken. Such measures typically involve applying a higher threshold of stringency to reject a hypothesis in order to compensate for the multiple comparisons being made. In this situation, the power analysis should reflect the multiple testing approach to be used. Thus, for example, a given study may be well powered to detect a certain effect size when only one test is to be made, but the same effect size may have much lower power if several tests are to be performed.

A Priori vs. Post Hoc Analysis

Power analysis can either be done before or after data is collected. A priori power analysis is conducted prior to the research study, and is typically used to determine an appropriate sample size to achieve adequate power. Post-hoc power analysis is conducted after a study has been completed, and uses the obtained sample size and effect size to determine what the power was in the study, assuming the effect size in the sample is equal to the effect size in the population. Whereas the utility of prospective power analysis in experimental design is universally accepted, the usefulness of retrospective techniques is controversial.

Application

Funding agencies, ethics boards and research review panels frequently request that a researcher perform a power analysis, for example to determine the minimum number of animal test subjects needed for an experiment. If a study is inadequately powered, then, in frequentist statistics, there is little point in completing the research, as it is unlikely to allow one to choose between hypotheses at the desired significance level. By contrast, in Bayesian statistics, any properly-conducted experiment is valuable, as the data is used in the context of all data collected, and allows one to update one's beliefs via Bayesian inference, regardless of how little is collected. However, even in Bayesian statistics, power is a useful measure of how much a given experiment size can be expected to refine one's beliefs.

SAMPLE SIZE

The sample size of a statistical sample is the number of observations that constitute it. It is typically denoted n, a positive integer. Typically, all else being equal, a larger sample size leads to increased precision in estimates of various properties of the population, though the results will become less accurate if there is a systematic error in the experiment. This can be seen in such statistical rules as the law of large numbers and the central limit theorem. Repeated measurements and replication of independent samples are often required in measurement and experiments to reach a desired precision. A typical example would be when a statistician wishes to estimate the arithmetic mean of a quantitative random variable. Assuming that they have a random sample with independent observations, and also that the variability of the population is known, then the standard error of the sample mean is given by the formula:

$$\sigma / \sqrt{n}.$$

It is easy to show that as n becomes very large, this variability becomes small. This leads to more sensitive hypothesis tests with greater statistical power and smaller confidence intervals.

Required Sample Sizes for Hypothesis Tests

A common problem facing statisticians is calculating the sample size required to yield a certain power for a test, given a predetermined Type I error rate α. A typical example for this is as follows:

Let X_i, i = 1, 2..., n be independent observations taken from a normal distribution with unknown mean ì and known variance σ^2.

Let us consider two hypotheses, a null hypothesis:

$H_0{:}\mu = 0$

and an alternative hypothesis:

$H_a{:}\mu = \mu^*$

for some 'smallest significant difference' $\mu^* > 0$. This is the smallest value for which we care about observing a difference. Now, if we wish to

- Reject H_0 with a probability of at least $1-\beta$ when H_a is true

- Reject H_0 with probability α when H_0 is true, then we need the following:

If z_α is the upper α percentage point of the standard normal distribution, then

$$\Pr(\overline{x} > z_\alpha \sigma / \sqrt{n} \setminus H_0 \text{true}) = \alpha$$

and so

'Reject H_0 if our sample average ($\overline{x}$) is more than $z_\alpha \sigma \setminus \sqrt{n}$'

is a decision rule which satisfies (2).

Now we wish for this to happen with a probability at least 1–β when H_a is true. In this case, our sample average will come from a Normal distribution with mean μ^*.

Therefore we require,

$$\Pr(\overline{x} > z_\alpha \sigma / \sqrt{n} \setminus H_0 \text{true}) \geq 1 - \beta$$

Through careful manipulation, this can be shown to happen when,

$$n \geq \left(\frac{\Phi^{-1}(1-\beta) + z_\alpha}{\mu^* / \sigma} \right)$$

where Φ is the normal cumulative distribution function.

Stratified Sample Size

With more complicated sampling techniques, such as Stratified sampling, the sample can often be split up into sub-samples. Typically, if there are k such sub-samples (from k different strata) then each of them will have a sample size n_i, i = 1, 2..., k. These n_i must conform to the rule that $n_1 + n_2 + ... + n_k = n$ (i.e. that the total sample size is given by the sum of the sub-sample sizes). Selecting these n_i optimally can be done in various ways, using Neyman's optimal allocation.

Leslie Kish, there are many reasons to do this; that is to take sub-samples from distinct sub-populations or "strata" of the original population: to decrease variances of sample estimates, to use partly non-random methods, or to study strata individually. A useful, partly non-random method would be to sample individuals where easily accessible, but, where not, sample clusters to save travel costs.

In general, for H strata, a weighted sample mean is,

$$\bar{x}_w = \sum_{h=1}^{H} W_h \bar{x}_h,$$

with,

$$\mathrm{Var}(\bar{x}_w) = \sum_{h=1}^{H} W_h^2 \mathrm{Var}(\bar{x}_h),$$

The weights, W(h), frequently, but not always, represent the proportions of the population elements in the strata, and W(h)=N(h)/N. For a fixed sample size, that is n=Sum{n(h)},

$$\mathrm{Var}(\bar{x}_w) = \sum_{h=1}^{H} W_h^2 \mathrm{Var}(h)\left(\frac{1}{n_h} - \frac{1}{N_h}\right),$$

which can be made a minimum if the sampling rate within each stratum is made proportional to the standard deviation within each stratum: $n_h / N_h = kS_h$.

An "optimum allocation" is reached when the sampling rates within the strata are made directly proportional to the standard deviations within the strata and inversely proportional to the square roots of the costs per element within the strata:

$$\frac{n(h)}{N(h)} = \frac{KS(h)}{\sqrt{C(h)}},$$

or, more generally, when

$$n(h) = \frac{K'W(h)S(h)}{\sqrt{C(h)}}.$$

SURVEY METHODOLOGY

SAMPLING

Sampling is that part of statistical practice concerned with the selection of an unbiased or random subset of individual observations within a population of individuals intended to yield some knowledge about the population of concern, especially for the purposes of making predictions based on statistical inference. Sampling is an important aspect of data collection.

Researchers rarely survey the entire population for two reasons: the cost is too high, and the population is dynamic in that the individuals making up the population may change over time. The three main advantages of sampling are that the cost is lower, data collection is faster, and since the data set is smaller it is possible to ensure homogeneity and to improve the accuracy and quality of the data.

Each observation measures one or more properties of observable bodies distinguished as independent objects or individuals. In survey sampling, survey weights can be applied to the data to adjust for the sample design. Results from probability theory and statistical theory are employed to guide practice. In business and medical research, sampling is widely used for gathering information about a population.

Process

The sampling process comprises several stages:

- Defining the population of concern
- Specifying a sampling frame, a set of items or events possible to measure
- Specifying a sampling method for selecting items or events from the frame
- Determining the sample size
- Implementing the sampling plan
- Sampling and data collecting
- Reviewing the sampling process

Population Definition

Successful statistical practice is based on focused problem definition. In sampling, this includes defining the population from which our sample is drawn. A population can be defined as including all people or items with the characteristic one wishes to understand. Because there is very rarely enough time or money to gather information from everyone or everything in a population, the goal becomes finding a representative sample of that population. Sometimes that which defines a population is obvious. For example, a manufacturer needs to decide whether a batch of material from production is of high enough quality to be released to the customer, or should be sentenced for scrap or rework due to poor quality. In this case, the batch is the population.

Although the population of interest often consists of physical objects, sometimes we need to sample over time, space, or some combination of these dimensions. For instance, an investigation of supermarket staffing could examine checkout line length at various times, or a study on endangered penguins might aim to understand their usage of various hunting grounds over time. For the time dimension, the focus may be on periods or discrete occasions.

In other cases, our 'population' may be even less tangible. For example, Joseph Jagger studied the behaviour of roulette wheels at a casino in Monte Carlo, and used this to identify a biased wheel. In this case, the 'population' Jagger wanted to investigate was the overall behaviour of the wheel while his 'sample' was formed from observed results from that wheel. Similar considerations arise when taking repeated measurements of some physical characteristic such as the electrical conductivity of copper.

This situation often arises when we seek knowledge about the cause system of which the observed population is an outcome. In such cases, sampling theory may treat the observed population as a sample from a larger 'superpopulation'. For example, a researcher might study the success rate of a new 'quit smoking' programme on a test group of 100 patients, in order to predict the effects of the programme if it were made available nationwide. Here the superpopulation is "everybody in the country, given access to this treatment" - a group which does not yet exist, since the programme isn't yet available to all.

Note also that the population from which the sample is drawn may not be the same as the population about which we actually want information. Often there is large but not complete overlap between these two groups due to frame issues etc.. Sometimes they may be entirely separate - for instance, we might study rats in order to get a better understanding of human health, or we might study records from people born in 2008 in order to make predictions about people born in 2009.

Time spent in making the sampled population and population of concern precise is often well spent, because it raises many issues, ambiguities and questions that would otherwise have been overlooked at this stage.

STRATIFIED SAMPLING

In statistics, stratified sampling is a method of sampling from a population. When sub-populations vary considerably, it is advantageous to sample each subpopulation independently. Stratification is the process of grouping members of the population into relatively homogeneous subgroups before sampling.The strata should be mutually exclusive: every element in the population must be assigned to only one stratum. The strata should also be collectively exhaustive: no population element can be excluded. Then random or systematic sampling is applied within each stratum. This often improves the representativeness of the sample by reducing sampling error. It can produce a weighted mean that has less variability than the arithmetic mean of a simple random sample of the population.

Stratified Sampling Strategies

- Proportionate allocation uses a sampling fraction in each of the strata that is proportional to that of the total population. If the population consists of 60% in the male stratum and 40% in the female stratum, then the relative size of the two samples should reflect this proportion.
- *Optimum allocation*: Each stratum is proportionate to the standard deviation of the distribution of the variable. Larger samples are taken in the strata with the greatest variability to generate the least possible sampling variance.

A real-world example of using stratified sampling would be for a political survey. If the respondents needed to reflect the diversity of the population, the researcher would specifically seek to include participants of various minority groups such as race or religion, based on their proportionality to the total population. A stratified survey could thus claim to be more representative of the population than a survey of simple random sampling or systematic sampling.

Similarly, if population density varies greatly within a region, stratified sampling will ensure that estimates can be made with equal accuracy in different parts of the region, and that comparisons of sub-regions can be made with equal statistical power. For example, in Ontario a survey taken throughout the province might use a larger sampling fraction in the less populated north, since the disparity in population between north and south is so great that a sampling fraction based on the provincial sample as a whole might result in the collection of only a handful of data from the north. Randomized stratification can also be used to improve population representativeness in a study.

Disadvantages

It is not useful when there are no similar subgroups. It cannot be used when amount of data in subgroups is not equal but total data in a subgroup are of equal importance as it gives more importance to subgroups with more data.

OPINION POLL

An opinion poll is a survey of public opinion from a particular sample. Opinion polls are usually designed to represent the opinions of a population by conducting a series of questions and then extrapolating generalities in ratio or within confidence intervals.

The first known example of an opinion poll was a local straw poll conducted by The Harrisburg Pennsylvanian in 1824, showing Andrew Jackson leading John Quincy Adams by 335 votes to 169 in the contest for the United States Presidency. Such straw votes gradually became more popular, but they remained local, usually city-wide phenomena. In 1916, the Literary Digest embarked on a national survey and correctly predicted Woodrow Wilson's election as president. Mailing out millions of postcards and simply counting the returns, the Digest correctly called the following four presidential elections.

In 1936 however the Digest came unstuck. Its 2.3 million "voters" constituted a huge sample; however they were generally more affluent Americans who tended to have Republican sympathies. The Literary Digest was ignorant of this new bias. The week before election day, it reported that Alf Landon was far more popular than Franklin D. Roosevelt. At the same time, George Gallup conducted a far smaller, but more scientifically-based survey, in which he polled a demographically representative sample. Gallup correctly predicted Roosevelt's landslide victory. The Literary Digest soon went out of business, while polling started to take off.

Elmo Roper was another American pioneer in political forecasting using scientific polls. He predicted the reelection of President Franklin D. Roosevelt three times, in 1936, 1940, and 1944. Louis Harris had been in the field of public opinion since 1947 when he joined the Elmo Roper firm, then later became partner.

Gallup launched a subsidiary in the United Kingdom, where it correctly predicted Labour's victory in the 1945 general election, in contrast with virtually all other commentators, who expected a victory for the Conservative Party, led by Winston Churchill.

By the 1950s, various types of polling had spread to most democracies. In Iraq, surveys conducted soon after the 2003 war aimed to measure the feelings of Iraqi citizens regarding Saddam Hussein, post-war conditions, and the presence of US forces.

Sample and Polling Methods

Opinion polls for many years were maintained through telecommunications or in person-to-person contact. Methods and techniques vary, though they are widely accepted in most areas. Verbal, ballot, and processed types can be conducted efficiently, contrasted with other types of surveys, systematics. Opinion polling developed into popular applications through popular thought, although response rates for some surveys declined. Also, the following has also led to differentiating results: Some polling organizations, such as and Angus Reid Strategies, YouGov and Zogby use Internet surveys, where a sample is drawn from a large panel of volunteers, and the results are weighed to reflect the demographics of the population of interest. This is in contrast to popular web polls that draw on whoever wishes to participate, rather than a scientific sample of the population, and are therefore not generally considered professional.

Tracking Polls

A tracking poll is a poll repeated at intervals generally averaged over a trailing window. For example, a weekly tracking poll uses the data from the past week and discards older data.

A key benefit of tracking polls is that the trend of a tracking poll corrects for bias: regardless of whether a poll consistently over or underestimates opinion, the trend correctly reflects increases or decreases.

A caution is that estimating the trend is more difficult and error-prone than estimating the level – intuitively, if one estimates the change, the difference between two numbers X and Y, then one has to contend with the error in both X and Y – it is not enough to simply take the difference, as the change may be random noise. A rough guide is that if the change in measurement falls outside the margin of error, it is worth attention.

Potential for Inaccuracy

Polls based on samples of populations are subject to sampling error which reflects the effects of chance and uncertainty in the sampling process. The uncertainty is often expressed as a margin of error. The margin of error is usually defined as the radius of a confidence interval for a particular statistic from a survey. One example is the per cent of people who prefer product A versus product B. When a single, global margin of error is reported for a survey, it refers to the maximum margin of error for all reported percentages using the full sample from the survey.

If the statistic is a percentage, this maximum margin of error can be calculated as the radius of the confidence interval for a reported percentage of 50%. Others suggest that a poll with a random sample of 1,000 people has margin of sampling error of 3% for the estimated percentage of the whole population.

A 3% margin of error means that if the same procedure is used a large number of times, 95% of the time the true population average will be within the 95% confidence interval of the sample estimate plus or minus 3%. The margin of error can be reduced by using a larger sample, however if a pollster wishes to reduce the margin of error to 1% they would need a sample of around 10,000 people. In practice pollsters need to balance the cost of a large sample against the reduction in sampling error and a sample size of around 500–1,000 is a typical compromise for political polls.

Another way to reduce the margin of error is to rely on poll averages. This makes the assumption that the procedure is similar enough between many different polls and uses the sample size of each poll to create a polling average. An example of a polling average can be found here: 2008 Presidential Election polling average. Another source of error stems from faulty demographic models by pollsters who weigh their samples by particular variables such as party identification in an election. For example, if you assume that the breakdown of the US population by party identification has not changed since the previous presidential election, you may underestimate a victory or a defeat of a particular party candidate that saw a surge or decline in its party registration relative to the previous presidential election cycle.

Over time, a number of theories and mechanisms have been offered to explain erroneous polling results. Some of these reflect errors on the part of the pollsters; many of them are statistical in nature. Others blame the respondents for not giving candid answers; these can be more controversial.

Nonresponse Bias

Since some people do not answer calls from strangers, or refuse to answer the poll, poll samples may not be representative samples from a population. Because of this selection bias, the characteristics of those who agree to be interviewed may be markedly different from those who decline. That is, the actual sample is a biased version of the universe the pollster wants to analyse.

In these cases, bias introduces new errors, one way or the other, that are in addition to errors caused by sample size. Error due to bias does not become smaller with larger sample sizes, because taking a larger sample size simply repeats the same mistake on a larger scale.

If the people who refuse to answer, or are never reached, have the same characteristics as the people who do answer, then the final results should be unbiased. If the people who do not answer have different opinions then there is bias in the results.

In terms of election polls, studies suggest that bias effects are small, but each polling firm has its own techniques for adjusting weights to minimize selection bias.

Response Bias

Survey results may be affected by response bias, where the answers given by respondents do not reflect their true beliefs. This may be deliberately engineered by unscrupulous pollsters in order to generate a certain result or please their clients, but more often is a result of the detailed wording or ordering of questions.

Respondents may deliberately try to manipulate the outcome of a poll by e.g. advocating a more extreme position than they actually hold in order to boost their side of the argument or give rapid and ill-considered answers in order to hasten the end of their questioning. Respondents may also feel under social pressure not to give an unpopular answer.

For example, respondents might be unwilling to admit to unpopular attitudes like racism or sexism, and thus polls might not reflect the true incidence of these attitudes in the population.

In American political parlance, this a phenomenon is often referred to as the Bradley Effect. If the results of surveys are widely publicized this effect may be magnified - a phenomenon commonly referred to as the spiral of silence.

Wording of Questions

It is well established that the wording of the questions, the order in which they are asked and the number and form of alternative answers offered can influence results of polls. For instance, the public is more likely to indicate support for a person who is described by the operator as one of the "leading candidates".

This support itself overrides subtle bias for one candidate, as is lumping some candidates in an "other" category or vice versa. Thus comparisons between polls often boil down to the wording of the question.

On some issues, question wording can result in quite pronounced differences between surveys. This can also, however, be a result of legitimately conflicted feelings or evolving attitudes, rather than a poorly constructed survey.

A common technique to control for this bias is to rotate the order in which questions are asked. Many pollsters also split-sample. This involves having two different versions of a question, with each version presented to half the respondents.

The most effective controls, used by attitude researchers, are:

- Asking enough questions to allow all aspects of an issue to be covered and to control effects due to the form of the question, the adequacy of the number being established quantitatively with psychometric measures such as reliability coefficients, and
- Analyzing the results with psychometric techniques which synthesize the answers into a few reliable scores and detect ineffective questions.

These controls are not widely used in the polling industry.

Coverage Bias

Another source of error is the use of samples that are not representative of the population as a consequence of the methodology used, as was the experience of the Literary Digest in 1936. For example, telephone sampling has a built-in error because in many times and places, those with telephones have generally been richer than those without. In some places many people have only mobile telephones. Because pollsters cannot call mobile phones, these individuals will never be included in the polling sample. If the subset of the population without cell phones differs markedly from the rest of the population, these differences can skew the results of the poll.

Polling organizations have developed many weighting techniques to help overcome these deficiencies, to varying degrees of success. Studies of mobile phone users by the Pew Research Centre in the US concluded that"cell-only respondents are different from landline respondents in important ways, they were neither numerous enough nor different enough on the questions we examined to produce a significant change in overall general population survey estimates when included with the landline samples and weighted US Census parametres on basic demographic characteristics." This issue was first identified in 2004, but came to prominence only during the 2008 US presidential election. In previous elections, the proportion of the general population using cell phones was small, but as this proportion has increased, the worry is that polling only landlines is no longer representative of the general population. In 2003, a 2.9% of households were wireless compared to 12.8 in 2006. This results in"coverage error". Many polling organisations select their sample by dialling random telephone numbers; however, there is a clear tendency for polls which included mobile phones in their sample to show a much larger lead for Obama than polls that did not.

The potential sources of bias are:

- Some households use cellphones only and have no landline. This tends to include minorities and younger voters; and occurs more frequently ir metropolitan areas. Men are more likely to be cellphone-only compared to women.

- Some people may not be contactable by landline from Monday to Friday and may be contactable only by cellphone.
- Some people use their landlines only to access the Internet, and answer calls only to their cellphones.

Some polling companies have attempted to get around that problem by including a"cellphone supplement". There are a number of problems with including cellphones in a telephone poll:

- It is difficult to get co-operation from cellphone users, because in many parts of the US, users are charged for both outgoing and incoming calls. That means that pollsters have had to offer financial compensation to gain co-operation.
- US federal law prohibits the use of automated dialling devices to call cellphones. Numbers therefore have to be dialled by hand, which is more time-consuming and expensive for pollsters.

An oft-quoted example of opinion polls succumbing to errors was the UK General Election of 1992. Despite the polling organizations using different methodologies virtually all the polls in the lead up to the vote, and to a lesser extent exit polls taken on voting day, showed a lead for the opposition Labour party but the actual vote gave a clear victory to the ruling Conservative party. In their deliberations after this embarrassment the pollsters advanced several ideas to account for their errors, including.

Late swing

Voters who changed their minds shortly before voting tended to favour the Conservatives, so the error was not as great as it first appeared.

Nonresponse Bias

Conservative voters were less likely to participate in surveys than in the past and were thus under-represented.

The Shy Tory Factor

The Conservatives had suffered a sustained period of unpopularity as a result of economic difficulties and a series of minor scandals, leading to a spiral of silence in which some Conservative supporters were reluctant to disclose their sincere intentions to pollsters.

The relative importance of these factors was, and remains, a matter of controversy, but since then the polling organizations have adjusted their methodologies and have achieved more accurate results in subsequent elections.

METHODS OF DATA COLLECTION

QUESTIONNAIRES

Questionnaires are one of the most popular methods of conducting scholarly research. They provide a convenient way of gathering information from a target population.

Advantages and Disadvantages of Written Questionnaires

Questionnaires are easy to analyse, and most statistical analysis software can easily process them. They are cost effective when compared to face-to-face interviews, mostly because of the costs associated with travel time. This is especially true for studies involving large sample sizes and large geographic areas. Written questionnaires become even more cost effective as the number of research questions increases.

Questionnaires are familiar to most people. Nearly everyone has had some experience completing questionnaires and they generally do not make people apprehensive. They are less intrusive than telephone or face-to-face surveys. When respondents receive a questionnaire in the mail, they are free to complete it on their own time-table. Unlike other research methods, the respondent is not interrupted by the research instrument. On the other hand, questionnaires are simply not suited for some people. For example, a written survey to a group of poorly educated people might not work because of reading skill problems. More frequently, some people are turned off by written questionnaires because of misuse.

Written questionnaires reduce interviewer bias because there is uniform question presentation. Unlike in-person interviewing, there are no verbal or visual clues to influence a respondent to answer in a particular way. Many investigators have reported that interviewer voice inflections and mannerisms can bias responses. Written surveys are not subject to this bias because there is no interviewer. On the other hand, the lack of an interviewer limits the researcher's ability to probe responses. Structured questionnaires often lose the "flavour of the response", because respondents often want to qualify their answers. By allowing frequent space for comments, the researcher can partially overcome this disadvantage.

A common criticism of mail surveys is that they often have low response rates. Low response is the curse of statistical analysis, and it can dramatically lower confidence in the results. While response rates vary widely from one questionnaire to another, well-designed studies consistently produce high response rates.

When returned questionnaires arrive in the mail, it's natural to assume that the respondent is the same person you sent the questionnaire to. A number of researchers have reported that this may not actually be the case. Many times business questionnaires get handed to other employees for completion. Housewives sometimes respond for their husbands. Kids respond as a prank. For a variety of reasons, the respondent may not be who you think it is. In a summary of five studies sponsored by the British Government, Scott reports that up to ten per cent of the returned questionnaires had been completed by someone other than the intended person.

Response Rate

Response rate is the single most important indicator of how much confidence can be placed in the results of a mail survey. A low response rate can be devastating to the reliability of a study. Fortunately, "low response rates are not an inherent shortcoming of mail surveys", and the researcher must do everything possible to maximize response. Much of the research in questionnaire methodology has centred around techniques to maximize response. However, Jones and Lang point out that increasing the response rate does not necessarily improve the precision of survey results.

Following up on Nonrespondents

One of the most powerful tool for increasing response is to use follow-ups or reminders. "Traditionally, between 5 and 65 per cent of those sent questionnaires respond without follow-up reminders. These rates are too low to yield confident results". The need to follow up on nonrespondents is clear.

Researchers can increase the response from follow-up attempts by including another copy of the questionnaire. The most important consideration is that the investigator "designs the follow-up procedure by taking into consideration the unique characteristics of the people in the sample." The most successful follow-ups have been achieved by phone calls.

Many researchers have examined whether postcard follow-ups are effective in increasing response. The vast majority of these studies show that a follow-up postcard increases response rate, and a meta-analysis by Fox, Crask, and Kim reveals an aggregate gain of 3.5 per cent. The postcard serves as an effective reminder for subjects who have forgotten to complete the survey.

Nonresponse Bias

Many studies have attempted to determine if there is a difference between respondents and nonrespondents. Some researchers have reported that people who respond to surveys answer questions differently than those who do not. Others have found that late responders answer differently than early responders, and that the differences may be due to the different levels of interest in the subject matter. One researcher, who examined a volunteer organization, reported that those more actively involved in the organization were more likely to respond.

Demographic characteristics of nonrespondents have been investigated by many researchers. Most studies have found that nonresponse is associated with low education. However, one reseacher reported that demographic characteristics such as age, education, and employment status were the same for respondents and nonrespondents. Another study found that nonrespondents were more often single males.

Most researchers view nonresponse bias as a continuum, ranging from fast responders to slow responders. In fact, one study used extrapolation to estimate the magnitude of bias created by nonresponse. Another group of researchers argue that nonresponse should not be viewed as a continuum, and "that late respondents do not provide a suitable basis for estimating the characteristics of nonrespondents".

Goal Definition

Most problems with questionnaires can be traced back to the design phase of the project. Well-defined goals are the best way to assure a good questionnaire design. One of the best ways to clarify the study goals is to decide how the information will be used.. Study goals should be committed to writing. When the goals of a study can be expressed in a few clear and concise sentences, the design of the questionnaire becomes considerably easier. The questionnaire is developed to directly address the goals of the study.

One important way to assure a successful survey is to include other experts and relevant decision-makers in the questionnaire design process. Their suggestions will improve the questionnaire and they will subsequently have more confidence in the results.

General Layout and Format Considerations

The physical appearance of a written survey may largely determine if the respondent will return it. Therefore, it is important to use professional production methods for the questionnaire—either desktop publishing or typesetting and keylining. Every questionnaire should have a title that is short and meaningful to the respondent. The rationale is that a questionnaire with a title will be perceived as more credible than one without.

Well-designed questionnaires include clear and concise instructions on how they should be completed. These must be very easy to understand, so use short sentences and basic vocabulary. The questionnaire itself should have the return address printed on it since questionnaires often get separated from the reply envelopes.

Questionnaires should use simple and direct language. The questions must be clearly understood by the respondent, and have the same meaning that the researcher intended. The wording of a question should be simple, to the point, and familiar to the target population. Surprisingly, several researchers have found that longer questions elicit more information than shorter ones, and that the information tends to be more accurate. However, it is generally accepted that questionnaire items should be simply stated and as brief as possible. The rationale is that this will reduce misunderstandings and make the questionnaire appear easier to complete. One way to eliminate misunderstandings is to emphasize crucial words in each item by using bold, italics or underlining.

Uncommon words, jargon, and abbreviations may be included in a questionnaire provided that they are familiar to the population being investigated. Slang is often ambiguous, and should be excluded from all questionnaires.

Questionnaires should leave adequate space for respondents to make comments. One criticism of questionnaires is their inability to retain the "flavour" of a response. Leaving space for comments will provide valuable information not captured by the response categories. Leaving white space also makes the questionnaire look easier and this might increase response.

Researchers should design the questionnaire so it holds the respondent's interest. The goal is to make the respondent want to complete the questionnaire. One way to keep a questionnaire interesting is to provide variety in the type of items used. Varying the questioning format will also prevent respondents from falling into "response sets".

The Order of the Questions

Questionnaires should begin with a few non-threatening and easy to answer items. If the first items are too difficult or threatening, there is little chance that the person will complete the questionnaire. People generally look at the first few questions before deciding whether or not to complete the questionnaire. The researcher can encourage response by starting with a few interesting and nonthreatening questions.

Likewise, the most important items should appear in the first half of the questionnaire. Respondents often send back partially completed questionnaires. By putting the most important items near the beginning, the partially completed questionnaires will still contain important information.

Items on a questionnaire should be grouped into logically coherent parts. Grouping questions that are similar will make the questionnaire easier to complete, and the respondent will feel more comfortable. Questions that use the same response formats, or those that cover a specific topic, should appear together.

Each question should follow comfortably from the previous question. Writing a questionnaire is similar to writing anything else. Transitions between questions should be smooth. Questionnaires that jump from one unrelated topic to another feel disjointed and are not likely to produce high response rates.

Most investigators have found that the order in which questions are presented can affect the way that people respond. One study reported that questions in the latter half a questionnaire were more likely to be omitted, and contained fewer extreme responses. Carp suggested that it may be necessary to prevent general questions before specific ones in order to avoid response contamination. McFarland reported that when specific questions were asked before general questions, respondents tended to exhibit greater interest in the general questions. A few researchers, however, have found that question-order does not effect responses. Bradburn and Mason reported that interviews involving self-reports and self-evaluations were unaffected by question order. Clancey and Wachsler found that responses to questions were similar regardless of where the questions appeared in a questionnaire. Bishop et al. reported that question-order effects existed in interviews, but not in written surveys. Ayidiya and McClendon reported mixed results, where some questions were subject to order effects, and other similar questions were not.

Anonymity and Confidentiality

As a general rule, long questionnaires get less response than short questionnaires. However, some studies have shown that the length of a questionnaire does not necessarily affect response. "Seemingly more important than length is question content." A subject is more likely to respond if they are involved and interested in the research topic. Questions should be meaningful and interesting to the respondent.

Colour of the Paper

One study found that the colour of the paper. Nevertheless, Berdie, Anderson and Neibuhr suggest that colour might make the survey more appealing. Another early study examined the ink and paper colour combinations that provide the greatest legibility. The authors suggest three different ink colours for white paper: black, grass green, and lustre blue. The only other recommended combination is black ink on yellow paper. Some investigators have examined the effect of using a green paper compared to white paper. Two studies reported no significant differences in response rates, while another reported a 9.1 per cent difference. A meta-analysis of these studies calculated an average aggregate increase of 2.0 per cent when using a green questionnaire.

Incentives

Many researchers have examined the effect of providing

a variety of nonmonetary incentives to subjects. These include token gifts such as small packages of coffee, ball-point pens, postage stamps, or key rings, trading stamps, participation in a raffle or lottery, or a donation to a charity in the respondent's name. Generally, nonmonetary incentives have resulted in an increased response.

There can be little doubt that monetary incentives increase response. Only a few investigators have reported no increase in response. The overwhelming majority have reported increased response by including monetary incentives.

Church conducted of meta-analysis of 38 prior studies that used some form of an incentive. Monetary and nonmonetary incentives were effective only when enclosed with the survey. The promise of an incentive for a returned questionnaire was not effective in increasing response. The average increase in response rate for monetary and nonmonetary incentives was 19.1 per cent and 7.9 per cent, respectively.

Many researchers have found that higher monetary incentives generally work better than smaller ones. Armstrong proposed a diminishing return model, where increasing the amount of the incentive would have a decreasing effect on response rate. A meta-analysis performed by Fox, Crask, and Kim applied Armstrong's diminishing return model to fifteen studies. An incentive of 25¢ increased the response rate by an average of 16 per cent, and $1 increased the response by 31 per cent.

It is not known whether the effects of incentives disappear after follow-up mailings. Kephart and Bressler found that a 25¢ incentive significantly increased response, however, the effect disappeared after one follow-up mailing. Another study using a 25¢ incentive reported a significant difference, and the difference continued to be significant even after three follow-up mailings. James and Bolstein reported that four mailings without an incentive produced a better response than one mailing with an incentive. However, incentives of $1 and $2 with follow-ups produced a significantly better response than the same number of follow-ups with no incentive. Nederhof used a ball-point pen as an incentive and reported that "the effect of nonmonetary incentives on response rates disappears after the first mailing."

It is not clear whether offering to share the results of the research provides sufficient incentive to affect response. Mullner, Levy, Byre, and Matthews report that mentioning the offer in a cover letter did not increase response, while two older studies found that it did.

Notification of a Cutoff Date

Several researchers have examined the effect of giving subjects a deadline for responding While a deadline will usually reduce the time from the mailing until the returns begin arriving, it appears that it does not increase response, and may even reduce the response. One possible explanation is that a cutoff date might dissuade procrastinators from completing the questionnaire after the deadline has past. A meta-analysis by Fox, Crask and Kim revealed an aggregate increase in response rate of 1.7 per cent, which was not significant.

Reply Envelopes and Postage

A good questionnaire makes it convenient for the respondent to reply. Mail surveys that include a self-addressed stamped reply envelope get better response than business reply envelopes, although they are more expensive since you also pay for the non-respondents. Some investigators have suggested that people might feel obligated to complete the questionnaire because of the guilt associated with throwing away money--that is, the postage stamp. Others have pointed out that using a business reply permit might suggest advertising to some people. Another possibility is that a business reply envelope might be perceived as less personal.

Armstrong and Lusk performed a meta-analysis on 34 studies comparing stamped versus business reply postage. They calculated that stamped reply envelopes had a 9 per cent greater aggregate effect than business reply envelopes. In a subsequent meta-analysis on nine studies, Fox, Crask, and Kim reported an aggregate effect of 6.2 per cent.

The Outgoing Envelope and Postage

There have been several researchers that examined whether there is a difference in response between first class postage versus bulk rate.. A meta-analysis of these studies revealed a small, but significant, aggregate difference of 1.8 per cent. Envelopes with bulk mail permits might be perceived as"junk mail", unimportant, or less personal and thus will be reflected in a lower response rates.

A few researchers have also examined whether metreed mail or stamps work better on the outgoing envelope. The results of these studies suggest a small increase in response favouring a stamped envelope. A meta-analysis of these studies revealed that the aggregate difference was slightly less than one per cent. Many researchers have reported increased response rates by using registered, certified, or special delivery mail to send the questionnaire. The wisdom of using these techniques must be weighed against the consequences of angering respondents that make a special trip to the post office, only to find a questionnaire.

It is not clear whether a typed or hand-addressed envelope would affect response. One study, conducted at the University of Minnesota, reported that students responded better to hand-addressed postcards, while professors responded better to typed addresses. This researcher could find no studies that examined whether gummed labels would have a deleterious effect on response rate, although we might predict that response rate would be less for gummed labels because they have the appearance of less personalization.

This researcher could also find no studies that examined whether the colour of the envelope affects response rate. First impressions are important, and the respondent's first impression of the study usually comes from the envelope containing the survey. Therefore, we might predict that colour would have a positive impact on response because of its uniqueness.

The "Don't Know", "Undecided", and "Neutral" Response Options

Response categories are developed for questions in order

to facilitate the process of coding and analysis. Many studies have looked at the effects of presenting a "don't know" option in attitudinal questions. The "don't know" option allows respondents to state that they have no opinion or have not thought about a particular issue.

Holdaway found that the physical placement of the "undecided" category could change response patterns. Respondents were more likely to choose the "undecided" category when it was off to the side of the scale. This study also reported different response patterns depending on whether the midpoint was labeled "undecided" or "neutral".

Bishop also found that the physical location of the middle alternative can make a difference in responses, and that placing the middle option at the last position in the question increased the percentage of respondents who selected it by over 9 per cent. Bishop states that "offering respondents a middle alternative in a survey question will generally make a significant difference in the ceases that would be drawn." The middle option of an attitudinal scale attracts a substantial number of respondents who might be unsure of their opinion.

Poe et al. studied the "don't know" option for factual questions. Unlike attitude questions, respondents might legitimately not know the answer to a factual question. Their findings suggest that the "don't know" option should not be included in factual questions. Questions that excluded the "don't know" option produced a greater volume of accurate data. They found no difference in response rate depending on the inclusion or exclusion of the "don't know" option. Poe's finding directly contradict several previous authors who advocate including a "don't know" response category when there is any possibility that the respondent may not know the answer to a question.

Question Wording

The wording of a question is extremely important. Researchers strive for objectivity in surveys and, therefore, must be careful not to lead the respondent into giving the answer a desired answer. Unfortunately, the effects of question wording are one of the least understood areas of questionnaire research.

Many investigators have confirmed that slight changes in the way questions are worded can have a significant impact on how people respond. Several authors have reported that minor changes in question wording can produce more than a 25 per cent difference in people's opinions.

One important area of question wording is the effect of the interrogation and assertion question formats. The interrogation format asks a question directly, where the assertion format asks subjects to indicate their level of agreement or disagreement with a statement. Schuman and Presser reported no significant differences between the two formats, however, other researchers hypothesized that the interrogation format is more likely to encourage subjects to think about their answers. Petty, Rennier and Cacioppo found that the interrogation format caused greater polarization in subjects' responses, suggesting that there was greater cognition than the assertion format.

Other investigators have looked at the effects of modifying adjectives and adverbs. Words like usually, often, sometimes, occasionally, seldom, and rarely are "commonly" used in questionnaires, although it is clear that they do not mean the same thing to all people. Simpson and a replication by Hakel looked at twenty modifying adjectives and adverbs. These researchers found that the precise meanings of these words varied widely between subjects, and between the two studies. However, the correlation between the two studies with respect to the relative ranking of the words was.99.

John Hoyt conducted a study on how people interpret quantifying adjectives. The results show that some of the adjectives had high variability and others had low variability. The following adjectives were found to have highly variable meanings: a clear mandate, most, numerous, a substantial majority, a minority of, a large proportion of, a significant number of, many, a considerable number of, and several. Other adjectives produced less variability and generally had shared meaning. These were: lots, almost all, virtually all, nearly all, a majority of, a consensus of, a small number of, not very many of, almost none, a damn few, hardly any, a couple, and a few.

Sponsorship

There have been several studies to determine if the sponsor of a survey might affect response rate. The overwhelming majority of these studies have clearly demonstrated that university sponsorship is the most effective. A meta-analysis of these studies revealed an aggregate increase in response rate of 8.9 per cent. Dillman suggested that this may be due to the past benefits that the respondent has received from the university. Another possibility is that a business sponsor implies advertising or sales to potential respondents.

Prenotification Letters

Many researchers have studied prenotification letters to determine if they increase response rate. A meta-analysis of these studies revealed an aggregate increase in response rate of 7.7 per cent. Dillman proposed that prenotification letters might help to establish the legitimacy of a survey, thereby contributing to a respondent's trust. Another possibility is that a prenotification letter builds expectation, and reduces the possibility that a potential respondent might disregard the survey when it arrives.

The prenotification letter should address five items:

1. Briefly describe why the study is being done.
2. Identify the sponsors.
3. Explain why the person receiving the pre-letter was chosen.
4. Justify why the respondent should complete the questionnaire.
5. Explain how the results will be used.

Cover Letters

The cover letter is an essential part of the survey. To a large degree, the cover letter will affect whether or not the respondent completes the questionnaire. It is important to maintain a friendly tone and keep it as short as possible. The importance of the cover letter should not be underestimated. It provides an opportunity to persuade the respondent to complete the survey. If the questionnaire can be completed in less than fifteen minutes, the response rate can be increased by mentioning this in the cover letter.

Flattering the respondent in the cover letter does not seem to affect response Altruism or an appeal to the social utility of a study has occasionally been found to increase response, but more often, it is not an effective motivator.

The cover letter should address seven items:

1. Briefly describe why the study is being done.
2. Identify the sponsors.
3. Mention the incentive.
4. Mention inclusion of a stamped, self-addressed return envelope.
5. Encourage prompt response without using deadlines.
6. Describe the confidentiality/anonymity policy.
7. Give the name and phone number of someone thcy can call.

Personalization in a Cover Letter

There are no definitive answers whether or not to personalize cover letters. Some researchers have found that personalized cover letters can be detrimental to response when anonymity or confidentiality are important to the respondent.

The literature regarding personalization are mixed. Some researchers have found that personalized cover letters with hand-written signatures helped response rates. Other investigators, however, have reported that personalization has no effect on response.

Signature on the Cover Letter

The signature of the person signing the cover letter has been investigated by several researchers. Ethnic sounding names and the status of the researcher do not affect response. One investigator found that a cover letter signed by the owner of a marina produced better response than one signed by the sales manager. The literature is mixed regarding whether a hand-written signature works better than one that is mimeographed. Two researchers reported that mimeographed signatures worked as well as a hand-written one, while another reported that hand-written signatures produced better response. Another investigator found that cover letters signed with green ink increased response by over 10 per cent.

Postscript on the Cover Letter

It is commonly believed that a handwritten postscript in the cover letter might increase response. One older study did find an increase in response, however, two more recent studies found no significant difference.

Questionnaire Construction

A questionnaire is a series of questions asked to individuals to obtain statistically useful information about a given topic. When properly constructed and responsibly administered, questionnaires become a vital instrument by which statements can be made about specific groups or people or entire populations.

Questionnaires are frequently used in quantitative marketing research and social research. They are a valuable method of collecting a wide range of information from a large number of individuals, often referred to as respondents. Adequate questionnaire construction is critical to the success of a survey. Inappropriate questions, incorrect ordering of questions, incorrect scaling, or bad questionnaire format can make the survey valueless, as it may not accurately reflect the views and opinions of the participants. A useful method for checking a questionnaire and making sure it is accurately capturing the intended information is to pretest among a smaller subset of target respondents.

Questionnaire Construction Issues

- Know how you will use the results of your research before you start. If, for example, the results won't influence your decision or you can't afford to implement the findings or the cost of the research outweighs its usefulness, then save your time and money; don't bother doing the research.

- The research objectives and frame of reference should be defined beforehand, including the questionnaire's context of time, budget, manpower, intrusion and privacy.
- How and from where you select the respondents will determine whether you will be able to generalize your findings to the larger population.
- The nature of the expected responses should be defined and retained for interpretation of the responses, be it preferences, facts, beliefs, feelings, descriptions of past behaviour, or standards of action.
- Unneeded questions are an expense to the researcher and an unwelcome imposition on the respondents. All questions should contribute to the objective(s) of the research.
- If you"research backwards" and determine what you want to say in the report then even though you don't know the exact answers yet, you will be certain to ask all the questions you need - and only the ones you need - in such a way to write your report.
- The topics should fit the respondents' frame of reference. Their background may affect their interpretation of the questions. Respondents should have enough information or expertise to answer the questions truthfully.
- The type of scale, index, or typology to be used shall be determined.
- The level of measurement you use will determine what you can do with and conclude from the data. If the response option is yes/no then you will only know how many or what per cent of your sample answered yes/no. You cannot, however, conclude what the average respondent answered.
- The types of questions should fit the statistical data analysis techniques available and your goals.

- Questions and prepared responses to choose from should be neutral as to intended outcome. A biased question or questionnaire encourages respondents to answer one way rather than another. Even questions without bias may leave respondents with expectations.
- The order or "natural" grouping of questions is often relevant. Prior previous questions may bias later questions.
- The wording should be kept simple: no technical or specialized words.
- The meaning should be clear. Ambiguous words, equivocal sentence structures and negatives may cause misunderstanding, possibly invalidating questionnaire results. Double negatives should be reworded as positives.
- If a survey question actually contains more than one issue, the researcher will not know which one the respondent is answering. Care should be taken to ask one question at a time.
- The list of possible responses should be collectively exhaustive. Respondents should not find themselves with no category that fits their situation. One solution is to use a final category for "other ________".
- The possible responses should also be mutually exclusive. Categories should not overlap. Respondents should not find themselves in more than one category, for example in both the "married" category and the "single" category - there may be need for a "not living with spouse" category.
- Writing style should be conversational, yet concise and accurate and appropriate to the target audience.
- Many people will not answer personal or intimate questions. For this reason, questions about age, income, marital status, etc. are generally placed at the end of the survey. This way, even if the respondent refuses to answer these "personal" questions, he/she will have already answered the research questions.

- "Loaded" questions evoke emotional responses and may skew results.
- Presentation of the questions on the page and use of white space, colours, pictures, charts, or other graphics may affect respondent's interest or distract from the questions.
- Numbering of questions may be helpful.
- Questionnaires can be administered by research staff, by volunteers or self-administered by the respondents. Clear, detailed instructions are needed in either case, matching the needs of each audience.

Table. Methods of collection

Method	Benefits/Cautions
Postal	This method has a low cost. Survey participants can choose to remain anonymous. It is not labour intensive.
Telephone	Questionnaires can be conducted swiftly. Rapport with respondents High response rate Be careful that your sampling frame doesn't skew your sample, For example, if you select the phone numbers from a phone book, you are necessarily excluding people who only have a mobile phone, those who requested an unpublished phone number, and individuals who have recently moved to the area because none of these people will be in the book.
Electronic	This method has a low cost, and on most surveys costs nothing for the participants and little for the surveyors. Questionnaires can be conducted swiftly. Survey participants can choose to remain anonymous. It is not labour intensive. Questions can be more detailed, as opposed to the limits of paper or telephones. This method works well if your survey contains several branching questions.

	Sample may "self select" and thus not be representative of the population.
Personally Administered	Questions can be more detailed, as opposed to the limits of paper or telephones. Rapport with respondents High response rate Usually a convenience sample so you cannot generalize your results.

Types of Questions

- *Contingency questions*: A question that is answered only if the respondent gives a particular response to a previous question. This avoids asking questions of people that do not apply to them.
- *Matrix questions*: Identical response categories are assigned to multiple questions. The questions are placed one under the other, forming a matrix with response categories along the top and a list of questions down the side. This is an efficient use of page space and respondents' time.
- *Closed ended questions*: Respondents' answers are limited to a fixed set of responses. Most scales are closed ended. Other types of closed ended questions include:
  - *Yes/no questions*: The respondent answers with a "yes" or a "no".
  - *Multiple choice*: The respondent has several option from which to choose.
  - *Scaled questions*: Responses are graded on a continuum. Examples of types of scales include the Likert scale, semantic differential scale, and rank-order scale.
- *Open ended questions*: No options or predefined categories are suggested. The respondent supplies their own answer without being constrained by a fixed set of possible responses.

  Examples of types of open ended questions include:

- *Completely unstructured*: For example, "What is your opinion of questionnaires?"
- *Word association*: Words are presented and the respondent mentions the first word that comes to mind.
- *Sentence completion*: Respondents complete an incomplete sentence. For example, "The most important consideration in our decision to buy a new house is..."
- *Story completion*: Respondents complete an incomplete story.
- *Picture completion*: Respondents fill in an empty conversation balloon.
- *Thematic apperception test*: Respondents explain a picture or make up a story about what they think is happening in the picture

Question Sequence

- Questions should flow logically from one to the next.
- The researcher must ensure that the answer to a question is not influenced by previous questions.
- Questions should flow from the more general to the more specific.
- Questions should flow from the least sensitive to the most sensitive.
- Questions should flow from factual and behavioural questions to attitudinal and opinion questions.
- Questions should flow from unaided to aided questions.
- The three stage theory, initial questions should be screening and rapport questions. Then in the second stage you ask all the product specific questions. In the last stage you ask demographic questions.

INTERVIEWS

An interview is a specialised type of communication, usually verbal, between two or more people and is carried out for a specific purpose. It is different from an ordinary conversation in that its form and purpose is structured.

The interview may be carried out for a number of reasons, for example:

- *To select someone for a job*: Personnel selection
- *To collect information*: Market or social research
- *To assist someone,*: A clinical or counselling interview

For an interview to have the best chance of success, the interviewer should usually show warmth and responsiveness. This can be seen as a genuine interest in the person being interviewed. They should show understanding, and not stop the person being interviewed from expressing their thoughts and feelings. Finally, the interviewer should not allow their own wishes, reactions or opinions to influence the outcome of the interview. From this you can see that interviewing is a skilled activity that takes experience and practice.

Planning an Interview

If you are going to carry out an interview, you need to think about the steps involved. Some preparation must be done before the interview to make sure that you get what you need from it, and some thought given afterwards to the information gathered:

- Decide on the purpose of the interview. For example, are you interviewing someone for a job? Are you trying to find out someone's opinion about something? Are you trying to help someone with a problem?
- Decide what kind of information you need to get from the interview to achieve the purpose. You should have a list of specific goals. If you were interviewing someone for a job, you would want to find out whether they were suited to the type of work and would fit in with the rest of the staff.
- Decide what questions are you going to ask. You should draw up a list of questions so that the answers help you to achieve your goals. For example, if you were interviewing someone for the job of a postal worker, you might want to find out whether they were fit enough to carry a heavy sack and walk the streets.

- Carry out the interview. If you were interviewing someone for a job, you should be able to form a fair and honest assessment of the person being interviewed.
- Study the answers to your questions. Make sure that your goals have been achieved. If not, find out more information.
- Make a decision about the purpose of the interview. For example, the person interviewed has been successful and will be offered the job.

Personnel Selection Interviews

Purpose

A personnel selection interview has three purposes:

1. To get information from candidates about their abilities and ambitions;
2. To assess the likelihood of the candidates fitting in well with future colleagues;
3. To give information to the candidates to ensure that they are sufficiently informed about the job to decide whether they wish to carry on with their application.

Questions

All questions asked at interview must be relevant to the post, and should not stray into areas that employment law does not allow, such as those that might lead to discrimination on the grounds of gender, race or disability. If you draw up a job description of the activities involved in doing the job, and a 'person specification' that covers what experience, skills and abilities, training, education and qualifications a suitable candidate should have, you will be able to look for matches in a fair and objective way. When short-listing candidates for interview, you should do it on the basis of this matching process. Candidates have the right to ask why they were not short-listed or offered a job and therefore you must keep proper records of the questions asked and the selection criteria for this purpose. These must be kept for 6 months by law.

Format

Most interviews, including selection interviews, fall into four phases of welcome, collecting information, supplying information and parting. After this, you decide who to appoint, take up references, and offer the chosen candidate the job.

Welcome - The interviewer, or a panel of interviewers, usually greets the candidate, chats informally and explains briefly the procedure of the interview. The aim is to make the candidate relax. Collecting information - This is where you collect information about how the candidate matches the person specification.

All candidates should be asked more or less the same questions, and these should cover:

1. Work history, duties, likes, dislikes, achievements, working conditions, level of earnings, reasons for changing job, type of job desired;
2. Education and training, best and poorest subjects, grades, extra-curricular activities, training beyond undergraduate level;
3. Personal factors such as interests, hobbies, family status and commitments, geographical mobility, flexibility.

Supplying information - You give information to the candidate. The candidate may have questions about the demands of the job, the work environment, etc. and should be given the opportunity to ask them. Parting - The candidate leaves, usually with the promise of being informed of the results of the interview as soon as possible. It is good practice to offer expenses to candidates, especially those who are on low incomes or who are just starting on their career.

Conventions

- The interview will typically last between 10 and 60 minutes; the more important the job, the longer the interview. For some very senior posts, or for those with very specialist requirements, the interview and selection process can last several days.
- The interview will consist mainly of the interviewer,

or the panel of interviewers, asking carefully selected and relevant questions, and then listening to the answers. Somebody should be responsible for recording the candidate's answers.

- The interview is usually a formal occasion in which both parties are formally dressed, behave politely and are not interrupted.
- The interview can take place across a desk or table, which makes note taking easy but can be intimidating, especially if there is a panel of interviewers on one side and the candidate on the other. It is more relaxing to sit at right angles to a candidate, perhaps in easy chairs or next to a low coffee table.

Interviewing in Market, Product or Social Research

Purpose

Interviews may be used in market research, consumer-product evaluation, social research on attitudes, or before any change is made in equipment or in working methods. It is also possible to reveal design faults in a product by talking to the users.

Methods of Data Collection

The Personal Interview Method

The personal interview is the most frequently used method. It is a direct form of investigation where trained interviewers get information from selected individuals. A formal questionnaire is usually used for the interview. The place in which the interview is conducted depends on the subject and on the method of sampling. It may take place in the street or it may be a 'Hall Test', that takes place in a town hall or other public building. If you want to speak to elderly or disabled people, this is best done in their homes or some place that they visit such as a lunch club. It should be by appointment only; never just knock on a door and expect to be let in. Children should always be accompanied if they are carrying out questionnaires in homes.

The Focused Interview Method

The focused interview differs from the personal interview in that respondents are encouraged to talk freely, while the interviewer reports what they say. They may even record it on a tape for later analysis. To keep the interview to the point, guiding questions are sometimes put to the respondent. Often, more information can be obtained this way, than when detailed, fixed questions are asked.

Disadvantages of personal and focused interviews:

1. There is great danger that the interviewer, when recording the answers, will interpret them in their own way.
2. The interpretation of the interviews by the researcher is also very difficult and gives an opportunity for personal bias to distort the findings.
3. Statistical analysis of the findings is either very difficult or impossible since the information may not be easy to quantify or code.
4. The interview takes a long time, which increases the cost per interview.
5. There is a high proportion of irrelevant information in the data.

The Telephone Interview Method

This is similar to the personal interview but obviously takes place over the telephone. Again the respondents are asked a set list of questions relevant to the study. This method is becoming very common for market research, as well as being used by service companies, such as banks, who want to make contact with their customers, either to improve services or to sell additional ones.

Advantages:

- It is a quick method for conducting a number of interviews within a short time.
- The interviewers can be supervised easily.

- The cost per interview is low.
- The sampling can be spread over the country and travelling is eliminated.
- People who might otherwise be inaccessible, can be interviewed, since the interview can be very brief and arranged for a time that is convenient to the respondent.

Disadvantages:

- Telephone subscribers may not be representative of the general population, Mobile phone numbers may be used which do not give information about the location of the respondent.
- Only a short questionnaire can be used.
- Observation is not possible, so that the interviewers have to rely totally on what the respondent tells them.
- The times during the day when respondents can be called are limited, for example to office hours, or early evening, and it is difficult to predict such times. Calling during meals or when people are watching TV can lead to negative responses.
- 'Call-backs' have to be made when the number is engaged.

The Panel Method

The panel method is used to study changes over time. A panel of the same respondents are used and they are questioned about the same sort of thing over a period of time. There are several types of panel including the consumer-purchasing panel, the consumer-product testing panel, or the television audience panel. The panel is often recruited by means of personal interviews of a cross-section of the population. The respondents are given diaries in which they enter, for example, every time they buy one of the products being surveyed. They return the diaries at regular intervals. Alternatively, the panel may be interviewed about the relevant facts periodically. This method has been successfully adopted for radio, television and opinion research.

Advantages:

- The method is especially useful for research into trends, as the same individuals are questioned over a period of time.
- Data collected over a period of time can be accumulated and the factors underlying the change can be analysed.
- The case histories of panel members can be established to give relevant background material to responses.
- The panel can sometimes be used for enquiries on other subjects, provided that these are not likely to affect the reliability of the panel for its main purpose.

Disadvantages:

- Individuals may leave the panel.
- If people refuse to join the panel it may no longer represent a target population.
- Being a member of the panel over a long period of time may affect the opinions and behaviour of panelists, so that their responses may no longer be representative of the population at large.
- The original recruiting drive is usually expensive so investment takes a long time to yield returns.
- Panel members are usually rewarded in some small way, which adds to the overall cost.

The Group Interview Method

A small and carefully selected group of people is invited to a discussion on whatever topic is under review. A questionnaire may be provided, but more usually, the group is encouraged to discuss the matter freely, following a basic agenda. The discussion may be recorded on tape, if the respondents agree, or an observer may be present to take notes. The interviewer's task is to remain in the background and to intervene only to bring the discussion back to the point.

Advantages:

- Group interviews are appropriate in research concerned with motives and opinions where such factors as social status and acceptance are involved. Such factors are brought out through the dynamic group situation.

- The group interview is relatively inexpensive as one interviewer can listen to up to ten people at a time.
- The free discussion of the group on a topic can provide valuable information for pilot studies
- The spontaneity of the discussion may produce information and attitudes that cannot be obtained by other methods.

Disadvantages:

- It is usually very doubtful whether such a group can be regarded as really representative of the population at large.
- Statistical analysis of the material is usually difficult, if not impossible.
- The influence of the more vocal group members on group opinion is hard to estimate.
- In the group situation, people may assume roles and behaviour that are not characteristic of their usual behaviour.
- Some groups are difficult to assemble, for example, managing directors.

Self-administered and Group-administered Questionnaires

The interviewer is often a person in authority such as a teacher. They briefly explain the purpose and requirements of the survey to the respondent, or group of respondents, and then leaves them alone to complete the questions. The method usually gives a high response rate and a minimum of interviewer bias. It has the benefit of a degree of interviewer assessment of the respondents, a better explanation to the respondents and personal contact.

For groups of respondents assembled together, the interviewer distributes the questionnaire to the assembly or reads aloud each question for immediate completion. All respondents then answer each question in the same order.

Groups of forty can be handled in this way, but they can affect answers by copying, talking and asking questions.

Format of the Interview

The following stages usually occur:

- Decide on the aims of the study and what you are trying to investigate - usually called the 'hypothesis' or 'null hypothesis'. For example, 'men are more interested in sport than women'.
- Review the relevant literature and discuss with other people. This includes deciding how the data will be analysed, and making sure that the information is collected in a suitable format.
- Design the study, making the hypothesis specific to the situation. For example, 'men are more interested in playing golf than women'.
- Compose the interview questions that will bring out the information that you need for your study.
- Carry out a small test to make sure that you have phrased the questions adequately and modify them if you need to.
- Select a sample of subjects to be approached.
- Collect your data.
- Sort out and process your data. This can include giving codes to the answers so that they can be put on a computer spreadsheet for analysis by a statistical package.
- Do the statistical analysis.
- Put all of the results together and see what they are telling you. This is the part where the hypothesis is tested to see, for example, if men statistically do play more golf than women.
- Write up the results, relating the findings to other research, drawing ceases and interpretations.

Anonymity

Data obtained by means of questionnaires is confidential, in the sense that no responses or findings should ever be published which could be traced back to particular individuals. This is a requirement of the Data Protection Act. In enlisting co-operation for any survey, respondents are usually given this assurance and a guarantee of anonymity. This is often crucial in obtaining frank and revealing responses. Where possible, therefore, you should not ask respondents to put their names on, or to sign, their questionnaires. If you need to maintain a check on non-respondents, the questionnaires can be numbered and cross-referenced back to individuals.

DOCUMENTATION

Documentation may refer to the process of providing evidence or to the communicable material used to provide such documentation. Documentation may also refer to tools aiming at identifying documents or to the field of study devoted to the study of documents and bibliographies.

Subfields of documentation include:

- Medical documentation
- Technical documentation
- Legal documentation
- Administrative documentation
- Historical documentation

Documentation in Computer Science:

- Architectural and Design documentation.
- Technical Documentation.
- User Documentation.
- System Documentation.
- Marketing Documentation.

There are various types of Documentation Tools which are available for this purpose.

Documentation understood as document is any communicable material used to explain some attributes of an object, system or procedure. It is often used to mean engineering documentation or software documentation, which is usually paper books or computer readable files that describe the structure and components, or on the other hand, operation, of a system/product. A professional whose field and work is documentation used to be termed a documentalist. Normally, documentalists are trained or have a background in both a specific subject and in the field of documentation. A person who more or less exclusively writes technical documentation is called a technical writer. Technical writers are similarly trained or have a background in technical writing, along with some knowledge of the subject(s) they are documenting. Often, though, they collaborate with subject matter experts, such as engineers.

Common types of computer hardware/software documentation include online help, FAQs, how-tos, and user guides. The term RTFM is often used colloquially in regard to such documentation, especially to computer hardware and software user guides.

A common type of software document frequently written by software engineers in the simulation industry is the SDF. While developing the software for a simulator, which can range from embedded avionics devices to 3D terrain databases by way of full motion control systems, the engineer keeps a notebook detailing the development lifecycle of the project. The notebook can contain a requirements part, an interface part detailing the communication interface of the software, a notes part to detail the proof of concept attempts to track what worked or didn't work in solving certain problems, and a testing part to detail how the software will be tested to prove conformance to the requirements of the contract.

The end result is a detailed description of how the software is designed, how to build and install the software on the target device, and any known weaknesses in the design of the software.

This document will allow future developers and maintainers of the trainer to come up to speed on the software design in as short a time as possible and have a documented reference when modifying code or searching for bugs.

Principles

While associated ISO standards are not easily available publicly, a guide from other sources for this topic may serve the purpose. David Berger has provided several principles of document writing, regarding the terms used, procedure numbering and even lengths of sentences, etc..

The following is a list of guides dealing with each specific field and type:

- Documentation in health care
- Thesis writing,,
- *Further information*: Dissertation
- Papers for academic journal publishing

Procedures and Techniques

The procedures of documentation vary from one sector, or one type, to another. In general, these may involve document drafting, formatting, submitting, reviewing, approving, distributing, repositing and tracking, etc., and are convened by associated SOPs in a regulatory industry.

OBSERVATION

Observation:

- Observation is a method of data gathering in which a qualified person watches, or walks through, the actual processing associated with a system
- Best for studying processes, e.g. manufacturing
- Useful for studying the work flow through an office for example
- Could be active or passive

Non-behavioural observation:

- Record analysis:
- Analysis of historical or current records and public or private records.
- Physical condition analysis
- Audits of merchandise availability, studies of plant safety compliance, etc.
- Process or activity analysis
- Time/motion studies, financial flows in a banking system, paper flow in office systems, etc.

Behavioural observation:

- *Nonverbal analysis*: E.g., Monitoring eye movement in user-interface studies.

- *Linguistic analysis*: E.g., study of a sales presentation's content or the study of what, how, and how much information is conveyed in a training situation.
- *Extralinguistic analysis*: E.g., study of the linguistic content of the interaction between supervisors and subordinates.
- *Spatial analysis*: E.g., a study of how salespeople physically approach customers.

Advantages of the Observational Method

- Collect the original data at the time it occurs
- Secure information that participants would ignore because it's so common it is not seen as relevant
- Only method available to collect certain types of data
- Capture the whole event as it occurs in its natural environment
- Subjects seem to accept an observational intrusion better than they respond to questioning

Limitations of the Observational Method

- Observer or recording equipment must be at the scene of the event when it takes place
- Slow process
- Expensive process
- Most reliable results are restricted to information that can be learned by overt action or surface indicators
- Research environment is more likely suited to subjective assessment and recording of data than to quantification of events
- Limited as a way to learn about the past
- Cannot observe rationale for actions, only actions themselves

6

Scaling

CONCEPT

Scaling is the branch of measurement that involves the construction of an instrument that associates qualitative constructs with quantitative metric units. Scaling evolved out of efforts in psychology and education to measure "unmeasurable" constructs like authoritarianism and self esteem. In many ways, scaling remains one of the most arcane and misunderstood aspects of social research measurement. And, it attempts to do one of the most difficult of research tasks — measure abstract concepts. Most people don't even understand what scaling is. The basic idea of scaling is described in General Issues in Scaling, including the important distinction between a scale and a response format. Scales are generally divided into two broad categories: unidimensional and multidimensional. The unidimensional scaling methods were developed in the first half of the twentieth century and are generally named after their inventor.

We'll look at three types of unidimensional scaling methods here:

1. Thurstone or Equal-Appearing Interval Scaling
2. Likert or "Summative" Scaling
3. Guttman or "Cumulative" Scaling

In the late 1950s and early 1960s, measurement theorists developed more advanced techniques for creating multidimensional scales. Although these techniques are not considered here, you may want to look at the method of concept mapping that relies on that approach to see the power of these multivariate methods.

TYPES OF SCALING

The various types of scaling techniques used in research can be classified into.

Two categories:

1. Comparative scales, and
2. Non-comparative scales.

In comparative scaling, the respondent is asked to compare one object with another. For example, the researcher can ask the respondents whether they prefer brand A or brand B of a detergent. On the other hand, in non-comparative scaling respondents need only evaluate a single object. Their evaluation is independent of the other object which the researcher is studying. Respondents using a non-comparative scale employ whatever rating standard seems appropriate to them. Non-comparative techniques consist of continuous and itemized rating scales.

RATING SCALE

A rating scale is a set of categories designed to elicit information about a quantitative or a qualitative attribute. In the social sciences, common examples are the Likert scale and 1-10 rating scales in which a person selects the number which is considered to reflect the perceived quality of a product.

A rating scale is an instrument that requires the rater to assign the rated object that have numerals assigned to them.

TYPES OF RATING SCALES

All the rating scales can be classified into one of the following four classifications:

1. Some data are measured at the nominal level. That is, any numbers used are mere labels: they express no mathematical properties. Examples are SKU inventory codes and UPC bar codes.
2. Some data are measured at the ordinal level. Numbers indicate the relative position of items, but not the magnitude of difference.
   One example is a Likert scale:
   Statement: we could not live without computer.

Response options:
- Strongly Disagree
- Disagree
- Agree
- Strongly Agree

3. Some data are measured at the interval level. Numbers indicate the magnitude of difference between items, but there is no absolute zero point. Examples are attitude scales and opinion scales.
4. Some data are measured at the ratio level. Numbers indicate magnitude of difference and there is a fixed zero point. Ratios can be calculated. Examples include: age, income, price, costs, sales revenue, sales volume, and market share.

More than one rating scale is required to measure an attitude or perception due to the requirement for statistical comparisons between the categories in the polytomous Rasch model for ordered categories.

In terms of Classical test theory, more than one question is required to obtain an index of internal reliability such as Cronbach's alpha, which is a basic criterion for assessing the effectiveness of a rating scale and, more generally, a psychometric instrument.

RANKING SCALE

A measurement type for which the relative values of data are defined solely in terms of being lesser, equal to or greater as compared with other data on the ordinal scale. These characteristics may arise from categorical rating scales, or from converting interval scale data to become ranked data.

MULTIDIMENSIONAL SCALING

Multidimensional scaling is a set of related statistical techniques often used in information visualization for exploring similarities or dissimilarities in data. MDS is a special case of ordination.

An MDS algorithm starts with a matrix of item–item similarities, then assigns a location to each item in N-dimensional space, where N is specified a priori. For sufficiently small N, the resulting locations may be displayed in a graph or 3D visualisation.

TYPES

MDS algorithms fall into a taxonomy, depending on the meaning of the input matrix:

Classical Multidimensional Scaling

Also known as Torgerson Scaling or Torgerson-Gower scaling – takes an input matrix giving dissimilarities between pairs of items and outputs a coordinate matrix whose configuration minimizes a loss function called strain.

Metric Multidimensional Scaling

A superset of classical MDS that generalizes the optimization procedure to a variety of loss functions and input matrices of known distances with weights and so on.

A useful loss function in this context is called stress which is often minimized using a procedure called Stress Majorization.

Non-metric Multidimensional Scaling

In contrast to metric MDS, non-metric MDS both finds a non-parametric monotonic relationship between the dissimilarities in the item-item matrix and the Euclidean distance between items, and the location of each item in the low-dimensional space.

The relationship is typically found using isotonic regression:

- Louis Guttman's smallest space analysis is an example of a non-metric MDS procedure.

Generalized Multidimensional Scaling

An extension of metric multidimensional scaling, in which the target space is an arbitrary smooth non-Euclidean space. In case when the dissimilarities are distances on a surface and the target space is another surface, GMDS allows finding the minimum-distortion embedding of one surface into another.

DETAILS

The data to be analysed is a collection of we objects on which a distance function is defined,

$\delta_{i,j}$:= distance between i th and j th objects.

These distances are the entries of the dissimilarity matrix:

$$\Delta := \begin{pmatrix} \delta_{1,1} & \delta_{1,2} & \cdots & \delta_{1,I} \\ \delta_{2,1} & \delta_{2,2} & \cdots & \delta_{2,I} \\ \vdots & \vdots & & \vdots \\ \delta_{I,1} & \delta_{I,2} & \cdots & \delta_{I,I} \end{pmatrix}.$$

The goal of MDS is, given Δ, to find I vectors $x_1,...x_I \in \mathbb{R}^N$ such that,

$$\|x_i - x_j\| \approx \delta_{i,j} \text{ for all } i, j \in I,$$

where $\|.\|$ is a vector norm. In classical MDS, this norm is the Euclidean distance, but more generally it may be a metric or arbitrary distance function.

In other words, MDS attempts to find an embedding from the objects into R^N such that distances are preserved. If the dimension N is chosen to be 2 or 3, we may plot the vectors x_i to obtain a visualization of the similarities between the objects.

Note that the vectors x_i are not unique: with the Euclidean distance, they may be arbitrarily translated and rotated since these transformations do not change the pairwise distances,

$$\|x_i - x_j\|.$$

There are various approaches to determining the vectors x_i. Usually, MDS is formulated as an optimization problem, where $(x_1,...x_I)$ is found as a minimizer of some cost function, for example,

$$\min_{(x_1,...x_I)} \sum_{i<j} \left(\|x_i - x_j\| - \delta_{i,j}\right)^2.$$

A solution may then be found by numerical optimization techniques. For some particularly chosen cost functions, minimizers can be stated analytically in terms of matrix eigendecompositions.

PROCEDURE

There are several steps in conducting MDS research:

- *Formulating the problem*: What variables do you want to compare? How many variables do you want to compare? More than 20 is often considered cumbersome. Less than 8 will not give valid results. What purpose is the study to be used for?
- *Obtaining Input Data*: Respondents are asked a series of questions. For each product pair they are asked to rate similarity. The first question could be for Coke/Pepsi for example, the next for Coke/Hires rootbeer, the next for Pepsi/Dr Pepper, the next for Dr Pepper/Hires rootbeer, etc. The number of questions is a function of the number of brands and can be calculated as $Q = N(N - 1)/ 2$ where Q is the number of questions and N is the number of brands. This approach is referred to as the "Perception data: direct approach". There are two other approaches. There is the "Perception data: derived approach" in which products are decomposed into attributes which are rated on a semantic differential scale. The other is the "Preference data approach" in which respondents are asked their preference rather than similarity.
- *Running the MDS statistical programme*: Software for running the procedure is available in many software for statistics. Often there is a choice between Metric MDS, and Nonmetric MDS.
- *Decide number of dimensions*: The researchers must decide on the number of dimensions they want the computer to create. The more dimensions, the better the statistical fit, but the more difficult it is to interpret the results.
- *Mapping the results and defining the dimensions*: The statistical programme will map the results. The map will plot each product. The proximity of products to each other indicate either how similar they are or how preferred they are, depending on which approach was used. The dimensions must be labelled

by the researcher. This requires subjective judgement and is often very challenging. The results must be interpreted.

- *Test the results for reliability and Validity*: Compute R-squared to determine what proportion of variance of the scaled data can be accounted for by the MDS procedure. An R-square of.6 is considered the minimum acceptable level. An R-square of.8 is considered good for metric scaling and.9 is considered good for non-metric scaling. Other possible tests are Kruskal's Stress, split data tests, data stability tests and test-retest reliability.
- *Report the results comprehensively*: Along with the mapping, at least distance measure and reliability should be given. It is also very advisable to give the algorithm which is often definde by the programme used, if you have given a start configuration or had a random choice, the number of runs, the assessment of dimensionality, the Monte Carlo method results, the number of iterations, the assessment of stability, and the proportional variance of each axis.

APPLICATIONS

Applications include scientific visualisation and data mining in fields such as cognitive science, information science, psychophysics, psychometrics, marketing and ecology. New applications arise in the scope of autonomous wireless nodes which populate a space or an area. MDS may apply as a real time enhanced approach to monitoring and managing such populations.

Marketing

In marketing, MDS is a statistical technique for taking the preferences and perceptions of respondents and representing them on a visual grid, called perceptual maps.

Comparison and Advantages

Potential customers are asked to compare pairs of

products and make judgements about their similarity. Whereas other techniques obtain underlying dimensions from responses to product attributes identified by the researcher, MDS obtains the underlying dimensions from respondents' judgments about the similarity of products. This is an important advantage. It does not depend on researchers' judgments. It does not require a list of attributes to be shown to the respondents. The underlying dimensions come from respondents' judgments about pairs of products. Because of these advantages, MDS is the most common technique used in perceptual mapping.

DESIGNING QUESTIONNAIRE

Most problems with questionnaire analysis can be traced back to the design phase of the project. Well-defined goals are the best way to assure a good questionnaire design. When the goals of a study can be expressed in a few clear and concise sentences, the design of the questionnaire becomes considerably easier. The questionnaire is developed to directly address the goals of the study.

One of the best ways to clarify your study goals is to decide how you intend to use the information. Do this before you begin designing the study. This sounds obvious, but many researchers neglect this task. Why do research if the results will not be used? Be sure to commit the study goals to writing. Whenever you are unsure of a question, refer to the study goals and a solution will become clear. Ask only questions that directly address the study goals. Avoid the temptation to ask questions because it would be "interesting to know".

As a general rule, with only a few exceptions, long questionnaires get less response than short questionnaires. Keep your questionnaire short. In fact, the shorter the better. Response rate is the single most important indicator of how much confidence you can place in the results. A low response rate can be devastating to a study. Therefore, you must do everything possible to maximize the response rate. One of the most effective methods of maximizing response is to shorten the questionnaire.

If your survey is over a few pages, try to eliminate questions. Many people have difficulty knowing which questions could be eliminated. For the elimination round, read each question and ask, "How am I going to use this information?" If the information will be used in a decision-making process, then keep the question... it's important. If not, throw it out.

One important way to assure a successful survey is to include other experts and relevant decision-makers in the questionnaire design process. Their suggestions will improve the questionnaire and they will subsequently have more confidence in the results.

Formulate a plan for doing the statistical analysis during the design stage of the project. Know how every question will be analysed and be prepared to handle missing data. If you cannot specify how you intend to analyse a question or use the information, do not use it in the survey.

Make the envelope unique. We all know how important first impressions are. The same holds true for questionnaires. The respondent's first impression of the study usually comes from the envelope containing the survey. The best envelopes are coloured, hand-addressed and use a commemorative postage stamp. Envelopes with bulk mail permits or gummed labels are perceived as unimportant. This will generally be reflected in a lower response rate.

Provide a well-written cover letter. The respondent's next impression comes from the cover letter. The importance of the cover letter should not be underestimated. It provides your best chance to persuade the respondent to complete the survey.

Give your questionnaire a title that is short and meaningful to the respondent. A questionnaire with a title is generally perceived to be more credible than one without.

Include clear and concise instructions on how to complete the questionnaire. These must be very easy to understand, so use short sentences and basic vocabulary. Be sure to print the return address on the questionnaire itself.

Begin with a few non-threatening and interesting items. If the first items are too threatening or "boring", there is little chance that the person will complete the questionnaire. People generally look at the first few questions before deciding whether or not to complete the questionnaire. Make them want to continue by putting interesting questions first.

Use simple and direct language. The questions must be clearly understood by the respondent. The wording of a question should be simple and to the point. Do not use uncommon words or long sentences. Make items as brief as possible. This will reduce misunderstandings and make the questionnaire appear easier to complete. One way to eliminate misunderstandings is to emphasize crucial words in each item by using bold, italics or underlining.

Leave adequate space for respondents to make comments. One criticism of questionnaires is their inability to retain the "flavour" of a response. Leaving space for comments will provide valuable information not captured by the response categories. Leaving white space also makes the questionnaire look easier and this increases response.

Place the most important items in the first half of the questionnaire. Respondents often send back partially completed questionnaires. By putting the most important items near the beginning, the partially completed questionnaires will still contain important information.

Hold the respondent's interest. We want the respondent to complete our questionnaire. One way to keep a questionnaire interesting is to provide variety in the type of items used. Varying the questioning format will also prevent respondents from falling into "response sets".

At the same time, it is important to group items into coherent categories. All items should flow smoothly from one to the next. If a questionnaire is more than a few pages and is held together by a staple, include some identifying data on each page. Pages often accidentally separate. Provide incentives as a motivation for a properly completed questionnaire. What does the respondent get for completing your questionnaire? Altruism is rarely an effective motivator. Attaching a dollar bill to the questionnaire works well. If the information you are collecting is of interest to the respondent, offering a free summary report is also an excellent motivator. Whatever you choose, it must make the respondent want to complete the questionnaire.

Use professional production methods for the questionnaire—either desktop publishing or typesetting and keylining. Be creative. Try different coloured inks and paper. The object is to make your questionnaire stand out from all the others the respondent receives.

Make it convenient. The easier it is for the respondent to complete the questionnaire the better. Always include a self-addressed postage-paid envelope. Envelopes with postage stamps get better response than business reply envelopes.

The final test of a questionnaire is to try it on representatives of the target audience. If there are problems with the questionnaire, they almost always show up here. If possible, be present while a respondent is completing the questionnaire and tell her that it is okay to ask you for clarification of any item. The questions she asks are indicative of problems in the questionnaire.

INTERVIEWING

An interview is a conversation between two or more people where questions are asked by the interviewer to obtain information from the interviewee.

INTERVIEWING SKILLS

- An interview is a 2-way communication; however, it should be controlled by the interviewer
- Every interviewee is a guest in your organization and should be treated in such a manner
- Always welcome the interviewees with a warm greeting
- Encourage interviewees to respond positively and share the information
- It is always better to take notes during Interview
- Good interviews flow smoothly when both the interviewer and the candidate take part in an information exchange

TYPES OF DIFFICULT INTERVIEWS

- Some interviewees demand a particularly focused interviewing techniques.
- In order to get an accurate assessment of a candidate's ability, the interviewer's ability to handle different types of candidate is very important
- Before Interviewing, develop an understanding of the following types of candidates:
  - Nervous candidate
  - Uncommunicative candidate
  - Talkative candidate

HANDLING A NERVOUS CANDIDATE

- Give them an especially warm greeting
- Engage in more small talk than usual
- Point out various facilities or areas of interest within your organization
- Start with specific, fact-based questions that are easy for the candidate to answer and unlikely to be stressful
- Speak slowly in a relaxed, informal manner

HANDLING AN UNCOMMUNICATIVE CANDIDATE

- Many reserved or uncommunicative candidates simply need to be encouraged to share their thoughts
- Using silence can be effective
- If the candidate is having trouble in answering questions related to their strengths and weaknesses, tell them that you will give them some time to think about it and come back to the question later

HANDLING A TALKATIVE CANDIDATE

- Candidates who talk too much, often about things unrelated to the job or interview can be challenging
- Tell the candidate that you will be following a structure, and stress on the time available for each part of the interview

- When necessary, remind the candidate of the time limits
- Redirect the conversation as politely as possible

CONDUCTING THE INTERVIEW

There are 3 steps to follow while conducting an Interview:

1. Open the Interview
2. Gather Information
3. Close the Interview

OPENING AN INTERVIEW

- While opening an interview, your purpose is to put both you and candidate at ease, and set the stage for an open conversation
- There are 3 steps you should complete when opening the interview:
  - Build rapport
  - State the agenda
  - Ask for acceptance

GATHERING INFORMATION

- Gathering Information represents 70 to 80 per cent of the interview
- There are 3 steps you should complete when gathering information from the interviewee:
  - Ask lead questions
  - Ask follow-up questions
  - Transition to the next subject

CLOSING AN INTERVIEW

- The close of the interview is used to indicate to the candidate that the information-gathering portion is complete and the interview is about to wind down.
- Take the following 4 steps when closing an interview:
  - Ask for and answer questions
  - Promote the organization and the job
  - Outline next steps
  - Thank the candidate

EVALUATION OF CANDIDATES

- *Manage your bias*:
  - Interviewer should be very careful to identify and overcome any biases
  - Bias is a form of extreme generalization. You may generalize that a candidate lacks written communication skills because of last two people hired from the same college had poor written communication skil
- 2 steps to evaluate the candidate:
  - Summarize the interview
  - Score the candidate

EFFECTIVE COMMUNICATION TECHNIQUES

Effective communication techniques include:

- Active Listening
- Nonverbal behaviour
- Verbal devices

COMPARATIVE AND NONCOMPARATIVE SCALING

With comparative scaling, the items are directly compared with each other. In noncomparative scaling each item is scaled independently of the others.

COMPOSITE MEASURES

Composite measures of variables are created by combining two or more separate empirical indicators into a single measure. Composite measures measure complex concepts more adequately than single indicators, extend the range of scores available and are more efficient at handling multiple items. In addition to scales, there are two other types of composite measures. Indexes are similar to scales except multiple indicators of a variable are combined into a single measure. The index of consumer confidence, for example, is a combination of several measures of consumer attitudes. A typology is similar to an index except the variable is measured at the nominal level. Indexes are constructed by accumulating scores assigned to individual attributes, while scales are constructed through the assignment of scores to patterns of attributes. While indexes and scales provide measures of a single dimension, typologies are often employed to examine the intersection of two or more dimensions. Typologies are very useful analytical tools and can be easily used as independent variables, although since they are not unidimensional it is difficult to use them as a dependent variable.

DATA TYPES

The type of information collected can influence scale construction.

Different types of information are measured in different ways:

- Some data are measured at the nominal level. That is, any numbers used are mere labels: they express no mathematical properties. Examples are SKU inventory codes and UPC bar codes.
- Some data are measured at the ordinal level. Numbers indicate the relative position of items, but not the magnitude of difference. An example is a preference ranking.
- Some data are measured at the interval level. Numbers indicate the magnitude of difference between items, but there is no absolute zero point. Examples are attitude scales and opinion scales.
- Some data are measured at the ratio level. Numbers indicate magnitude of difference and there is a fixed zero point. Ratios can be calculated. Examples include: age, income, price, costs, sales revenue, sales volume, and market share.

SCALE CONSTRUCTION DECISIONS

- What level of data is involved?
- What will the results be used for?
- Should you use a scale, index, or typology?
- What types of statistical analysis would be useful?

- Should you use a comparative scale or a noncomparative scale?
- How many scale divisions or categories should be used?
- Should there be an odd or even number of divisions?
- What should the nature and descriptiveness of the scale labels be?
- What should the physical form or layout of the scale be?
- Should a response be forced or be left optional?

COMPARATIVE SCALING TECHNIQUES

- *Pairwise comparison scale*: A respondent is presented with two items at a time and asked to select one. This is an ordinal level technique when a measurement model is not applied. Krus and Kennedy elaborated the paired comparison scaling within their domain-referenced model. The Bradley–Terry–Luce model can be applied in order to derive measurements provided the data derived from paired comparisons possess an appropriate structure. Thurstone's Law of comparative judgment can also be applied in such contexts.
- *Rasch model scaling*: Respondents interact with items and comparisons are inferred between items from the responses to obtain scale values. Respondents are subsequently also scaled based on their responses to items given the item scale values. The Rasch model has a close relation to the BTL model.
- *Rank-order scale*: A respondent is presented with several items simultaneously and asked to rank them. This is an ordinal level technique.
- *Bogardus social distance scale*: Measures the degree to which a person is willing to associate with a class or type of people. It asks how willing the respondent is to make various associations. The results are reduced to a single score on a scale. There are also non-comparative versions of this scale.

- *Q-Sort scale*: Up to 140 items are sorted into groups based a rank-order procedure.
- *Guttman scale*: This is a procedure to determine whether a set of items can be rank-ordered on a unidimensional scale. It utilizes the intensity structure among several indicators of a given variable. Statements are listed in order of importance. The rating is scaled by summing all responses until the first negative response in the list. The Guttman scale is related to Rasch measurement; specifically, Rasch models bring the Guttman approach within a probabilistic framework.
- *Constant sum scale*: A respondent is given a constant sum of money, script, credits, or points and asked to allocate these to various items. This is an ordinal level technique.
- *Magnitude estimation scale*: In a psychophysics procedure invented by S. S. Stevens people simply assign numbers to the dimension of judgment. The geometric mean of those numbers usually produces a power law with a characteristic exponent. In cross-modality matching instead of assigning numbers, people manipulate another dimension, such as loudness or brightness to match the items. Typically the exponent of the psychometric function can be predicted from the magnitude estimation exponents of each dimension.

NON-COMPARATIVE SCALING TECHNIQUES

- *Continuous rating scale*: Respondents rate items by placing a mark on a line. The line is usually labeled at each end. There are sometimes a series of numbers, called scale points, under the line. Scoring and codification is difficult.
- *Likert scale*: Respondents are asked to indicate the amount of agreement or disagreement on a five- to nine-point scale. The same format is used for multiple

questions. This categorical scaling procedure can easily be extended to a magnitude estimation procedure that uses the full scale of numbers rather than verbal categories.

- *Phrase completion scales*: Respondents are asked to complete a phrase on an 11-point response scale in which 0 represents the absence of the theoretical construct and 10 represents the theorized maximum amount of the construct being measured. The same basic format is used for multiple questions.
- *Semantic differential scale*: Respondents are asked to rate on a 7 point scale an item on various attributes. Each attribute requires a scale with bipolar terminal labels.
- *Stapel scale*: This is a unipolar ten-point rating scale. It ranges from +5 to "5 and has no neutral zero point.
- *Thurstone scale*: This is a scaling technique that incorporates the intensity structure among indicators.
- *Mathematically derived scale*: Researchers infer respondents' evaluations mathematically. Two examples are multi dimensional scaling and conjoint analysis.

SCALE EVALUATION

Scales should be tested for reliability, generalizability, and validity. Generalizability is the ability to make inferences from a sample to the population, given the scale you have selected. Reliability is the extent to which a scale will produce consistent results. Test-retest reliability checks how similar the results are if the research is repeated under similar circumstances. Alternative forms reliability checks how similar the results are if the research is repeated using different forms of the scale. Internal consistency reliability checks how well the individual measures included in the scale are converted into a composite measure.

Scales and indexes have to be validated. Internal validation checks the relation between the individual measures included in the scale, and the composite scale itself. External validation checks the relation between the composite scale and other indicators of the variable, indicators not included in the scale. Content validation checks how well the scale measures what is supposed to measure. Criterion validation checks how meaningful the scale criteria are relative to other possible criteria. Construct validation checks what underlying construct is being measured. There are three variants of construct validity. They are convergent validity, discriminant validity, and nomological validity. The coefficient of reproducibility indicates how well the data from the individual measures included in the scale can be reconstructed from the composite scale.

7

Sampling Designs

In the theory of finite population sampling, a sampling design specifies for every possible sample its probability of being drawn. Mathematically, a sampling design is denoted by the function $P(S)$ which gives the probability of drawing a sample S.

TYPES OF SAMPLING

We may then consider different types of probability samples. Although there are a number of different methods that might be used to create a sample, they generally can be grouped into one of two categories: *probability samples* or *non-probability* samples.

PROBABILITY SAMPLES

The idea behind this type is random selection. More specifically, each sample from the population of interest has a known probability of selection under a given sampling plan..

SIMPLE RANDOM SAMPLING

The most widely known type of a random sample is the simple random sample (SRS). This is characterized by the fact that the probability of selection is the same for every case in the population. Simple random sampling is a method of selecting n units from a population of size N such that every possible sample of size an has equal chance of being drawn.

An example may make this easier to understand. Imagine you want to carry out a survey of 100 voters in a small town with a population of 1,000 eligible voters. With a town this size, there are "old-fashioned" ways to draw a sample. For example, we could write the names of all voters on a piece of paper, put all pieces of paper into a box and draw 100 tickets at random. You shake the box, draw a piece of paper and set it aside, shake again, draw another, set it aside, etc. until we had 100 slips of paper. These 100 form our sample. And this sample would be drawn through a simple random sampling procedure - at each draw, every name in the box had the same probability of being chosen.

In real-world social research, designs that employ simple random sampling are difficult to come by. We can imagine some situations where it might be possible - you want to interview a sample of doctors in a hospital about work conditions. So you get a list of all the physicians that work in the hospital, write their names on a piece of paper, put those pieces of paper in the box, shake and draw. But in most real-world instances it is impossible to list everything on a piece of paper and put it in a box, then randomly draw numbers until desired sample size is reached. There are many reasons why one would choose a different type of probability sample in practice.

STRATIFIED RANDOM SAMPLING

In this form of sampling, the population is first divided into two or more mutually exclusive segments based on some categories of variables of interest in the research. It is designed to organize the population into homogenous subsets before sampling, then drawing a random sample within each subset. With stratified random sampling the population of N units is divided into subpopulations of units respectively. These subpopulations, called *strata*, are non-overlapping and together they comprise the whole of the population. When these have been determined, a sample is drawn from each, with a separate draw for each of the different strata. The sample sizes within the strata are denoted by respectively. If a SRS is taken within each stratum, then the whole sampling procedure is described as stratified random sampling.

The primary benefit of this method is to ensure that cases from smaller strata of the population are included in sufficient numbers to allow comparison. An example makes it easier to understand. Say that you're interested in how job satisfaction varies by race among a group of employees at a firm. To explore this issue, we need to create a sample of the employees of the firm.

However, the employee population at this particular firm is predominantly white:

- *African-American*: 9%
- *Asian*: 10%
- *Latino*: 6%
- *White*: 75%

If we were to take a simple random sample of employees, there's a good chance that we would end up with very small numbers of Blacks, Asians, and Latinos. That could be disastrous for our research, since we might end up with too few cases for comparison in one or more of the smaller groups.

Rather than taking a simple random sample from the firm's population at large, in a stratified sampling design, we ensure that appropriate numbers of elements are drawn from each racial group in proportion to the percentage of the population as a whole. Say we want a sample of 1000 employees - we would stratify the sample by race then randomly draw out 750 employees from the White group, 90 from the African American, 100 from the Asian, and 60 from the Latino. This yields a sample that is proportionately representative of the firm as a whole. Stratification is a common technique.

There are many reasons for this, such as:

- If data of known precision are wanted for certain subpopulations, than each of these should be treated as a population in its own right.
- Administrative convenience may dictate the use of stratification, for example, if an agency administering a survey may have regional offices, which can supervise the survey for a part of the population.
- Sampling problems may be inherent with certain sub populations, such as people living in institutions.
- Stratification may improve the estimates of characteristics of the whole population. It may be

possible to divide a heterogeneous population into sub-populations, each of which is internally homogenous. If these strata are homogenous, i.e., the measurements vary little from one part to another; a precise estimate of any stratum mean can be obtained from a small sample in that stratum. The estimate can then be combined into a precise estimate for the whole population.

- There is also a statistical advantage in the method, as a stratified random sample nearly always results in a smaller variance for the estimated mean or other population parametres of interest.

SYSTEMATIC SAMPLING

This method of sampling is at first glance very different from SRS. In practice, it is a variant of simple random sampling that involves some listing of elements - every nth element of list is then drawn for inclusion in the sample. Say you have a list of 10,000 people and you want a sample of 1,000.

Creating such a sample includes three steps:

1. Divide number of cases in the population by the desired sample size. In this example, dividing 10,000 by 1,000 gives a value of 10.
2. Select a random number between one and the value attained in Step 1. In this example, we choose a number between 1 and 10 - say we pick 7.
3. Starting with case number chosen in Step 2, take every tenth record.

More generally, suppose that the N units in the population are ranked 1 to N in some order. To select a sample of n units, we take a part at random, from the 1st k units and take every k-th part thereafter.

The advantages of systematic sampling method over simple random sampling include:

1. It is easier to draw a sample and often easier to execute without mistakes. This is a particular advantage when the drawing is done in the field.
2. Intuitively, you might think that systematic sampling

might be more precise than SRS. In effect it stratifies the population into n strata, consisting of the 1st k units, the 2nd k units, and so on. Thus, we might expect the systematic sample to be as precise as a stratified random sample with one part per stratum. The difference is that with the systematic one the units occur at the same relative position in the stratum whereas with the stratified, the position in the stratum is determined separately by randomization within each stratum.

CLUSTER SAMPLING

In some instances the sampling part consists of a group or cluster of smaller units that we call elements or subunits. There are two main reasons for the widespread application of cluster sampling.

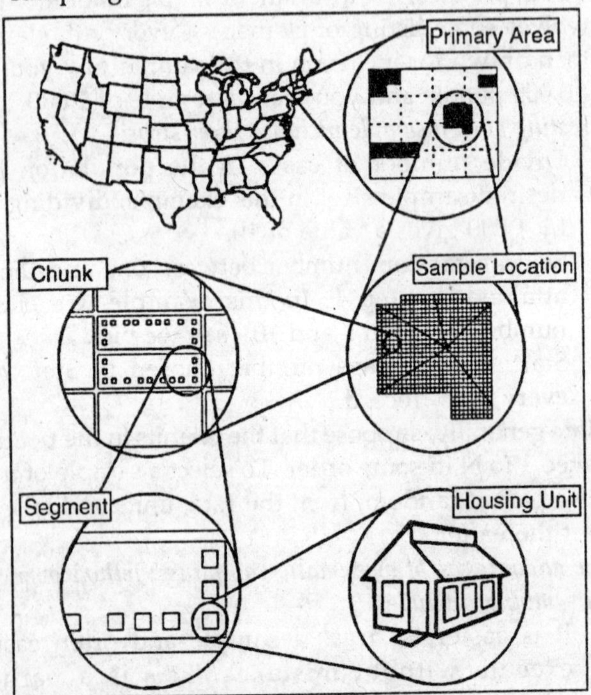

Although the first intention may be to use the elements as sampling units, it is found in many surveys that no reliable list of elements in the population is available and that it would be prohibitively expensive to construct such a list. In many countries there are no complete and updated lists of the people, the houses or the farms in any large geographical region.

Even when a list of individual houses is available, economic considerations may point to the choice of a larger cluster unit. For a given size of sample, a small part usually gives more precise results than a large unit. For example a SRS of 600 houses covers a town more evenly than 20 city blocks containing an average of 30 houses apiece. But greater field costs are incurred in locating 600 houses and in traveling between them than in covering 20 city blocks. When cost is balanced against precision, the larger part may prove superior.

Important things about cluster sampling:

- Most large scale surveys are done using cluster sampling;
- Clustering may be combined with stratification, typically by clustering within strata;
- In general, for a given sample size n cluster samples are less accurate than the other types of sampling in the sense that the parametres you estimate will have greater variability than an SRS, stratified random or systematic sample.

NON-PROBABILITY SAMPLING

Social research is often conducted in situations where a researcher cannot select the kinds of probability samples used in large-scale social surveys. For example, say you wanted to study homelessness - there is no list of homeless individuals nor are you likely to create such a list. However, you need to get some kind of a sample of respondents in order to conduct your research. To gather such a sample, you would likely use some form of non-probability sampling.

To reiterate, the primary difference between probability methods of sampling and non-probability methods is that in the latter you do not know the likelihood that any element of a population will be selected for study. There are four primary types of non-probability sampling methods:

AVAILABILITY SAMPLING

Availability sampling is a method of choosing subjects who are available or easy to find. This method is also sometimes referred to as haphazard, accidental, or convenience sampling. The primary advantage of the method is that it is very easy to carry out, relative to other methods. A researcher can merely stand out on his/her favourite street corner or in his/her favourite tavern and hand out surveys. One place this used to show up often is in university courses. Years ago, researchers often would conduct surveys of students in their large lecture courses. For example, all students taking introductory sociology courses would have been given a survey and compelled to fill it out. There are some advantages to this design - it is easy to do, particularly with a captive audience, and in some schools you can attain a large number of interviews through this method.

The primary problem with availability sampling is that you can never be certain what population the participants in the study represent. The population is unknown, the method for selecting cases is haphazard, and the cases studied probably don't represent any population you could come up with.

However, there are some situations in which this kind of design has advantages - for example, survey designers often want to have some people respond to their survey before it is given out in the "real" research setting as a way of making certain the questions make sense to respondents. For this purpose, availability sampling is not a bad way to get a group to take a survey, though in this case researchers care less about the specific responses given than whether the instrument is confusing or makes people feel bad,

Despite the known flaws with this design, it's remarkably common. Ask a provocative question, give telephone number and web site address, announce results of poll. This method provides some form of statistical data on a current issue, but it is entirely unknown what population the results of such polls represents. At best, a researcher could make some cond-itional statement about people who are watching CNN at a particular point in time who cared enough about the issue in question to log on or call in.

QUOTA SAMPLING

Quota sampling is designed to overcome the most obvious flaw of availability sampling. Rather than taking just anyone, you set quotas to ensure that the sample you get represents certain characteristics in proportion to their prevalence in the population.

Note that for this method, you have to know something about the characteristics of the population ahead of time. Say you want to make sure you have a sample proportional to the population in terms of gender - you have to know what percentage of the population is male and female, then collect sample until yours matches. Marketing studies are particularly fond of this form of research design.

The primary problem with this form of sampling is that even when we know that a quota sample is representative of the particular characteristics for which quotas have been set, we have no way of knowing if sample is representative in terms of any other characteristics. If we set quotas for gender and age, we are likely to attain a sample with good representativeness on age and gender, but one that may not be very representative in terms of income and education or other factors.

Moreover, because researchers can set quotas for only a small fraction of the characteristics relevant to a study quota sampling is really not much better than availability sampling. To reiterate, you must know the characteristics of the entire population to set quotas; otherwise there's not much point to setting up quotas.

Finally, interviewers often introduce bias when allowed to self-select respondents, which is usually the case in this form of research. In choosing males 18-25, interviewers are more likely to choose those that are better-dressed, seem more approachable or less threatening. That may be understandable from a practical point of view, but it introduces bias into research findings.

PURPOSIVE SAMPLING

Purposive sampling is a sampling method in which elements are chosen based on purpose of the study. Purposive sampling may involve studying the entire population of some limited group or a subset of a population. As with other non-probability sampling methods, purposive sampling does not produce a sample that is representative of a larger population, but it can be exactly what is needed in some cases - study of organization, community, or some other clearly defined and relatively limited group.

SNOWBALL SAMPLING

Snowball sampling is a method in which a researcher identifies one member of some population of interest, speaks to him/her, then asks that person to identify others in the population that the researcher might speak to. This person is then asked to refer the researcher to yet another person, and so on. Snowball sampling is very good for cases where members of a special population are difficult to locate. For example, several studies of Mexican migrants in Los Angeles have used snowball sampling to get respondents.

The method also has an interesting application to group membership - if you want to look at pattern of recruitment to a community organization over time, you might begin by interviewing fairly recent recruits, asking them who introduced them to the group. Then interview the people named, asking them who recruited them to the group.

The method creates a sample with questionable representativeness. A researcher is not sure who is in the sample. In effect snowball sampling often leads the researcher into a realm he/she knows little about. It can be difficult to determine how a sample compares to a larger population. Also, there's an issue of who respondents refer you to - friends refer to friends, less likely to refer to ones they don't like, fear, etc.

THEORY OF ESTIMATION

Estimation theory is a branch of statistics and signal processing that deals with estimating the values of parametres based on measured/empirical data. The parametres describe an underlying physical setting in such a way that the value of the parametres affects the distribution of the measured data. An estimator attempts to approximate the unknown parametres using the measurements.

For example, it is desired to estimate the proportion of a population of voters who will vote for a particular candidate. That proportion is the unobservable parametre; the estimate is based on a small random sample of voters.

Or, for example, in radar the goal is to estimate the location of objects by analyzing the received echo and a possible question to be posed is "where are the airplanes?" To answer where the airplanes are, it is necessary to estimate the distance the airplanes are at from the radar station, which can provide an absolute location if the absolute location of the radar station is known.

In estimation theory, it is assumed that the desired information is embedded in a noisy signal. Noise adds uncertainty, without which the problem would be deterministic and estimation would not be needed.

ESTIMATION PROCESS

The entire purpose of estimation theory is to arrive at an estimator, and preferably an implementable one that could actually be used. The estimator takes the measured data as input and produces an estimate of the parametres.

It is also preferable to derive an estimator that exhibits optimality. Estimator optimality usually refers to achieving minimum average error over some class of estimators, for example, a minimum variance unbiased estimator. In this case, the class is the set of unbiased estimators, and the average error measure is variance. However, optimal estimators do not always exist.

These are the general steps to arrive at an estimator:

- In order to arrive at a desired estimator for estimating a single or multiple parametres, it is first necessary to determine a model for the system. This model should incorporate the process being modeled as well as points of uncertainty and noise. The model describes the physical scenario in which the parametres apply.

- After deciding upon a model, it is helpful to find the limitations placed upon an estimator. This limitation, for example, can be found through the Cramér-Rao bound.
- Next, an estimator needs to be developed or applied if an already known estimator is valid for the model. The estimator needs to be tested against the limitations to determine if it is an optimal estimator.
- Finally, experiments or simulations can be run using the estimator to test its performance.

After arriving at an estimator, real data might show that the model used to derive the estimator is incorrect, which may require repeating these steps to find a new estimator. A non-implementable or infeasible estimator may need to be scrapped and the process started anew. In summary, the estimator estimates the parametres of a physical model based on measured data.

BASICS

To build a model, several statistical "ingredients" need to be known. These are needed to ensure the estimator has some mathematical tractability instead of being based on "good feel". The first is a set of statistical samples taken from a random vector (RV) of size *N*. Put into a vector,

$$x = \begin{pmatrix} x[0] \\ x[1] \\ \vdots \\ x[N-1] \end{pmatrix}$$

Secondly, we have the corresponding *M* parametres,

$$\theta = \begin{pmatrix} \theta_1 \\ \theta_2 \\ \vdots \\ \theta_M \end{pmatrix}$$

which need to be established with their probability density function or probability mass function

$$p(x|\theta).$$

It is also possible for the parametres themselves to have a probability distribution. It is then necessary to define the Bayesian probability

$$\pi(\theta).$$

After the model is formed, the goal is to estimate the parametres, commonly denoted $\hat{\theta}$, where the "hat" indicates the estimate.

One common estimator is the minimum mean squared error estimator, which utilizes the error between the estimated parametres and the actual value of the parametres

$$e = \hat{\theta} - \theta$$

as the basis for optimality. This error term is then squared and minimized for the MMSE estimator.

ESTIMATORS

Commonly-used estimators and estimation methods, and topics related to them:

- Maximum likelihood estimators
- Bayes estimators
- Method of moments estimators
- Cramér-Rao bound
- Minimum mean squared error, also known as Bayes least squared error
- Maximum a posteriori
- Minimum variance unbiased estimator
- Best linear unbiased estimator
- Unbiased estimators.
- Particle filter
- Markov chain Monte Carlo
- Kalman filter
- Ensemble Kalman filter
- Wiener filter

APPLICATIONS

Numerous fields require the use of estimation theory. *Some of these fields include*:

- Interpretation of scientific experiments
- Signal processing
- Clinical trials
- Opinion polls
- Quality control
- Telecommunications
- Project management
- Software engineering
- Control theory
- Network intrusion detection system
- Orbit Determination

Measured data are likely to be subject to noise or uncertainty and it is through statistical probability that optimal solutions are sought to extract as much information from the data as possible.

T, F, Z, TEST

T-TEST

A t-test is any statistical hypothesis test in which the test statistic follows a Student's t distribution if the null hypothesis is supported. It is most commonly applied when the test statistic would follow a normal distribution if the value of a scaling term in the test statistic were known.

When the scaling term is unknown and is replaced by an estimate based on the data, the test statistic follows a Student's t distribution.The t-statistic was introduced in 1908 by William Sealy Gosset, a chemist working for the Guinness brewery in Dublin, Ireland.

Gosset had been hired due to Claude Guinness's innovative policy of recruiting the best graduates from Oxford and Cambridge to apply biochemistry and statistics to Guinness' industrial processes. Gosset devised the t-test as a way to cheaply monitor the quality of stout. He published the test in Biometrika in 1908, but was forced to use a pen name by his employer, who regarded the fact that they were using statistics as a trade secret. In fact, Gosset's identity was unknown to fellow statisticians.

Among the most frequently used t-tests are:

- A one-sample location test of whether the mean of a normally distributed population has a value specified in a null hypothesis.
- A two sample location test of the null hypothesis that the means of two normally distributed populations are equal. All such tests are usually called Student's t-tests, though strictly speaking that name should only be used if the variances of the two populations are also assumed to be equal; the form of the test used when this assumption is dropped is sometimes called Welch's t-test. These tests are often referred to as"unpaired" or"independent samples" t-tests, as they are typically applied when the statistical units underlying the two samples being compared are non-overlapping.
- A test of the null hypothesis that the difference between two responses measured on the same statistical part has a mean value of zero. For example, suppose we measure the size of a cancer patient's tumor before and after a treatment. If the treatment is effective, we expect the tumor size for many of the patients to be smaller following the treatment. This is often referred to as the"paired" or"repeated measures" t-test:
- A test of whether the slope of a regression line differs significantly from 0.

Most *t*-test statistics have the form $T = Z/s$, where Z and s are functions of the data. Typically, Z is designed to be sensitive to the alternative hypothesis, whereas s is a scaling parametre that allows the distribution of T to be determined.

As an example, in the one-sample *t*-test Z is $\sqrt{n}\overline{X}/\sigma$, where $\overline{X}$ is the sample mean of the data, n is the sample size, and ó is the population standard deviation of the data; s in the one-sample *t*-test is $\hat{\sigma}/\sigma$, where $\hat{\sigma}$ is the sample standard deviation.

The assumptions underlying a t-test are that:

- Z follows a standard normal distribution under the null hypothesis
- ps^2 follows a ÷^{2} distribution with p degrees of freedom under the null hypothesis, where p is a positive constant
- Z and s are independent.

In a specific type of *t*-test, these conditions are consequences of the population being studied, and of the way in which the data are sampled. For example, in the *t*-test comparing the means of two independent samples, the following assumptions should be met:

- Each of the two populations being compared should follow a normal distribution.
- If using Student's original definition of the t-test, the two populations being compared should have the same variance. If the sample sizes in the two groups being compared are roughly equal, Student's original t-test is highly robust to the presence of unequal variances. Welch's t-test is insensitive to equality of the variances regardless of whether the sample sizes are similar.
- The data used to carry out the test should be sampled independently from the two populations being compared. This is in general not testable from the data, but if the data are known to be dependently sampled, then the classical t-tests discussed here may give misleading results.

Two sample t-tests for a difference in mean can be either unpaired or paired. Paired t-tests are a form of blocking, and have greater power than unpaired tests when the paired units are similar with respect to"noise factors" that are independent of membership in the two groups being compared. In a different context, paired t-tests can be used to reduce the effects of confounding factors in an observational study.

The unpaired, or"independent samples" t-test is used when two separate independent and identically distributed samples are obtained, one from each of the two populations being compared. For example, suppose we are evaluating the effect of a medical treatment, and we enroll 100 subjects into our study, then randomize 50 subjects to the treatment group and 50 subjects to the control group. In this case, we have two independent samples and would use the unpaired form of the t-test.

The randomization is not essential here - if we contacted 100 people by phone and obtained each person's age and gender, and then used a two-sample t-test to see whether the mean ages differ by gender, this would also be an independent samples t-test, even though the data are observational.

Dependent samples t-tests typically consist of a sample of matched pairs of similar units, or one group of units that has been tested twice. A typical example of the repeated measures t-test would be where subjects are tested prior to a treatment, say for high blood pressure, and the same subjects are tested again after treatment with a blood-pressure lowering medication.

A dependent t-test based on a"matched-pairs sample" results from an unpaired sample that is subsequently used to form a paired sample, by using additional variables that were measured along with the variable of interest. The matching is carried out by identifying pairs of values consisting of one observation from each of the two samples, where the pair is similar in terms of other measured variables. This approach is often used in observational studies to reduce or eliminate the effects of confounding factors.

Explicit expressions that can be used to carry out various t-tests. In each case, the formula for a test statistic that either exactly follows or closely approximates a t-distribution under the null hypothesis is given. Also, the appropriate degrees of freedom is given in each case. Each of these statistics can be used to carry out either a one-tailed test or a two-tailed test.

Once a t value is determined, a p-value can be found using a table of values from Student's t-distribution. If the calculated p-value is the threshold chosen for statistical significance, then the null hypothesis is rejected in favour of the alternative hypothesis.

In testing the null hypothesis that the population mean is equal to a specified value μ0, one uses the statistic,

$$t = \frac{\overline{x} - \mu_0}{\frac{s}{\sqrt{n}}},$$

where s is the sample standard deviation of the sample and n is the sample size. The degrees of freedom used in this test is n – 1.

Suppose one is fitting the model,

$$Y_i = \alpha + \beta x_i + \varepsilon_i,$$

where x_i, $i = 1..., n$ are known, α and β are unknown, and ε_i are independent normally distributed random errors with expected value 0 and unknown variance σ^2, and Y_i, $i = 1..., n$ are observed. It is desired to test the null hypothesis that the slope β is equal to some specified value β_0.

Let,

$$\hat{\alpha}, \hat{\beta} = \text{least – squares estimates},$$

$$SE_{\hat{\alpha}}, SE_{\hat{\beta}} = \text{the s tan dard error of least – squares estimates.}$$

Then,

$$t_{score} = \frac{\hat{\beta} - \beta_0}{SE_{\hat{\beta}}}$$

has a *t*-distribution with $n - 2$ degrees of freedom if the null hypothesis is true.

The standard error of the angular coefficient:

$$SE_{\hat{\beta}} = \frac{\sqrt{\frac{\sum_{i=1}^{n}(Y_i - \hat{y}_i)^2}{n-2}}}{\sqrt{\sum_{i=1}^{n}(x_i - \overline{x})^2}}$$

can be written in terms of the residuals. Let

$$\hat{\varepsilon}_i = Y_i - \hat{y}_i = Y_i - (\hat{\alpha} + \hat{\beta}x_i) = \text{residuals} = \text{estimated errors},$$

$$SSE = \sum_{i=1}^{n} \hat{\varepsilon}_i^2 = \text{sum of squares of residuals.}$$

Then t_{score} is given by:

$$t_{score} = \frac{(\hat{\beta} - \beta_0)\sqrt{n-2}}{\sqrt{SSE / \sum_{i=1}^{n}(x_i - \bar{x})^2}}.$$

The *t*-test provides an exact test for the equality of the means of two normal populations with unknown, but equal, variances. The Welch's *t*-test is a nearly-exact test for the case where the data are normal but the variances may differ. For moderately large samples, the *t*-test becomes very similar to the Z-test, and is therefore robust to moderate violations of the normality assumption for moderate or large sample sizes.

For exactness, the *t*-test and Z-test require normality of the sample means, and the *t*-test additionally requires that the sample variance follows a scaled $\times^2$ distribution, and that the sample mean and sample variance be statistically independent. Normality of the individual data values is not required if these conditions are met.

By the central limit theorem, sample means of moderately large samples are often well-approximated by a normal distribution even if the data are not normally distributed. For non-normal data, the distribution of the sample variance may deviate substantially from a χ^2 distribution.

However, if the sample size is large Slutsky's theorem implies that the distribution of the sample variance has little effect on the distribution of the test statistic. If the data are substantially non-normal and the sample size is small, the *t*-test can give misleading results.

When the normality assumption does not hold, a non-parametric alternative to the *t*-test can often have better statistical power.

For example, for two independent samples when the data distributions are asymmetric or the distributions have large tails, then the Mann-Whitney U test can have higher power than the *t*-test. The usual choices for non-parametric location tests are the Mann–Whitney U test for independent samples, and the binomial test or the Wilcoxon signed-rank test for paired samples.

One-way analysis of variance generalizes the two-sample *t*-test when the data belong to more than two groups.

F-TEST

An F-test is any statistical test in which the test statistic has an F-distribution under the null hypothesis. It is most often used when comparing statistical models that have been fit to a data set, in order to identify the model that best fits the population from which the data were sampled. Exact *F-tests* mainly arise when the models have been fit to the data using least squares. The name was coined by George W. Snedecor, in honour of Sir Ronald A. Fisher. Fisher initially developed the statistic as the variance ratio in the 1920s.

Examples of F-tests include:

- The hypothesis that the means of several normally distributed populations, all having the same standard deviation, are equal. This is perhaps the best-known F-test, and plays an important role in the analysis of variance.
- The hypothesis that a proposed regression model fits the data well.
- The hypothesis that a data set in a regression analysis follows the simpler of two proposed linear models that are nested within each other.
- Scheffé's method for multiple comparisons adjustment in linear models.

An F-test of the null hypothesis that two populations have the same variance is a standard statistical procedure. However this F-test was diagnosed as being extremely sensitive to non-normality. Alternatives, which mainly or completely avoid the potential for erroneous ceases if data are not from normal distributions, are Levene's test, Bartlett's test, and the Brown–Forsythe test.

In contrast, the other F-tests described in this substance are much more robust to violations of the normality assumption, and so are still recommended procedures.

Most F-tests arise by considering a decomposition of the variability in a collection of data in terms of sums of squares.

The test statistic in an F-test is the ratio of two scaled sums of squares reflecting different sources of variability. These sums of squares are constructed so that the statistic tends to be greater when the null hypothesis is not true. In order for the statistic to follow the F-distribution under the null hypothesis, the sums of squares should be statistically independent, and each should follow a scaled chi-squared distribution. The latter condition is guaranteed if the data values are independent and normally distributed with a common variance

The F-test in one-way analysis of variance is used to assess whether the expected values of a quantitative variable within several pre-defined groups differ from each other. For example, suppose that a medical trial compares four treatments.

The ANOVA F-test can be used to assess whether any of the treatments is on average superior, or inferior, to the others versus the null hypothesis that all four treatments yield the same mean response. This is an example of an"omnibus" test, meaning that a single test is performed to detect any of several possible differences.

Alternatively, we could carry out pairwise tests among the treatments. The advantage of the ANOVA F-test is that we do not need to pre-specify which treatments are to be compared, and we do not need to adjust for making multiple comparisons.

The disadvantage of the ANOVA F-test is that if we reject the null hypothesis, we do not know which treatments can be said to be significantly different from the others - if the F-test is performed at level α we cannot state that the treatment pair with the greatest mean difference is significantly different at level α..

The formula for the one-way ANOVA F-test statistic is,

$$F = \frac{\text{explained variance}}{\text{unexplained variance}},$$

or

$$F = \frac{\text{between} - \text{group variability}}{\text{with} - \text{group variability}}.$$

The "explained variance", or "between-group variability" is,

$$\sum_i n_i(\bar{Y}_{i.} - \bar{Y})^2 / (K-1)$$

where $\bar{Y}_i$ denotes the sample mean in the ith group, n_i is the number of observations in the ith group, and Y denotes the overall mean of the data.

The "unexplained variance", or "within-group variability" is,

$$\sum_{ij} (Y_{ij} - \bar{Y}_i.)^2 / (N-K),$$

where Y_{ij} is the jth observation in the ith out of *K* groups and *N* is the overall sample size. This F-statistic follows the F-distribution with $K-1$, $N-K$ degrees of freedom under the null hypothesis. The statistic will be large if the between-group variability is large relative to the within-group variability, which is unlikely to happen if the population means of the groups all have the same value.

Note that when there are only two groups for the one-way ANOVA F-test, F = t2 where t is the Student's t statistic.

Consider two models, 1 and 2, where model 1 is'nested' within model 2. That is, model 1 has p1 parametres, and model 2 has p2 parametres, where p2 > p1, and for any choice of parametres in model 1, the same regression curve can be achieved by some choice of the parametres of model 2. The model with more parametres will always be able to fit the data at least as well as the model with fewer parametres. Thus typically model 2 will give a better fit to the data than model 1. But one often wants to determine whether model 2 gives a significantly better fit to the data. One approach to this problem is to use an F test.

If there are n data points to estimate parametres of both models from, then one can calculate the F statistic, given by,

$$F = \frac{\left(\frac{RSS_1 - RSS_2}{p_2 - p_1}\right)}{\left(\frac{Rss_2}{n - p_2}\right)}$$

where RSSi is the residual sum of squares of model i. If your regression model has been calculated with weights, then replace RSSi with χ 2, the weighted sum of squared residuals. Under the null hypothesis that model 2 does not provide a significantly better fit than model 1, F will have an F distribution, with degrees of freedom. The null hypothesis is rejected if the F calculated from the data is greater than the critical value of the F distribution for some desired false-rejection probability. The test is a likelihood ratio test.

Z-TEST

A Z-test is any statistical test for which the distribution of the test statistic under the null hypothesis can be approximated by a normal distribution. Due to the central limit theorem, many test statistics are approximately normally distributed for large samples. Therefore, many statistical tests can be performed as approximate Z-tests if the sample size is not too small. In addition, some statistical tests, such as comparisons of means between two samples, or a comparison of the mean of one sample to a given constant, are exact Z-tests under certain assumptions.

The most general way to obtain a Z-test is to define a numerical test statistic that can be calculated from a collection of data, such that the sampling distribution of the statistic is approximately normal under the null hypothesis. Statistics that are averages of approximately independent data values are generally well-approximated by a normal distribution. An example of a statistic that would not be well-approximated by a normal distribution would be an extreme value such as the sample maximum.

If T is a statistic that is approximately normally distributed under the null hypothesis, the next step in performing a Z-test is to determine the expected value θ of T under the null hypothesis, and then obtain an estimate s of the standard deviation of T. We then calculate the standard score $Z = (T - \theta)/ s$, from which one-tailed and two-tailed p-values can be calculated as $\Phi(-|Z|)$ and $2\Phi(-|Z|)$, respectively, where Φ is the standard normal cumulative distribution function.

The term Z-test is often used to refer specifically to the one-sample location test comparing the mean of a set of measurements to a given constant.

If the observed data X1..., Xn are:

- Uncorrelated,
- Have a common mean μ, and
- Have a common variance σ^2, then the sample average X has mean μ and variance σ^2/n. If our null hypothesis is that the mean value of the population is a given number μ_0, we can use X $-\mu_0$ as a test-statistic, rejecting the null hypothesis if X $-\mu_0$ is large.

To calculate the standardized statistic $Z = (X - \mu_0)/s$, we need to either know or have an approximate value for σ^2, from which we can calculate $s^2 = \sigma^2/n$. In some applications, σ^2 is known, but this is uncommon. If the sample size is moderate or large, we can substitute the sample variance for σ^2, giving a *plug-in* test.

The resulting test will not be an exact Z-test since the uncertainty in the sample variance is not accounted for — however, it will be a good approximation unless the sample size is small.

A t-test can be used to account for the uncertainty in the sample variance when the sample size is small and the data are exactly normal.

There is no universal constant at which the sample size is generally considered large enough to justify use of the plug-in test.

Typical rules of thumb range from 20 to 50 samples. For larger sample sizes, the t-test procedure gives almost identical p-values as the Z-test procedure.

Other location tests that can be performed as Z-tests are the two-sample location test and the paired difference test.

For the Z-test to be applicable, certain conditions must be met:

- Nuisance parametres should be known, or estimated with high accuracy. Z-tests focus on a single parametre, and treat all other unknown parametres as being fixed at their true values. In practice, due to Slutsky's theorem, "plugging in" consistent estimates of nuisance parametres can be justified. However if the sample size is not large enough for these estimates to be reasonably accurate, the Z-test may not perform well.

- The test statistic should follow a normal distribution. Generally, one appeals to the central limit theorem to justify assuming that a test statistic varies normally. There is a great deal of statistical research on the question of when a test statistic varies approximately normally. If the variation of the test statistic is strongly non-normal, a Z-test should not be used.

It is important to use estimates appropriate for the way the data were sampled. In the special case of Z-tests for the one or two sample location problem, the usual sample standard deviation is only appropriate if the data were collected as an independent sample.

In some situations, it is possible to devise a test that properly accounts for the variation in plug-in estimates of nuisance parametres, giving an exact test for finite samples. In the case of one and two sample location problems, a t-test does this. Non-parametric methods require weaker assumptions on the data, but their power is generally much lower than most Z-tests.

Location tests are the most familiar t-tests. Another class of Z-tests arises in maximum likelihood estimation of the parametres in a parametric statistical model. Maximum likelihood estimates are approximately normal under certain conditions, and their asymptotic variance can be calculated in terms of the Fisher information.

The maximum likelihood estimate divided by its standard error can be used as a test statistic for the null hypothesis that the population value of the parametre equals zero. More generally, if $\hat{\theta}$ is the maximum likelihood estimate of a parametre è, and è$_0$ is the value of è under the null hypothesis,

$$(\hat{\theta} - \theta_0)/SE(\hat{\theta})$$

can be used as a Z-test statistic.

When using a Z-test for maximum likelihood estimates, it is important to be aware that the normal approximation may be poor if the sample size is not sufficiently large. Although there is no simple, universal rule stating how large the sample size must be to use a Z-test, simulation can give a good idea as to whether a Z-test is appropriate in a given situation.

Z-tests are employed whenever it can be argued that a test statistic follows a normal distribution under the null hypothesis of interest.

Many non-parametric test statistics, such as U statistics, are approximately normal for large enough sample sizes, and hence are often performed as Z-tests.

CHI-SQUARE TEST

The chi-square (I) test is used to determine whether there is a significant difference between the expected frequencies and the observed frequencies in one or more categories.

Do the number of individuals or objects that fall in each category differ significantly from the number you would expect? Is this difference between the expected and observed due to sampling error, or is it a *real* difference?

Chi-Square Test Requirements:

- Quantitative data.
- One or more categories.
- Independent observations.
- Adequate sample size.
- Simple random sample.
- Data in frequency form.
- All observations must be used.

EXPECTED FREQUENCIES

When you find the value for chi square, you determine whether the observed frequencies differ significantly from the expected frequencies.

You find the expected frequencies for chi square in three ways:

- You hypothesize that all the frequencies are equal in each category. For example, you might expect that half of the entering freshmen class of 200 at Tech

College will be identified as women and half as men. You figure the *expected* frequency by dividing the number in the sample by the number of categories. In this exam pie, where there are 200 entering freshmen and two categories, male and female, you divide your sample of 200 by 2, the number of categories, to get 100 in each category.

- You determine the expected frequencies on the *basis of some prior knowledge*. Let's use the Tech College example again, but this time pretend we have prior knowledge of the frequencies of men and women in each category from last year's entering class, when 60% of the freshmen were men and 40% were women. This year you might expect that 60% of the total would be men and 40% would be women. You find the expected frequencies by multiplying the sample size by each of the hypothesized population proportions. If the freshmen total were 200, you would expect 120 to be men and 80 to be women. Now let's take a situation, find the expected frequencies, and use the chi-square test to solve the problem.

SITUATION

Thai, the manager of a car dealership, did not want to stock cars that were bought less frequently because of their unpopular colour.

The five colours that he ordered were red, yellow, green, blue, and white. Thai, the expected frequencies or number of customers choosing each colour should follow the percentages of last year.

She felt 20% would choose yellow, 30% would choose red, 10% would choose green, 10% would choose blue, and 30% would choose white.

She now took a random sample of 150 customers and asked them their colour preferences. The results of this poll are shown in Tableunder the column labeled _observed frequencies."

Table. Colour Preference for 150 customers for thai's superior car dealership

Category colour	Observed frequencies	Expected frequencies
Yallow	35	30
Red	50	45
Green	30	15
Blue	10	15
White	25	45

The expected frequencies in Table are figured from last year's percentages. Based on the percentages for last year, we would expect 20% to choose yellow. Figure the expected frequencies for yellow by taking 20% of the 150 customers, getting an expected frequency of 30 people for this category. For the colour red we would expect 30% out of 150 or 45 people to fall in this category.

Using this method, Thai figured out the expected frequencies 30, 45, 15, 15, and 45. Obviously, there are discrepancies between the colours preferred by customers in the poll taken by Thai and the colours preferred by the customers who bought their cars *last* year. Most striking is the difference in the green and white colours. If Thai were to follow the results of her poll, she would stock twice as many green cars than if she were to follow the customer colour preference for green based on last year's sales.

In the case of white cars, she would stock half as many this year. What to do??? Thai needs to know whether or not the discrepancies between last year's choices and this year's preferences on the basis of his poll demonstrate a *real* change in customer colour preferences. It could be that the differences are simply a result of the random sample she *chanced to* select. If so, then the population of customers really has not changed from last year as far as colour preferences go. The *null hypothesis* states that there is no significant difference between the expected and observed frequencies. The *alternative hypothesis* states they *are* different. The level of significance is set at.05 The chi-square formula used on these data is,

$$X^2 = \frac{(o - E)^2}{E}$$

where

O is the Odserved frequency in each category
E is the Expected frequency in the corresponding category is sum of
df is the "degree of freedom" (n-1)
X^2 is chi square

PROCEDURE

We are now ready to use our formula for X2 and find out if there *is* a significant difference between the observed and expected frequencies for the customers in choosing cars.

As suggested, set up a worksheet; then you will follow the directions to form the columns and solve the formula:

- Directions for Setting Up Worksheet for Chi Square

Category	O	E	(O-E)	$(O-E)^2$	$\frac{(O-E)^2}{E}$
Yellow	35	30	5	25	0.83
Red	50	45	5	25	0.56
Green	30	15	15	225	15
Blue	10	15	–5	25	1.67
White	25	45	–20	400	8.89

- After calculating the Chi Square value, find the *"Degrees of Freedom." Degrees of freedom* refers to the number of values that are free to vary after restriction has been placed on the data. For instance, if you have four numbers with the restriction that their sum has to be 50, then three of these numbers can be anything, they are free to vary, but the fourth number *definitely* is restricted. For example, the first three numbers could be 15, 20, and 5, adding up to 40; then the fourth number has to be 10 in order that they sum to 50. The degrees of freedom for these values are then three. The degrees of freedom here is defined as $N - 1$, the number in the group minus one restriction.

- Find the table value for Chi Square. Begin by finding the *df* found in step 2 along the left hand side of the table. Run your fingers across the proper row until you reach the predetermined level of significance at the column heading on the top of the table. The table value for Chi Square in the correct box of *4 df* and *P=.05* level of significance is 9.49.
- If the calculated chi-square value for the set of data you are analyzing is equal to or greater than the table value, reject the null hypothesis. *There IS a significant difference between the data sets that cannot be due to chance alone.* If the number you calculate is LESS than the number you find on the table, than you can probably say that any differences are due to chance alone. In this situation, the rejection of the null hypothesis means that the differences between the expected frequencies and the observed frequencies are not due to chance. That is, they are not due to chance variation in the sample Thai took; there is a real difference between them. Therefore, in deciding what colour autos to stock, it would be to Thai's advantage to pay careful attention to the results of her poll!

The steps in using the chi-square test may be summarized as fllows:

Chi-square test summary:

- Write the observed frequencies in columm O
- Figure the expected frequencies and write them in column E.
- Use the formula to find the chi-square value:
- Find the df.(N –1)
- Find the table value (consult the chi square table)
- If Your chi-square value is equal to or greater than the table value, reject the null hypothesis: differences in your data are not due to change alone

For example, the reason observed frequencies in a fruit fly genetic breeding lab did not match expected frequencies could be due to such influences as:

- Mate selection
- Too small of a sample size was used
- Incorrect identification of male or female flies
- The wrong genetic cross was sent from the lab
- The flies were mixed in the bottle

TABULATION

The most important thing about a table is that it should clearly communicate information. To achieve this there are certain conventions that must be followed.

Checklist:

- Tables must be clear and easy to read
- Must be ruled or presented as a computer generated table an of an appropriate size for the information.
- Must have a title which describes the data in the table. This title should be underlined or in bold type.
- Columns and rows should be clearly headed. When appropriate the left column or top row should contain the independent variable and the bottom row or right column should contain the dependent variable.
- Units should be displayed in column/row headings only.
- Missing values should be displayed as -, and zeros as 0. Thee should be no blanks in a table conveying experimental results.
- Numbers should be listed neatly each other and should be to the same number of decimal places.

Table. Showing Rate of Urine production Against Time

Time (min)	Rate of Urine Production (mL/min)
0	6.8
10	7.3
20	1.6
30	2.4
40	–
50	5.7

- All the numerical data must be recorded so that the units, tens, decimals points etc line up under each other.
- All information should be in the same units – corresponding to those in the heading,
- All information should be to the same number of decimal places and should reflect the degree of accuracy to which the readings were taken

Example:

Correct	Incorrect
15.6	15.6
5.0	5.0
125.2	125.2

Example: Measurements of 15mm, 1.7cm and 35mm were taken. One part should be chosen for representing information in the table.

Correct (cm)	Incorrect Length	Length
1.5	1.5mm	
1.7	1.7cm	
3.5	35mm	

Example: When averaging results the final average should reflect the degree of precision to which it was measured. I f four readings for length were recorded to 0.1 of a cm, then the average should be calculated to 0.1 of a cm.

Example: 1.7cm, 3.9cm, 3.1cm and 2.4 should be averaged as 2.8cm, not as the degree of precision to which the measurements were made was 0.1cm.

CODING

Coding refers to an analytical process in which data, often from interview transcripts or questionnaires, are categorised to facilitate analysis.

QUANTITATIVE APPROACH

The classification of information is an important step in

preparation of data for computer processing. Data which are coded usually come from questionnaires used in qualitative research in social sciences. Those data, usually measured and recorded as nominal or ordinal variables, are *coded* in order to be analysed by statistical software.

Questionnaire data can be *pre-coded* or *post-coded*: One code should apply to only one category and categories should be comprehensive. There should be clear guidelines for *coders* so that code is consistent in order to simplify classification.

QUALITATIVE APPROACH

For disciplines in which a qualitative format is preferential, including ethnography, humanistic geography or phenomenological psychology a varied approach to coding can be applied. Iain Hey Outlines a two step process beginning with basic coding in order to distinguish overall themes, followed by a more in depth, interpretive code in which more specific trends and patterns can be interpreted. The process can be done manually- which can be as simple as highlighting different concepts with different colours, or fed into a software package.

8

Report Writing

WRITING RESEARCH

Writing is easy. All you do is stare at a blank sheet of paper until drops of blood form on your forehead. — Gene Fowler

A major goal of this course is the development of effective technical writing skills. To help you become an accomplished writer, you will prepare several research papers based upon the studies completed in lab. Our research papers are not typical "lab reports." In a teaching lab a lab report might be nothing more than answers to a set of questions. Such an assignment hardly represents the kind of writing you might be doing in your eventual career.

Written and oral communications skills are probably the most universal qualities sought by graduate and professional schools as well as by employers. You alone are responsible for developing such skills to a high level.

LEARNING TECHNICAL WRITING

Before you begin your first writing assignment, please consult all of the following resources, in order to gain the most benefit from the experience.

- General form of a typical research article
- Specific guidelines (if any) for the assignment.
- McMillan, VE. "Writing Papers in the Biological Sciences, Third Ed." New York: Bedford/St. Martin's, 2001. ISBN 0-312-25857-7 (REQUIRED for Bios 211, 311, recommended for other science courses that include writing)

- Writing portfolio examples (pdf) As you polish up your writing skills please make use of the following resources
- Instructor feedback on previous assignments
- Common errors in student research papers
- Selected writing rules (somewhat less serious than the other resources)

For Biosciences majors the general guidelines apply to future course work, as can be seen by examining the guidelines for the advanced experimental sciences research paper. Instructions for authors from the Journal of Biological Chemistry editorial board may be helpful as well. Their statement of editorial policies and practices may give you an idea of how material makes its way into the scientific literature.

GENERAL FORM OF A RESEARCH PAPER

An objective of organizing a research paper is to allow people to read your work selectively. When we research a topic, we may be interested in just the methods, a specific result, the interpretation, or perhaps we just want to see a summary of the paper to determine if it is relevant to our study. To this end, many journals require the following parts, submitted in the order listed. There are variations of course. Some journals call for a combined results and discussion, for example, or include materials and methods after the body of the paper. The well known journal *Science* does away with separate parts altogether, except for the abstract. Your papers are to adhere to the form and style required for the Journal of Biological Chemistry, requirements that are shared by many journals in the life sciences.

General Style

Specific editorial requirements for submission of a manuscript will always supercede instructions in these general guidelines.

To make a paper readable:

- Print or type using a 12 point standard font, such as Times, Geneva, Bookman, Helvetica, etc.

- Text should be double spaced on 8 1/2" x 11" paper with 1 inch margins, single sided
- Number pages consecutively
- Start each new part on a new page
- Adhere to recommended page limits

Mistakes to avoid:

- Dividing a table or figure - confine each figure/table to a single page
- Submitting a paper with pages out of order

In all parts of your paper:

- Use normal prose including articles ("a", "the," etc.)
- Stay focused on the research topic of the paper
- Use paragraphs to separate each important point
- Indent the first line of each paragraph
- Present your points in logical order
- Use present tense to report well accepted facts - for example, 'the grass is green'
- Use past tense to describe specific results - for example, 'When weed killer was applied, the grass was brown'
- Avoid informal wording, don't address the reader directly, and don't use jargon, slang terms, or superlatives
- Avoid use of superfluous pictures - include only those figures necessary to presenting results

Title Page

Select an informative title as emphasised in the examples in your writing portfolio example package. Include the name(s) and addresses of all authors, and date submitted. "Biology lab #1" would not be an informative title, for example.

General Intent

An abstract is a concise single paragraph summary of completed work or work in progress. In a minute or less a reader can learn the rationale behind the study, general approach to the problem, pertinent results, and important ceases or new questions.

Writing an Abstract

Write your summary after the rest of the paper is completed. After all, how can you summarize something that is not yet written?

Economy of words is important throughout any paper, but especially in an abstract. However, use complete sentences and do not sacrifice readability for brevity.

You can keep it concise by wording sentences so that they serve more than one purpose.

For example, "In order to learn the role of protein synthesis in early development of the sea urchin, newly fertilized embryos were pulse-labeled with tritiated leucine, to provide a time course of changes in synthetic rate, as measured by total counts per minute (cpm)." This sentence provides the overall question, methods, and type of analysis, all in one sentence. The writer can now go directly to summarizing the results.

Summarize the study, including the following elements in any abstract:

Try to keep the first two items to no more than one sentence each:

- Purpose of the study - hypothesis, overall question, objective
- Model organism or system and brief description of the experiment
- Results, including specific data - if the results are quantitative in nature, report quantitative data; results of any statistical analysis shoud be reported
- Important ceases or questions that follow from the experiments.

Style:

- Single paragraph, and concise
- As a summary of work done, it is always written in past tense
- An abstract should stand on its own, and not refer to any other part of the paper such as a figure or table.

- Focus on summarizing results - limit background information to a sentence or two, if absolutely necessary
- What you report in an abstract must be consistent with what you reported in the paper
- Corrrect spelling, clarity of sentences and phrases, and proper reporting of quantities are just as important in an abstract as they are anywhere else

General Intent

The purpose of an introduction is to aquaint the reader with the rationale behind the work, with the intention of defending it. It places your work in a theoretical context, and enables the reader to understand and appreciate your objectives.

Writing an Introduction

The abstract is the only text in a research paper to be written without using paragraphs in order to separate major points. Approaches vary widely, however for our studies the following approach can produce an effective introduction.

- Describe the importance (significance) of the study - why was this worth doing in the first place? Provide a broad context.
- Defend the model - why did you use this particular organism or system? What are its advantages? You might comment on its suitability from a theoretical point of view as well as indicate practical reasons for using it.
- Provide a rationale. State your specific hypothesis(es) or objective(s), and describe the reasoning that led you to select them.
- Very briefy describe the experimental design and how it accomplished the stated objectives.

Style:

- Use past tense except when referring to established

facts. After all, the paper will be submitted after all of the work is completed.

- Organize your ideas, making one major point with each paragraph. If you make the four points, you will need a minimum of four paragraphs.
- Present background information only as needed in order support a position. The reader does not want to read everything you know about a subject.
- State the hypothesis/objective precisely - do not oversimplify.
- As always, pay attention to spelling, clarity and appropriateness of sentences and phrases.

Materials and Methods

There is no specific page limit, but a key concept is to keep this part as concise as you possibly can. People will want to read this material selectively.

The reader may only be interested in one formula or part of a procedure. Materials and methods may be reported under separate subheadings within this part or can be incorporated together.

General Intent

This should be the easiest part to write, but many students misunderstand the purpose. The objective is to document all specialized materials and general procedures, so that another individual may use some or all of the methods in another study or judge the scientific merit of your work.

It is not to be a step by step description of everything you did, nor is a methods part a set of instructions. In particular, it is not supposed to tell a story. By the way, your notebook should contain all of the information that you need for this part.

WRITING A MATERIALS AND METHODS PART

Materials:

- Describe materials separately only if the study is so complicated that it saves space this way.

- Include specialized chemicals, biological materials, and any equipment or supplies that are not commonly found in laboratories.
- Do not include commonly found supplies such as test tubes, pipet tips, beakers, etc., or standard lab equipment such as centrifuges, spectrophotometres, pipettors, etc.
- If use of a specific type of equipment, a specific enzyme, or a culture from a particular supplier is critical to the success of the experiment, then it and the source should be singled out, otherwise no.
- Materials may be reported in a separate paragraph or else they may be identified along with your procedures.
- In biosciences we frequently work with solutions - refer to them by name and describe completely, including concentrations of all reagents, and pH of aqueous solutions, solvent if non-aqueous.

Methods:

- Report the methodology
- Describe the mehodology completely, including such specifics as temperatures, incubation times, etc.
- To be concise, present methods under headings devoted to specific procedures or groups of procedures
- Generalize - report how procedures were done, not how they were specifically performed on a particular day. For example, report "samples were diluted to a final concentration of 2 mg/ml protein;" don't report that "135 microliters of sample one was diluted with 330 microliters of buffer to make the protein concentration 2 mg/ml." Always think about what would be relevant to an investigator at another institution, working on his/her own project.
- If well documented procedures were used, report the procedure by name, perhaps with reference, and that's all. For example, the Bradford assay is well

known. You need not report the procedure in full - just that you used a Bradford assay to estimate protein concentration, and identify what you used as a standard. The same is true for the SDS-PAGE method, and many other well known procedures in biology and biochemistry.

Style:

- It is awkward or impossible to use active voice when documenting methods without using first person, which would focus the reader's attention on the investigator rather than the work. Therefore when writing up the methods most authors use third person passive voice.
- Use normal prose in this and in every other part of the paper – avoid informal lists, and use complete sentences.

What to avoid:

- Materials and methods are not a set of instructions.
- Omit all explanatory information and background - save it for the discussion.
- Omit information that is irrelevant to a third party, such as what colour ice bucket you used, or which individual logged in the data.

Results: The page length of this part is set by the amount and types of data to be reported. Continue to be concise, using figures and tables, if appropriate, to present results most effectively.

General Intent

The purpose of a results part is to present and emphasise your findings. Make this part a completely objective report of the results, and save all interpretation for the discussion.

Writing a Results Part

Important: You must clearly distinguish material that would normally be included in a research article from any raw data or other material that would not be published. In fact, such material should not be submitted at all unless requested by the instructor.

Content:

- Summarize your findings in text and emphasise them, if appropriate, with figures and tables.
- In text, describe each of your results, pointing the reader to observations that are most relevant.
- Provide a context, such as by describing the question that was addressed by making a particular observation.
- Describe results of control experiments and include observations that are not presented in a formal figure or table, if appropriate.
- Analyse your data, then prepare the analysed (converted) data in the form of a figure (graph), table, or in text form.

What to avoid:

- Do not discuss or interpret your results, report background information, or attempt to explain anything.
- Never include raw data or intermediate calculations in a research paper.
- Do not present the same data more than once.
- Text should complement any figures or tables, not repeat the same information.
- Please do not confuse figures with tables - there is a difference.

Style:

- As always, use past tense when you refer to your results, and put everything in a logical order.
- In text, refer to each figure as "figure 1," "figure 2," etc.; number your tables as well
- Place figures and tables, properly numbered, in order at the end of the report (clearly distinguish them from any other material such as raw data, standard curves, etc.)
- If you prefer, you may place your figures and tables appropriately within the text of your results part.

Figures and tables:

- Either place figures and tables within the text of the result, or include them in the back of the report (following Literature Cited) - do one or the other
- If you place figures and tables at the end of the report, make sure they are clearly distinguished from any attached materials, such as raw data
- Regardless of placement, each figure must be numbered consecutively and complete with caption
- Regardless of placement, each table must be titled, numbered consecutively and complete with heading
- Each figure and table must be sufficiently complete that it could stand on its own, separate from text

Discussion

Journal guidelines vary. Space is so valuable in the Journal of Biological Chemistry, that authors are asked to restrict discussions to four pages or less, double spaced, typed. That works out to one printed page. While you are learning to write effectively, the limit will be extended to five typed pages. If you practice economy of words, that should bc plenty of space within which to say all that you need to say.

General Intent

The objective here is to provide an interpretation of your results and support for all of your ceases, using evidence from your experiment and generally accepted knowledge, if appropriate. The significance of findings should be clearly described.

Writing a Discussion

Interpret your data in the discussion *in appropriate depth.* This means that when you explain a phenomenon you must describe mechanisms that may account for the observation. If your results differ from your expectations, explain why that may have happened. If your results agree, then describe the theory that the evidence supported. It is never appropriate to simply state that the data agreed with expectations, and let it drop at that.

- Decide if each hypothesis is supported, rejected, or if you cannot make a decision with confidence. Do not simply dismiss a study or part of a study as "inconclusive."
- Research papers are not accepted if the work is incomplete. Draw what ceases you can based upon the results that you have, and treat the study as a finished work
- You may suggest future directions, such as how the experiment might be modified to accomplish another objective.
- Explain all of your observations as much as possible, *focusing on mechanisms.*
- Decide if the experimental design adequately addressed the hypothesis, and whether or not it was properly controlled.
- Try to offer alternative explanations if reasonable alternatives exist.
- One experiment will not answer an overall question, so keeping the big picture in mind, where do you go next? The best studies open up new avenues of research. What questions remain?
- Recommendations for specific papers will provide additional suggestions.

Style:

- When you refer to information, distinguish data generated by your own studies from published information or from information obtained from other students.
- Refer to work done by specific individuals (including yourself) in past tense.
- Refer to generally accepted facts and principles in present tense. For example, "Doofus, in a 1989 survey, *found* that anemia in basset hounds *was correlated* with advanced age. Anemia *is* a condition in which there *is* insufficient hemoglobin in the blood."

The biggest mistake that students make in discussions is to present a superficial interpretation that more or less re-states the results. It is necessary to suggest *why* results came out as they did, focusing on the mechanisms behind the observations.

Literature Cited

Please note that in the introductory laboratory course, you will not be required to properly document sources of all of your information. One reason is that your major source of information is this website, and websites are inappropriate as primary sources. Second, it is problematic to provide a hundred students with equal access to potential reference materials. You may nevertheless find outside sources, and you should cite any substances that the instructor provides or that you find for yourself.

List all literature cited in your paper, in alphabetical order, by first author. In a proper research paper, only primary literature is used. Be cautious about using web sites as references - anyone can put just about anything on a web site, and you have no sure way of knowing if it is truth or fiction. If you are citing an on line journal, use the journal citation. Some of your papers may not require references, and if that is the case simply state that "no references were consulted."

Writing Research Reports

After you have done your Market Research work, you have to write a report. However, the best research can get put aside without being read. Following are a few tips for writing a good Market Research Report that you can be proud of. The first thing you have to do is to get your reader's attention with a powerful headline and a good opening summary. If you fail to get your prospects' attention, you will fail to communicate and deliver the benefits of your research. Always remember that if your report is not read and action taken, your company will receive no benefits from all the research that you have done, and that's a pretty darn shame. But if you do the report right, you are probably about 70 per cent of the way to a promotion. So read on and pay attention. The trick is writing a research report that will grab the reader's attention without allowing his or her mind to wander even for a second.

Or worse: Making a copy mistake that turns her or him off entirely — and gets your research report instantly tossed into the nearest virtual or literal trash can. In a very real sense, your body copy is a minefield that must be navigated with the greatest of care: Every word, every sentence and paragraph of body copy represents the chance to either intensify your prospect's focus... or to completely lose him. But take care, in long research reports — the headline and opening summary represent only about 4 per cent of the total volume of the report copy required.

There's a lot of pages where you can loose your reader's attention. Lose him, even for a split second, and you've probably lost him — and your promotion — for good! There are three unforgivable sins that you must be aware of and avoid when writing your report.

Avoid the following three unforgivable sins when crafting your research report:

- Do not confuse your reader...
- Do not bore your reader,
- Do not set off his BS detector...

By following the seven simple rules, you can avoid all three dangers and produce a top quality Market Research Report.

Keep Your Report Logically Organized

Humans are NOT logical animals. But when reading or learning, they generally require that the material be presented in a clear, logical way. That generally means starting at point "A"... progressing to point "B"... moving on to point "C"... and so on, until you have reached your ultimate cease.

To do that, you must build your case logically and methodically — much like a mason builds a brick wall. You must lay a solid foundation of research and then build upon each completed analysis argument with the next... brick by brick... in a logical order, proving your research points.

Ask yourself, "What must our reader know first... second... third... and so on, in order to conclude that this research offers the opportunity of a lifetime?"

Keep the Report Moving

When a reader's eyes first fall upon your report, a little stopwatch starts ticking in his head. If at any point, he feels you're not moving along quickly enough, you will lose him. Creating a dynamic flow of information in your research report is absolutely essential for maximum readability. There are three ways to do it...

- Creating and following a "chain of logic" outline helps a lot in this regard — by ensuring that you make each point once, then move on. If prospects feel like you're going back over stuff you already covered, any sense of momentum you may have established is instantly destroyed.
- Check the momentum of each draft by reading it aloud. Mark the places where you — as a reader — begin to become distracted or bored. Once again, highlight any parts that begin to lose you. Each of these parts will kill readership and response if they're still there in the final draft. Edit them or delete them.
- Making each part of copy shorter than the one before is a great way to create momentum. For example — let's say you have to make ten analysis points in order to complete the report. You could spend 1 1/2 pages making your first analysis... 1 page making your second... 3/4 of a page making your third... 1/2 page making your fourth... and then wrap up the final six points in a series of bullets covering a single page.

Keep Your Report Simple

Never ask your prospect to work in order to figure out what you're saying. Two-dollar words, esoteric references and complex sentences are killers in research reports. Subtlety, nuance and complexity are for poets — NOT market reports!

Try to limit yourself to one complete, clearly presented thought per sentence. When you connect two thoughts in a sentence, make sure they connect directly and clearly with each other.

Also be sure to avoid inserting undeveloped or underdeveloped thoughts in sentences or paragraphs. They're like little boobytraps in the report. They stop readers cold.

Keep the Report Fat-Free

Readers should feel as though they're getting good value in return for the number of words they're made to read. Your challenge is to never use three words when two will do the job.

Here are four ways to say more with less:

- *Use more precise word choices*: When you fail to use the word that most precisely and accurately communicates a thought, you wind up using five, six or even ten words instead. When searching for the most precise word, checking synomyms in a thesaurus often gives you the answer.
- *Eliminate unnecessary words*: Here again, reading copy aloud really helps. Much of the time, for example, the word "that" is totally unnecessary. When in doubt, leave it out!
- *Avoid unhelpful repitition*: Repetition of key sales points — a USP or major benefit, for example — is a beautiful thing. Repeating minor thoughts only slows the copy and bores the reader.
- *Figures of speech can help you say more, faster*: If a pictures is worth a thousand words, metaphors, similes, and other figures of speech are as well.

Keep Your Report Believable

Your reader is already skeptical. Making grandiose claims that you can't (or don't) prove beyond the shadow of a doubt will only confirm what he or she already suspects: That you're full of beans. And this will get your promotion trashed in a heartbeat.

Keep Your Report Potent

One of the fastest ways to lose your prospect's attention is to fail to focus on his favourite subject: HIM or HER! The word "You" has been called the most powerful word in the English language — and for good reason. Finding ways to personalize the report — applying each passage as if had been written for the reader — is a key to keeping his attention.

Avoid Unintended Impressions.

Here's where insisting that friends read your report can pay huge dividends. By the time you're ready to stick a fork in your new promotion, you can almost recite it word for word — frontwards and backwards. That means you're too close to the report to catch things that may be misread... even things that may raise objections or implant an erroneous impression in your reader's mind.

HOW TO WRITE A SCHOLARLY RESEARCH REPORT

Researchers communicate their results and help accumulate knowledge through conference papers, reports, on-line journals and print journals. While there are many rewards for having research disseminated in a scholarly outlet, the preparation of a good research report is not a trivial task. The common parts of a research report along with frequently made mistakes.

While the emphasis here is on reports prepared for scholarly, peer-reviewed publication, these points are applicable to other forms of research reports. Dissertations and theses, for example, provide more detail than scholarly publications yet they adhere to the same basic scientific writing principles. Since all scientific research involves observation, description and analysis, points made in this substance are applicable to historical and descriptive, as well as to experimental, research.

More detail can be found in the *Publication Manual of the American Psychological Association*, proposed revisions to the manual and many research methods textbooks.

First Steps in Writing a Research Report

You should constantly think about writing your report at every stage of your research activities. The parts of the research report discussed next in this article come from the most-cited style source for educational and psychological literature - the *Publication Manual of the American Psychological Association*.

The *Publication Manual* provides detailed information about the entire process of publication — from organizing, writing, keying and submitting your manuscript, to seeing the accepted manuscript through production and publication.

Of special interest in the fourth edition are the updated parts on reporting statistics, writing without bias, preparing manuscripts with a word processor for electronic production and publishing research in accordance with ethical principles of scientific publishing.

You should have a copy. Plan your report to focus on a single important finding or highly related group of findings. In the process of analyzing your data, you probably uncovered many relationships and gained numerous insights into the problem.

Your journal submission, however, should contain only one key point. The point should be so fundamental that you should be able express it in one sentence or, at most, in a paragraph. If you have several key points, consider writing multiple manuscripts. When writing your manuscript, keep in mind that the purpose is to inform the readers of what you investigated, why and how you conducted your investigation, the results and your ceases. As the investigator and writer, your job is simply to report, not to convince and usually not to advocate. You must provide enough detail so readers can reach their own ceases about the quality of your research and the veracity of your ceases.

Parts of your Report

- *Title*: It is important that the title be both brief and descriptive of your research. Search engines will use the title to help locate your article. Readers make quick decisions as to whether they are going to invest the time to read your article largely based on the title. Thus, the title should not contain jargon or vernacular. Rather, the title should be short (generally 15 words or less) and clearly indicate what the study is about. If in doubt, try to specify the cause and effect relationship in your key point. Avoid trite and wasteful phrases such as "A study of..." or "An investigation to determine..."

- *Abstract*: The abstract serves two major purposes: it helps a person decide whether to read the paper, and it provides the reader with a framework for understanding the paper if they decide to read it. Thus, your abstract should describe the most important aspects of the study within the word-limit provided by the journal. As appropriate for your research, try to include a statement of the problem, the people you studied, the dependent and independent variables, the instruments, the design, major findings, and ceases. If pressed for space, concentrate on the problem and, especially, your findings.
- *Introduction*: You will usually start your report with a paragraph or two presenting the investigated problem, the importance of the study, and an overview of your research strategy. You do not need to label this part. Its position within the paper makes that obvious.

The introductory paragraphs are usually followed by a review of the literature. Show how your research builds on prior knowledge by presenting and evaluating what is already known about your research problem. Assume that the readers possess a broad knowledge of the field, but not the cited articles, books and papers. Discuss the findings of works that are pertinent to your specific issue. You usually will not need to elaborate on methods.

The goal of the introduction and literature review is to demonstrate "the logical continuity between previous and present work". This does not mean you need to provide an exhaustive historical review. Analyse the relationships among the related studies instead of presenting a series of seemingly unrelated abstracts or annotations. The introduction should motivate the study. The reader should understand why the problem was researched and why the study represents a contribution to existing knowledge. Unless the study is an evaluation of a programme, it is generally inappropriate to attempt to motivate the study based on its social importance.

Method: The method part includes separate descriptions of the sample, the materials, and the procedures. These are subtitled and may be augmented by further parts, if needed.

Describe your sample with sufficient detail so that it is clear what population(s) the sample represents. A discussion of how the sample was formed is needed for replicability and understanding your study. The APA Task Force on Statistical Inference points out "how a population is defined affects almost every cease about an article" (Wilkinson, et al., 1999). Convenience samples are not unusual in scientific inquiry; their use should not discourage you from seeking a publication outlet for your report.

A description of your instruments, including all surveys, tests, questionnaires, interview forms, and other tools used to provide data, should appear in the materials subpart. Evidence of reliability and validity should be presented. Since reliability is a property of scores from a specific use of a specific instrument for a specific population, you should provide reliability estimates based on your data.

The design of the study, whether it is a case study, a survey, a controlled experiment, a meta-analysis, or some other type of research, is conveyed through the procedures subsection. It is here that the activities of the researcher are described, such as what was said to the participants, how groups were formed, what control mechanisms were employed, etc. The description is sufficient if enough detail is present for the reader to replicate the essential elements of the study. It is important for the procedures to conform to ethical criteria for researchers.

Results: Present a summary of what you found in the results part. Here you should describe the techniques that you used, each analysis and the results of each analysis.

Start with a description of any complications, such as protocol violations and missing data that may have occurred. Examine your data for anomalies, such as outliers, points of high influence, miscoded data, and illogical responses. Use your common sense to evaluate the quality of your data and make adjustments if need be. Describe the process that you used in order to assure your readers that your editing was appropriate and purified rather than skewed your results.

With today's availability of statistical packages, it is fairly easy to use very sophisticated techniques to analyse your data. Understand the techniques you are using and the statistics that you are reporting. Try to use the simplest, appropriate technique for which you can meet the underlying assumptions.

If you are going to use inferential statistics, you should determine the power a priori based on your anticipated distribution, design, and definition of practical significance. This information must stem from your related literature and not the data that you collected. If you fail to reach statistical significance, then this analysis can be used to show that the finding does not stem from low power.

Where appropriate, compute and report effect sizes or, at a minimum, be sure you provide enough information so effect sizes can be computed. Effect sizes provide a common metric for evaluating results across studies and aid in the design of future studies.

They will be needed by anyone who attempts a quantitative synthesis of your study along with the others in your area of research. For most research reports, the results should provide the summary details about what you found rather than an exhaustive listing of every possible analysis and every data point. Use carefully planned tables and graphs. While tables and graphs should be self-explanatory, do not include a table or graph unless it is discussed in the report.

Limit them to those that help the reader understand your data as they relate to the investigated problem.

Discussion: At this point, you are the expert on your data set and an authority on the problem you addressed. In this part, discuss and interpret your data for the reader, tell the reader of the implications of your findings and make recommendations. Do not be afraid to state your opinions.

Many authors chose to begin the discussion part by highlighting key results. Return to the specific problem you investigated and tell the reader what you now think and why. Relate your findings to those of previous studies, by explaining relationships and supporting or disagreeing with what others have found. Describe your logic and draw your ceases. Be careful, however, not to over generalize your results. Your ceases should be warranted by your study and your data.

Be sure to recognize the limitations of your study. Try to anticipate the questions a reader will have and suggest what problems should be researched next in order to extend your findings into new areas.

References: There should be a one-to-one match between the references cited in the report and the references listed in the reference part.

PUBLISHING YOUR REPORT

If you intend to publish in a journal, these journals will be the most likely candidates. Review the target audience and publication guidelines for these journals to decide which is best suited to your research. Regardless of scholarly quality, a key question in any editor's mind will be whether your manuscript is suited to the journal's purpose and audience. When considering where to submit, note the style of the substances in the journal.

Remember that the review process is conducted by human staff, and so is a fallible process. Peters and Ceci (1982) made this point abundantly clear. They retyped just-published articles from prominent journals, and resubmitted them. All of these articles were rejected without it being noticed that they had just been published by the same journals.

Because of high rejection rates and the usual long length of time journals need to make a selection decision, it is tempting to submit a manuscript simultaneously to more than one journal. This, however, is clearly unethical. Most journals appropriately specify that manuscripts under consideration cannot be submitted elsewhere. The editors and reviewers will be taking a considerable amount of time examining your manuscript, usually as volunteers. You should expect your manuscript to be rejected when it is submitted for the first time. If a manuscript is rejected, you should evaluate the comments and then decide whether to revise, resubmit, or submit it elsewhere. In order to facilitate both your revision and its subsequent evaluation, a resubmission should be accompanied by a description of the issues raised in the review process and your manuscript modifications and other substantive reactions to them.

While very little has been written about ethical standards for authors in the education field, the *Uniform Requirements for Manuscripts Submitted to Biomedical Journals*, which have been adopted by more than 500 scientific and biomedical journals, address criteria for authorship, acknowledgments, redundant publication, competing manuscripts, and conflict of interest. A concise summary of the *Uniform Requirements* can be found in Syrett and Rudner (1996).

A key concept in the *Uniform Requirements* is that individuals identified as authors should have made significant contributions to the conception and design, or analysis and interpretation of data, or both; to drafting of the manuscript or revising it critically for intellectual content; and on final approval of the version of the manuscript to be considered for publication. Being an advisor or head of a research group, does not, in itself, warrant authorship credit.

9

Case Study Methodology

The goals and objectives were presented and explained in detail. The methodology to accomplish those goals and objectives will be examined. The reader will become familiar with the specific techniques that are used in the current study.

That methodology will follow the recommendation of Yin (1994) and has four stages:

- Design the case study,
- Conduct the case study,
- Analyse the case study evidence, and
- Develop the ceases, recommendations and implications.

The substance begins with an introduction, that includes some of the background information that is intended to inform the reader. Following that part, each step of the methodology will be explored in detail. Finally a summary will connect all the information in a concise manner.

INTRODUCTION

Case study is an ideal methodology when a holistic, in-depth investigation is needed (Feagin, Orum,and Sjoberg, 1991). Case studies have been used in varied investigations, particularly in sociological studies, but increasingly, in instruction. Yin, Stake, and others who have wide experience in this methodology have developed robust procedures. When these procedures are followed, the researcher will be following methods as well developed and tested as any in the scientific field. Whether the study is experimental or quasi-experimental, the data collection and analysis methods are known to hide some details. Case studies, on the other hand, are designed to bring out the details from the viewpoint of the participants by using multiple sources of data.

Yin (1993) has identified some specific types of case studies: *Exploratory, Explanatory,* and *Descriptive.* Stake (1995) included three others: *Intrinsic* - when the researcher has an interest in the case; *Instrumental* - when the case is used to understand more than what is obvious to the observer; *Collective* - when a group of cases is studied. Exploratory cases are sometimes considered as a prelude to social research. Explanatory case studies may be used for doing causal investigations. Descriptive cases require a descriptive theory to be developed before starting the project. Pyecha (1988) used this methodology in a special education study, using a pattern-matching procedure. In all of the types of case studies, there can be single-case or multiple-case applications.

Case study research is not sampling research; that is a fact asserted by all the major researchers in the field, including Yin, Stake, Feagin and others. However, selecting cases must be done so as to maximize what can be learned in the period of time available for the study.

The unit of analysis is a critical factor in the case study. It is typically a system of action rather than an individual or group of individuals. Case studies tend to be selective, focusing on one or two issues that are fundamental to understanding the system being examined.

Case studies are multi-perspectival analyses. This means that the researcher considers not just the voice and perspective of the actors, but also of the relevant groups of actors and the interaction between them. This one aspect is a salient point in the characteristic that case studies possess. They give a voice to the powerless and voiceless. When sociological investigations present many studies of the homeless and powerless, they do so from the viewpoint of the "elite". Case study is known as a triangulated research strategy. Snow and Anderson asserted that triangulation can occur with data, investigators, theories, and even methodologies. Stake (1995) stated that the protocols that are used to ensure accuracy and alternative explanations are called triangulation. The need for triangulation arises from the ethical need to confirm the validity of the processes. In case studies, this could be done by using multiple sources of data. The problem in case studies is to establish meaning rather than location.

Denzin (1984) identified four types of triangulation: *Data source triangulation,* when the researcher looks for the data to remain the same in different contexts; *Investigator triangulation,* when several investigators examine the same phenomenon; *Theory triangulation,* when investigators with different view points interpret the same results; and *Methodological triangulation,* when one approach is followed by another, to increase confidence in the interpretation.

The issue of generalization has appeared in the literature with regularity. It is a frequent criticism of case study research that the results are not widely applicable in real life. Yin in particular refuted that criticism by presenting a well constructed explanation of the difference between analytic generalization and statistical generalization: "In analytic generalization, previously developed theory is used as a template against which to compare the empirical results of the case study". The inappropriate manner of generalizing assumes that some *sample* of cases has been drawn from a larger universe of cases. Thus the incorrect terminology such as "small sample" arises, as though a single-case study were a single respondent.

Stake (1995) argued for another approach centreed on a more intuitive, empirically-grounded generalization. He termed it "naturalistic" generalization. His argument was based on the harmonious relationship between the reader's experiences and the case study itself. He expected that the data generated by case studies would often resonate experientially with a broad cross part of readers, thereby facilitating a greater understanding of the phenomenon.

Yin (1994) presented at least four applications for a case study model:

- To explain complex causal links in real-life interventions

- To describe the real-life context in which the intervention has occurred
- To describe the intervention itself
- To explore those situations in which the intervention being evaluated has no clear set of outcomes.

Information technologies involve all four of the categories, but this study will only report on the last two. Since the Levy (1988) case study of the University of Arizona, there has been very little literature relating to the pace of acquisition of information technology at institutions of higher education. For this reason, Levy (1988) conducted a case study after consulting with experts in the field and with senior case researchers. Their recommendation was to conduct an in-depth study of the institution using the case methodology. This study replicates and extends that study and thereby adds to the body of knowledge on the nature of information technology acquisition at universities.

Levy (1988) used a single-case design for the study at the University of Arizona. Single cases may be used to confirm or challenge a theory, or to represent a unique or extreme case. Single-case studies are also ideal for revelatory cases where an observer may have access to a phenomenon that was previously inaccessible.

These studies can be holistic or embedded, the latter occurring when the same case study involves more than one unit of analysis. Multiple-case studies follow a replication logic. This is not to be confused with sampling logic, where a selection is made out of a population, for inclusion in the study. This type of sample selection is improper in a case study. Each individual case study consists of a "whole" study, in which facts are gathered from various sources and ceases drawn on those facts.

As in all research, consideration must be given to construct validity, internal validity, external validity, and reliability. Levy (1988) established construct validity using the single-case exploratory design, and internal validity using the single-case explanatory design. Yin (1994) suggested using multiple sources of evidence as the way to ensure construct validity.

The current study used multiple sources of evidence; survey instruments, interviews, and documents. The specification of the unit of analysis also provides the internal validity as the theories are developed and data collection and analysis test those theories. External validity is more difficult to attain in a single-case study. Yin (1994) provided the assertion that external validity could be achieved from theoretical relationships, and from these generalizations could be made.

It is the development of a formal case study protocol that provides the reliability that is required of all research. The design of this case study closely follows that of the Levy study. The methodology selected by Levy (1988) was based on the seminal work by Yin (1984) and confirmed by Feagin, Orum, and Sjoberg (1991).

That single-case study methodology was used in the current study. Danziger (1985) has established the "context of use" as a mitigating factor in the study of computing in organizations. The "pattern matching" of acquisition and use established in other environments may be shown to be applicable in higher education. Listed six sources of evidence for data collection in the case study protocol: documentation, archival records, interviews, direct observation, participant observation, and physical artifacts. Not all need be used in every case study (Yin, 1994). In this study, the last three types of sources are not relevant, since they are related to direct sociological investigation, and are not used. For this case study, the researcher replicated Levy's (1988) study, but also adds to the field by examining aspects of client/server computing, the Internet. It is based on a modification of the methodology devised by Yin (1984).

Each stage of the methodology will consist of a discussion of procedures recommended in the literature, followed by a discussion of the application of those procedures in the proposed study:

- *Design the case study protocol*:
  - Determine the required skills
  - Develop and review the protocol

- *Conduct the case study*:
  - Prepare for data collection
  - Distribute questionnaire
  - Conduct interviews
- *Analyse case study evidence*:
  - Analytic strategy
- Develop ceases, recommendations, and implications based on the evidence

In the order in which they are executed in the current study. Each part begins with the procedures recommended in the literature, followed by the application of the recommended procedure in the current study.

DESIGN THE CASE STUDY PROTOCOL

The first stage in the case study methodology recommended by Yin (1994) is the development of the case study protocol.

This stage is composed of two subheadings: *Determine the Required Skills* and *Develop and Review the Protocol.*

Determine the Required Skills

Recommended Procedures

Yin (1994) suggested that the researcher must possess or acquire the following skills: the ability to ask good questions and to interpret the responses, be a good listener, be adaptive and flexible so as to react to various situations, have a firm grasp of issues being studied, and be unbiased by preconceived notions. The investigator must be able to function as a "senior" investigator.

Application of Recommended Procedures

This researcher has had thirty years of experience in both academic and administrative computing and was adequately prepared for the investigation. This researcher's training in systems analysis is adequate preparation for the project.

A draft of the protocol will be developed by the researcher. This follows extensive relevant readings on the topic which would help in developing the draft questions. Yin (1994) recommended that this be conducted in a seminar format if there are multiple investigators.

The purpose of the seminar or review, in the case of a single investigator, is to discover problems in the plans or any phase of the study design. If there is a team of investigators, the seminar format would perhaps highlight team-member incompatibilities and perhaps potentially productive partnerships amongst the members. If there are unreasonable or unattainable deadlines in the plan, this will most likely be discovered by the team.

Some of the early criticism of the case study as a research methodology was that it was unscientific in nature, and because replication was not possible. The literature contains major refutations by Yin, Stake, Feagin, and others whose work resulted in a suggested outline for what a case study protocol could include. Yin (1994) reminded the researcher that there is more to a protocol than the instrument. He asserted that the development of the rules and procedures contained in the protocol enhance the reliability of case study research. While it is desirable to have a protocol for all studies, Yin (1994) stated that it is essential in a multiple-case study.

The protocol should include the following parts:

- *An overview of the case study project*: This will include project objectives, case study issues, and presentations about the topic under study
- *Field procedures*: Reminders about procedures, credentials for access to data sources, location of those sources
- *Case study questions*: The questions that the investigator must keep in mind during data collection
- *A guide for the case study report*: The outline and format for the report.

The discipline imposed on the investigator by the protocol is important to the overall progress and reliability of the study. It helps keep the investigator's focus on the main tasks and goals, while the process of development brings out problems that would only be faced during the actual investigation. The overview of the project is a useful way to communicate with the investigator, while the field procedures are indispensable during data collection.

The case study questions are those under study, not those contained in the survey instrument. Each question should also have a list of probable sources.

The guide for the case study report is often omitted from case study plans, since investigators view the reporting phase as being far in the future. Yin (1994) proposed that the report be planned at the start. Case studies do not have a widely accepted reporting format - hence the experience of the investigator is a key factor.

Some researchers have used a journal format which was suitable for their work, but not necessarily for other studies. Indeed the case study at Fairfield University is not served by such a format, nor was the Levy (1988) study before it. The reason for the absence of a fixed reporting format is that each case study is unique. The data collection, research questions and indeed the unit of analysis cannot be placed into a fixed mold as in experimental research.

Application of Recommended Procedures

Yin (1984) presented three conditions for the design of case studies: a) the type of research question posed, b) the extent of control an investigator has over actual behavioural events, and c) the degree of focus on contemporary events. In the Levy (1988) study and this study, there are several "what" questions. This type of research question justifies an exploratory study.

Examples of such questions include:

- What patterns of acquisition emerge from the current computing environment and the perceived needs for computing?
- What patterns are revealed from historical inventory records?
- Was there any change in the perceived needs related to the Internet?
- What characteristics of the categories of computing use contribute to the patterns of acquisition?

- What managerial issues arise from the rapid acquisition of information technology and how important have those technologies become to the organization?
- Since replacement and enhancement of information technologies are projected to increase, what economic impact will that have on the planning and budgeting of the university?
- Was there any particular budgetary and/or systematic preparation for the implementation of client/server computing?
- What was the level of managerial commitment to information technology?
- What was the level of faculty commitment to information technology?
- What was the degree of decentralization/ decentralization of information technologies?
- What resources were or will be needed for conversion to a client/server environment?
- What additional resources will be needed now and in the future for university community access to the WWW?

The existence of several "how" questions in the questionnaires make the study explanatory as well, which is not uncommon.

Examples of such questions include:

- How do the respondents view the availability of computing resources in comparison to peer institutions?
- How are information technology resources allocated?
- How are information technology resources financed?
- How will the institution balance the need for technological changes with the need to continue the accomplishment of routine tasks?
- How does Fairfield University plan to meet current demand for service while preparing for strategic long term goals?

- How does the university evaluate the cost-benefit of its computing environment?

The researcher had no control over the behavioural events, which is a characteristic of case studies. The third condition, that was present in the Levy (1988) study and is evident in the current study, is that the events being examined are contemporary, although historic information was used. An empirical investigation of a contemporary phenomenon within its real-life context is one situation in which case study methodology is applicable. Yin (1994) cautioned that case study designs are not variants of other research designs.

Yin (1994) proposed five components of case studies:

- A study's questions,
- Its propositions, if any,
- Its unit(s) of analysis,
- The logic linking the data to the propositions, and
- The criteria for interpreting the findings.

The research questions framed as "who", "what", "where", "how", and "why" determine the relevant strategy to be used. In the Levy (1988) study and the current study, the nature of the questions lead to an explanatory-exploratory case study. The Levy (1988) study and this proposed study, both being exploratory, need not, and do not have a proposition (Yin, 1994). The unit of analysis in a case study could be "an individual, a community, an organization, a nation-state, an empire, or a civilization".

The Levy (1988) study used the case study organization as the unit of analysis. The linking of the data to the propositions and the criteria for interpretation of the findings are not well developed in case studies. However they are represented in the data analysis and report. Levy (1988) established the single-case explanatory- exploratory methodology as the most suitable choice for the investigation of information technology. The explanatory strategy came from the need to determine the extent to which the patterns of acquisition and use that were established in other environments were applicable to higher education environment also. The exploratory strategy was used to examine the economic aspects of information technologies. As a replication of the Levy study, this study also followed that methodology.

DATA COLLECTION, DISTRIBUTION OF THE QUESTIONNAIRE, AND CONDUCTING INTERVIEWS

Recommended Procedures

The second stage of the methodology recommended by Yin (1994) and which were used in the current study, is the Conduct of the case study. There are three tasks in this stage that must be carried out for a successful project: *Preparation for Data Collection, Distribution of the Questionnaire,* and *Conducting Interviews.* They are interrelated. Once the protocol has been developed and tested, it puts the project into the second phase - the actual execution of the plan. In this phase the primary activity is that of data collection.

The protocol described addresses the types of evidence that are available in the case organization. In case studies, data collection should be treated as a design issue that will enhance the construct and internal validity of the study, as well as the external validity and reliability.

Most of the field methods described in the literature treat data collection in isolation from the other aspects of the research process (Yin, 1994), but that would not be productive in case study research.

Yin (1994) identified six primary sources of evidence for case study research. The use of each of these might require different skills from the researcher.

Not all sources are essential in every case study, but the importance of multiple sources of data to the reliability of the study is well established.

The six sources identified by Yin (1994) are:

1. Documentation,
2. Archival records,
3. Interviews,
4. Direct observation,
5. Participant observation, and
6. Physical artifacts.

No single source has a complete advantage over the others; rather, they might be complementary and could be used in tandem. Thus a case study should use as many sources as are relevant to the study.

Table. Types of Evidence

Source of Evidence	Strengths	Weaknesses
Documentation	Stable - repeated review Unobtrusive - exist prior to case study Exact - names etc. Broad coverage - extended time span	Retrievability - difficult Biased selectivity Reporting bias - reflects author bias Access - may be blocked
Archival Records	Same as above Precise and quantitative	Same as above Privacy might inhibit access
Interviews	Targeted - focuses on case study topic Insightful - provides perceived causal inferences	Bias due to poor questions Response bias Incomplete recollection Reflexivity - interviewee expresses what interviewer wants to hear
Direct Observation	Reality - covers events in real time Contextual - covers event context	Time consuming Selectivity - might miss facts Reflexivity - observer's presence might cause change Cost - observers need time
Participant Observation	Same as above Insightful into interpersonal behavior	Same as above Bias due to investigator's actions
Physical Artifacts	Insightful into cultural features Insightful into technical operations	Selectivity Availability

Documents could be letters, memoranda, agendas, study reports, or any items that could add to the data base. The validity of the documents should be carefully reviewed so as to avoid incorrect data being included in the data base. One of the most important uses of documents is to corroborate evidence gathered from other sources. The potential for over-reliance on document as evidence in case studies has been criticized. There could be a danger of this occurrence if the investigator is inexperienced and mistakes some types of documents for unmitigated truth.

Archival records could be useful in some studies since they include service records, maps, charts, lists of names, survey data, and even personal records such as diaries. The investigator must be meticulous in determining the origin of the records and their accuracy.

Interviews are one of the most important sources of case study information. The interview could take one of several forms: open-ended, focused, or structured. In an open-ended interview, the researcher could ask for the informant's opinion on events or facts.

This could serve to corroborate previously gathered data. In a focused interview, the respondent is interviewed for only a short time, and the questions asked could have come from the case study protocol. The structured interview is particularly useful in studies of neighbourhoods where a formal survey is required. The use of tape recorders during the interviews is left to the discretion of the parties involved.

Direct observation in a case study occurs when the investigator makes a site visit to gather data. The observations could be formal or casual activities, but the reliability of the observation is the main concern. Using multiple observers is one way to guard against this problem.

Participant observation is a unique mode of observation in which the researcher may actually participate in the events being studied. This technique could be used in studies of neighbourhoods or organizations, and frequently in anthropological studies.

The main concern is the potential bias of the researcher as an active participant. While the information may not be available in any other way, the drawbacks should be carefully considered by the researcher. Physical artifacts could be any physical evidence that might be gathered during a site visit. That might include tools, art works, notebooks, computer output, and other such physical evidence.

Yin (1994) suggested three principles of data collection for case studies:

- Use multiple sources of data
- Create a case study database
- Maintain a chain of evidence

The rationale for using multiple sources of data is the triangulation of evidence. Triangulation increases the reliability of the data and the process of gathering it. In the context of data collection, triangulation serves to corroborate the data gathered from other sources.

The cost of using multiple sources and the investigator's ability to carry out the task, should be taken into account prior to deciding on the use of this technique. The data that are collected during this phase need to be organized and documented just as it is in experimental studies.

The two types of databases that might be required are the data and the report of the investigator. The design of the databases should be such that other researchers would be able to use the material based on the descriptions contained in the documentation.

All types of relevant documents should be added to the database, as well as tabular materials, narratives, and other notes. In recommending that a chain of evidence be maintained, Yin (1994) was providing an avenue for the researcher to increase the reliability of the study.

The procedure is to have an external observer follow the derivation of evidence from initial research questions to ultimate case study ceases. The case study report would have citations to the case study database where the actual evidence is to be found.

Application of Recommended Procedures

This study used the methodology established by Levy (1988) in his investigation of the impacts of information technology at the University of Arizona. The methodology recommended by Yin (1984) and others was adapted for use at Fairfield University. The questionnaire developed by Levy (1988) was modified for use at Fairfield University. The modifications were approved by Levy (1988). The modified instruments reflect both the current case organization and the technology environment under study. The modified instruments were tested on a group of individuals from the administration and from the faculty at Fairfield University, the case organization.

The results from the test group indicated that changes to the instruments would be beneficial, and these changes were made.

The remodified instruments were reviewed by Levy. King and Kraemer (1985) provided the logical categories for context of use in computing environments and were adapted by Levy in the 1988 study: *technological development, structural arrangements, socio-technical interface, political/economic environment,* and *benefits/problems.* Specific questionnaire items cover these areas. These categories were also employed in the analysis.

The primary data gathering was accomplished using the "Administrator Assessment of Computing" and the "Faculty Assessment of Computing" questionnaires developed for the Levy study, appropriately modified to reflect recent developments and concerns specific to Fairfield University. The purpose of the modifications to the instruments was to gather data on the client/server aspects of the computing environment, as well as the use of the Internet and the WWW. Permission to use the questionnaires from Levy's study was obtained.

Some of the items in the instruments that relate to each of the categories are:

- *Technological Development*:
  - There is considerable support for the acquisition of PC networks within our department/unit
  - More local area networks
  - Access to the Internet and WWW
  - Access to networked CD's from classroom
  - Ability to create class material for use on the WWW
  - Video Conference capability
  - Microcomputer classrooms for instruction only

   - More classrooms connected to networks
   - More instructional software
   - Support for WWW/Multimedia course development
   - Ability to transfer large files with sound, images, etc.
- *Structural Arrangements*:
   - University policy has provided effective guidelines for computing use in the university
   - The university's central administration has been equitable in allocating available resources for computing
   - Satisfied with our level of computing decisions
- *Socio-Technical Interface*:
   - Hands-on workshops designed specifically for faculty and research uses of information technology tools would be useful for me
   - Current support programmes
   - Sufficient data communications capabilities
   - Access to Internet, WWW, E-mail, from the Office
   - Access to Internet, WWW, E-mail, from the Classroom
   - Access to Internet, WWW, E-mail, from the Home
   - Use the services of an Instructional Computing group to help faculty use computing for instruction
   - Use the services of a Research Computing group to help faculty use computing for instruction
- *Political/Economic Environment*:
   - All students should have access to computing, regardless of the course in which they are enrolled
   - Faculty positions
   - Support positions
   - Plant and Equipment maintenance
   - Current instructional programmes

 - There is sufficient support for instructional computing in our department
- *Benefits/Problems*:
 - The scope of the work we are able to undertake is directly increased by the use if computing
 - Attracting undergraduate students
 - Attracting faculty
 - Able to adequately discuss needs with mainframe support staff
 - Satisfied with system response time
 - Satisfied with institutional data sets available for analysis

The questionnaires were distributed through the office of the Academic Vice President (AVP) to all full-time faculty and academic administrators, and specific others recommended by the deans and the AVP. This data gathering activity was co-sponsored by the Education Technology committee. The questionnaire for faculty was also distributed to the permanent faculty of the School of Engineering, although they are not full-time faculty.

They are heavy users of technology and their views were considered valuable. Including part-time faculty other than the School of Engineering, carried the risk of including several hundred instructors who teach in the School of Continuing Education and whose access to computing resources is limited. They are adjunct lecturers who could be classified as part-time instructors.

Their number is too large to warrant the potential distortion in the results. The completed questionnaires were returned to the office of the Academic Vice President. A reminder notice was sent to all faculty and administrators one week after the original contact, so as to encourage participation.

This action increased the response rate. The Educational Technology Committee made phone calls to colleagues to encourage participation. Levy (1988) used open-ended interviews as recommended by Yin (1984) to expand the depth of data gathering, and to increase the number of sources of information. In this study the researcher used the same interview questions and protocol that were used in the Levy study.

As in the Levy study, the survey was enhanced by interviews of key individuals so as to acquire information that might not have become available through the questionnaire. The interviews were conducted according to the interviewee's schedule and availability, as suggested by Feagin, Orum, and Sjoberg (1991). The list of those to be interviewed included the Academic Vice President, the Vice President of Administration, the Director of Telecommunications, the Deans of Arts and Sciences, Business, and Engineering, and the Chair of the academic Educational Technology committee. The interview protocol used by Levy (1988) was free form and followed the recommendations of Yin (1984). It was ideal for the case organization under study. The researcher is well qualified to conduct this form of inquiry.

The source of the quantitative data was various university records in the public domain. The historic financial information, Financial Statements, 1989-1995 was available through the appropriate university officers. Permission was obtained from the Fairfield University Controller, for use of the documents. The Long Range Planning Committee Report (1993) and the Computer User Group Report (1993) were the primary sources of information on future projections. Both the documents were available in the university Library. The academic Educational Technology Committee minutes would have been very informative for some of the historic and anecdotal issues, but were unavailable for non-committee use.

ANALYSE CASE STUDY EVIDENCE

The following discussion will present the *Analytic Strategy* that should be followed in the course of evaluating data gathered in the previous stage of the study. There are various viewpoints relating to this phase of the study, and one of them is that statistical robustness is not an absolute necessity in all case studies. This researcher will present the specific statistical techniques that will be used in this study later in the part.

"Data analysis consists of examining, categorizing, tabulating, or otherwise recombining the evidence to address the initial propositions of a study". The analysis of case study is one of the least developed aspects of the case study methodology. The researcher needs to rely on experience and the literature to present the evidence in various ways, using various interpretations.

This becomes necessary because statistical analysis is not necessarily used in all case studies. This case study employs a series of statistical tests to help in the presentation of the data to the reader.

However not all case studies lend themselves to statistical analysis, and in fact the attempt to make the study conducive to such analysis could inhibit the development of other aspects of the study. Miles and Huberman (1984) have suggested alternative analytic techniques of analysis in such situations, such as using arrays to display the data, creating displays, tabulating the frequency of events, ordering the information, and other methods. This must be done in a way that will not bias the results.

Yin (1994) suggested that every investigation should have a general analytic strategy, so as to guide the decision regarding what will be analysed and for what reason. He presented some possible analytic techniques: *pattern-matching*, *explanation-building*, and *time-series analysis*. In general, the analysis will rely on the theoretical propositions that led to the case study. If theoretical propositions are not present, then the researcher could consider developing a descriptive framework around which the case study is organized.

Trochim (1989) considered pattern-matching as one of the most desirable strategies for analysis. This technique compares an empirically based pattern with a predicted one. If the patterns match, the internal reliability of the study is enhanced. The actual comparison between the predicted and actual pattern might not have any quantitative criteria.

The discretion of the researcher is therefore required for interpretations. Explanation-building is considered a form of pattern-matching, in which the analysis of the case study is carried out by building an explanation of the case. This implies that it is most useful in explanatory case studies, but it is possible to use it for exploratory cases as well as part of a hypothesis-generating process.

Explanation-building is an iterative process that begins with a theoretical statement, refines it, revises the proposition, and repeating this process from the beginning. This is known to be a technique that is fraught with problems for the investigator. One of those problems is a loss of focus, although keeping this in mind protects the investigator from those problems.

Time-series analysis is a well-known technique in experimental and quasi-experimental analysis. It is possible that a single dependent or independent variable could make this simpler than pattern-matching, but sometimes there are multiple changes in a variable, making starting and ending points unclear. There are some things that the researcher must be careful to review to ensure that the analysis will be of high quality, including: showing that all relevant evidence was used, that all rival explanations were used, that the analysis addressed the most significant aspect of the case study, and that the researchers knowledge and experience are used to maximum advantage in the study.

APPLICATION OF RECOMMENDED PROCEDURE

The data analysis for the current case study follows the logical categories used in the Levy (1988) study, and was adapted from the categories developed by King and Kraemer (1985).

The categories are:

- Technological development
- Structural arrangements
- Socio-technical interface
- Political economic environment, and
- Benefits/problems.

Those categories were supported by the selection of indicators that were "functionally equivalent" items for each concept. Functional equivalence means that the same variable may be measured by a variety of different indicators, all of which have some bearing on the concept.

This researcher modified the Levy questionnaires to reflect current technology developments and items of interest to Fairfield University. All references to the University of Arizona were replaced by references to Fairfield University. Several items were added to gather data concerning the Internet and the WWW. A factor analysis was executed to determine if the current case population produced the same groupings as in the Levy study. Loehlin (1992) recommended an exploratory factor analysis for the type of data that was gathered in this study.

Some of the items added to the original instrument include:

- Current use/could use/would enhance future use
  - Internet resources (Gopher, FTP etc.)
  - World Wide Web (WWW) resources (Netscape, etc.)
  - Networked PC access from classroom
- The following contribute to the effectiveness of our work
  - Access to the Internet, WWW, Email from the office, classroom, and home
- These developments could be important in five years
  - Access to the Internet and WWW
  - Access to networked CD's from classroom
  - Ability to create class material for use on WWW
- High priority should be placed on the following
  - More powerful network servers
  - Microcomputer/Multimedia classrooms for instruction only
  - More classrooms connected to the network
  - Support for WWW/Multimedia course development
  - More instructional software
  - Ability to transfer large files with sound, images.
  - Ability to scan and store documents on WWW for instruction
- Table adding up to one hundred per cent

- Use of the Internet for: Instruction, Research, Professional Interest, Email, and Personal Interest/Surfing.

Aczel (1996) recommended cross tabulations to explore a hypothesis such as that relating to differences between faculty and administration within the King and Kraemer (1985) categories. The hypothesis was that there is no significant difference between the responses of the two groups of respondents with regard to the factors relating to the rate of technology acquisition. Cross tabulations were used to explore the differences in responses of the faculty by school.

Cross tabulations and the chi- square were computed to determine if the differences that appeared among the sub groups of the university community such as faculty and administrators, were significant. A contingency coefficient for each cross tabulation indicated the strength of the relationship. The Likert-type variables were analysed using frequency distributions.

The ordinal items in the questionnaires were analysed using the mean and median. For those items in the questionnaires that are common to the Levy study and the current case organization, a paired comparison of the sample populations was run. The statistical tests were the Cross tabulation and Chi square, so that inferences may be drawn about the comparison of the two very different institutions. Those inferences could lead to grounded theory regarding the aspects of information technology at universities of different sizes. The Chi-square was used to assess whether the differences that emerged were significant. All analyses were carried out using SPSSx version 7.1 on an IBM Pentium 75 megahertz PC compatible running Windows 95. These resources were available to the researcher at Fairfield University. The data capture was carried out on a DEC Vax 6430 using Accent R, creating a database and screen driven programmes. The researcher created the programmes to validate the data as it was entered so as to minimize data entry errors. There are hundreds of private colleges that are about the same size as Fairfield University.

By applying the case study to this type of institution, the analytic generalizations could be informative to other similar institutions. The literature has pointed to increasing costs and declining revenues. Those are issues that many higher education institutions face.

DEVELOP CEASES, RECOMMENDATIONS, AND IMPLICATIONS BASED ON THE EVIDENCE

Recommended Procedure

The reporting aspect of a case study is perhaps most important from the user perspective. It is the contact point between the user and the researcher. A well designed research project that is not well explained to the reader, will cause the research report to fall into disuse.

In this part, the researcher must refrain from technical jargon and resort to clear explanations. Those explanations are necessary to help the user understand the implications of the findings.

Application of Recommended Procedure

These results are presented not exclusively as statistical results, but with accompanying explanations of the meaning of those test results. In that way both the technical requirements and the informational needs are met.

Summary

The case study methodology has been subjected to scrutiny and criticism at various times since the 1930's. As a research tool, it has not been a choice that is listed in the major research texts in the social sciences. However, as this researcher has shown in this substance and in the preceding substance in this journal, case study is a reliable methodology when executed with due care.

The literature, while not extensive, contains specific guidelines for researchers to follow in carrying out case studies. Yin and Stake have designed protocols for conducting the case study, which enhance the reliability and validity of the investigation.

The current study followed the design used by Levy (1988) in his case study of the impacts of information technology at the University of Arizona. The survey instruments used by Levy (1988) were modified for use at Fairfield University. The modifications included replacing "Fairfield University" for references to the "University of Arizona", deleting environmental references not appropriate for Fairfield University, and adding items to the instruments for the purpose of gathering data on the client/server computing, the Internet, and the World Wide Web.

Once the instruments were modified and the testing completed, the surveys were distributed to the full-time faculty and educational administrators. One week after the initial distribution, a reminder was sent to the groups so as to encourage participation.

The analysis followed conventional analytic techniques using statistical as well as anecdotal analysis. Differences between the responses of the administrators and faculty were explored using cross tabulations. These differences were examined within the categories described by King and Kraemer (1985) and adapted for use by Levy (1988) in a case study of the University of Arizona. For the Likert-type variables frequency distributions were used to analyse the data. For those items where the original Levy (1988) instruments and the current instruments were identical, a cross tabulation and chi-square were executed to examine the significance of the differences, if any, between the groups. All these tests were run at Fairfield University using SPSSX version 7.1 on an IBM Pentium 75 megahertz PC compatible running Windows 95. This substance has presented the methodology that was used to conduct the current study. In a future edition of this journal, the results will be presented in accord with the goals and objectives of the study so as to confirm that what was proposed was in fact executed.

The ceases will also be presented in the subsequent substance, and will once again follow the goals and objectives outlined in the introductory substance and confirm that what was proposed was in fact accomplished.

FIVE MISUNDERSTANDINGS ABOUT CASE STUDY RESEARCH

When we first became interested in in-depth case-study research, we was trying to understand how power and rationality shape each other and form the urban environments in which we live. It was clear to me that in order to understand a complex issue like this, in-depth case-study research was necessary. It was equally clear, however, that our teachers and colleagues kept dissuading me from employing this particular research methodology. 'You cannot generalize from a single case', some would say, 'and social science is about generalizing.'

Others would argue that the case study may be well suited for pilot studies but not for full-fledged research plans. Others again would comment that the case study is subjective, giving too much scope for the researcher's own interpretations. Thus the validity of case studies would be wanting, they argued. At first, we did not know how to respond to such claims, which clearly formed the conventional wisdom about case-study research. We decided therefore to find out where the claims come from and whether they are correct.

CONVENTIONAL WISDOM ABOUT CASE-STUDY RESEARCH

Looking up 'case study' in the *Dictionary of Sociology* as a beginning, we found the following in full citation:

Case Study: The detailed examination of a single example of a class of phenomena, a case study cannot provide reliable information about the broader class, but it may be useful in the preliminary stages of an investigation since it provides hypotheses, which may be tested systematically with a larger number of cases. This description is indicative of the conventional wisdom of case-study research, which, if not directly wrong, is so oversimplified as to be grossly misleading. It is correct that the case study is a 'detailed examination of a single example', but as as suggested, look, it is not true that a case study 'cannot provide reliable information about the broader class'.

It is also correct that a case study *can* be used 'in the preliminary stages of an investigation' to generate hypotheses, but it is misleading to see the case study as a pilot method to be used only in preparing the real study's larger surveys, systematic hypotheses testing, and theory-building. The conventional view, a case and a case study cannot be of value in and of themselves; they need to be linked to hypotheses, following the well-known hypothetico-deductive model of explanation. Mattei Dogan and Dominique Pelassy (1990: 121) put it like this: 'one can validly explain a particular case only on the basis of general hypotheses. All the rest is uncontrollable, and so of no use'. Similarly, the early Donald Campbell did not mince words when he relegated single-case studies to the methodological trash heap: [S]uch studies have such a total absence of control as to be of almost no scientific value. ... Any appearance of absolute knowledge, or intrinsic knowledge about singular isolated objects, is found to be illusory upon analysis. ... It seems well-nigh unethical at the present time to allow, as theses or dissertations in education.

FIVE MISUNDERSTANDINGS ABOUT

Case-study research If you read such criticism of a certain methodology enough times, or if you hear your thesis advisers repeat it, you begin to believe it may be true. This is what happened to me, and it made me uncertain about case-study methodology. As we continued our research, however, we found out that Campbell had later made a 180-degree turn in his views of the case study and had become one of the strongest proponents of this method. We eventually found, with the help of Campbell's later works and other works like them, that the problems with the conventional wisdom about case-study research can be summarized in five misunderstandings or oversimplifications about the nature of such research:

- *Misunderstanding no. 1*: General, theoretical (context-independent) knowledge is more valuable than concrete, practical (contextdependent) knowledge.
- *Misunderstanding no. 2*: One cannot generalize on the basis of an individual case; therefore, the case study cannot contribute to scientific development.

- *Misunderstanding no. 3*: The case study is most useful for generating hypotheses, that is, in the first stage of a total research process, while other methods are more suitable for hypotheses testing and theory-building.
- *Misunderstanding no. 4*: The case study contains a bias towards verification, that is, a tendency to confirm the researcher's preconceived notions.
- *Misunderstanding no. 5*: It is often difficult to summarize and develop general propositions and theories on the basis of specific case studies. These five misunderstandings indicate that it is theory, reliability and validity that are at issue; in other words, the very status of the case study as a scientific method. In what follows, we shall focus on these five misunderstandings and correct them one by one. First, however, we shall outline the role of cases in human learning.

ROLE OF CASES IN HUMAN LEARNING

In order to understand why the conventional view of case-study research is problematic, we need to grasp the role of cases and theory in human learning. Here two points can be made.

First, the case study produces the type of context-dependent knowledge that research on learning shows to be necessary to allow people to develop from rule-based beginners to virtuoso experts.

Second, in the study of human affairs, there appears to exist only context-dependent knowledge, which thus presently rules out the possibility of epistemic theoretical construction. The full argument behind these two points can be found in Flyvbjerg (2001: chs 2–4).

For reasons of space, we can only give an outline of the argument here. At the outset, however, we can assert that if the two points are correct, it will have radical consequences for the conventional view of the case study in research and teaching. This view would then be problematic.

Phenomenological studies of human learning indicate that for adults there exists a qualitative leap in their learning process from the rulegoverned use of analytical rationality in beginners to the fluid performance of tacit skills in what Pierre Bourdieu (1977) calls virtuosos and Hubert and Stuart Dreyfus (1986) true human experts.

Here we may note that most people are experts in a number of everyday social, technical and intellectual skills like giving a gift, riding a bicycle or interpreting images on a television screen, while only few reach the level of true expertise for more specialized skills like playing chess, composing a symphony or flying a fighter jet. Common to all experts, however, is that they operate on the basis of intimate knowledge of several thousand concrete cases in their areas of expertise. Context-dependent knowledge and experience are at the very heart of expert activity.

Such knowledge and expertise also lie at the centre of the case study as a research and teaching method; or, to put it more generally still, as a method of learning. Phenomenological studies of the learning process therefore emphasize the importance of this and similar methods: it is only because of experience with cases that one can at all move from being a beginner to being an expert. If people were exclusively trained in context-independent knowledge and rules, that is, the kind of knowledge that forms the basis of textbooks and computers, they would remain at the beginner's level in the learning process.

This is the limitation of analytical rationality: it is inadequate for the best results in the exercise of a profession, as student, researcher or practitioner. In a teaching situation, well-chosen case studies can help the student achieve competence, while context-independent facts and rules will bring the student just to the beginner's level.

Only a few institutions of higher learning have taken the consequence of this. Harvard University is one of them. Here both teaching and research in the professional schools are modelled to a wide extent on the understanding that case knowledge is central to human learning.

At one stage in our research, we was invited to Harvard to learn about case methodology 'in action'. During our stay, it became clear to me that if we was going to aspire to become an expert in our field of expertise, and if we wanted to be an effective help to our students in their learning processes, we would need to master case methodology in research and teaching.

Our stay at Harvard also became a major step forward in shedding our uncertainties about the conventional wisdom about cases and case studies. At Harvard we found the literature and people who effectively argued, 'Forget the conventional wisdom, go ahead and do a case study'. We figured if it is good enough for Harvard, it is good enough for me, and we suggest others might reason like this, including whole institutions of learning. There is much to gain, for instance, by transforming the lecture format still dominant in most universities to one of case learning.

It is not that rule-based knowledge should be discounted: it is important in every area and especially to novices. But to make rule-based knowledge the highest goal of learning is regressive. There is a need for both approaches. The highest levels in the learning process, that is, virtuosity and true expertise, are reached only via a person's own experiences as practitioner of the relevant skills. Therefore, beyond using the case method and other experiential methods for teaching, the best that teachers can do for students in professional programmes is to help them achieve real practical experience; for example, via placement arrangements, internships, summer jobs, and the like.

For researchers, the closeness of the case study to real-life situations and its multiple wealth of details are important in two respects. First, it is important for the development of a nuanced view of reality, including the view that human behaviour cannot be meaningfully understood as simply the rule-governed acts found at the lowest levels of the learning process, and in much theory. Second, cases are important for researchers' own learning processes in developing the skills needed to do good research.

If researchers wish to develop their own skills to a high level, then concrete, context-dependent experience is just as central for them as to professionals learning any other specific skills. Concrete experiences can be achieved via continued proximity to the studied reality and via feedback from those under study. Great distance to the object of study and lack of feedback easily lead to a stultified learning process, which in research can lead to ritual academic blind alleys, where the effect and usefulness of research becomes unclear and untested.

As a research method, the case study can be an effective remedy against this tendency. The second main point in connection with the learning process is that there does not and probably cannot exist predictive theory in social science. Social science has not succeeded in producing general, context-independent theory and has thus in the final instance nothing else to offer than concrete, context-dependent knowledge.

And the case study is especially well suited to produce this knowledge. In his later work, Donald Campbell arrives at a similar cease, explaining how his work has undergone 'an extreme oscillation away from our earlier dogmatic disparagement of case studies'. In a logic that in many ways resembles that of the phenomenology of human learning, Campbell now explains: After all, man is, in his ordinary way, a very competent knower, and qualitative common-sense knowing is not replaced by quantitative knowing. ... This is not to say that such common-sense naturalistic observation is objective, dependable, or unbiased. But it is all that we have. It is the only route to knowledge – noisy, fallible, and biased though it be. (Campbell, 1975: 179, 191) Campbell is not the only example of a researcher who has altered his views about the value of the case study.

Hans Eysenck (1976: 9), who originally did not regard the case study as anything other than a method of producing anecdotes, later realised that 'sometimes we simply have to keep our eyes open and look carefully at individual cases – not in the hope of proving anything, but rather in the hope of learning something!' Proof is hard to come by in social science because of the absence of 'hard' theory, whereas learning is certainly possible. More recently, similar views have been expressed by Charles Ragin, Howard Becker and their colleagues in explorations of what the case study is and can be in social inquiry . As for predictive theory, universals and scientism, the study of human affairs is thus at an eternal beginning. In essence, we have only specific cases and context-dependent knowledge. The first of the five misunderstandings about the case study – that general theoretical (contextindependent) knowledge is more valuable than concrete, practical (context-dependent) knowledge – can therefore be revised as follows.

CASES AS 'BLACK SWANS'

The view that one cannot generalize on the basis of a single case is usually considered to be devastating to the case study as a scientific method. This second misunderstanding about the case study is typical among proponents of the natural science ideal within the social sciences. Yet even researchers who are not normally associated with this ideal may be found to have this viewpoint. Anthony Giddens, for example, Research which is geared primarily to hermeneutic problems may be of generalized importance in so far as it serves to elucidate the nature of agents' knowledgeability, and thereby their reasons for action, across a wide range of action-contexts.

Pieces of ethnographic research like ... say, the traditional small-scale community research of fieldwork anthropology – are not in themselves generalizing studies. But they can easily become so if carried out in some numbers, so that judgements of their typicality can justifiably be made. It is correct that one can generalize in the ways Giddens describes, and that often this is both appropriate and valuable. But it would be incorrect to assert that this is the only way to work, just as it is incorrect to conclude that one cannot generalize from a single case.

It depends upon the case one is speaking of, and how it is chosen. This applies to the natural sciences as well as to the study of human affairs. For example, Galileo's rejection of Aristotle's law of gravity was not based upon observations 'across a wide range', and the observations were not 'carried out in some numbers'.

The rejection consisted primarily of a conceptual experiment and later of a practical one. These experiments, with the benefit of hindsight, are self-evident. Nevertheless, Aristotle's view of gravity dominated scientific inquiry for nearly two thousand years before it was falsified. In his experimental thinking, Galileo reasoned as follows: if two objects with the same weight are released from the same height at the same time, they will hit the ground simultaneously, having fallen at the same speed.

If the two objects are then stuck together into one, this object will have double the weight and will according to the Aristotelian view therefore fall faster than the two individual objects. This cease operated in a counter-intuitive way for Galileo. The only way to avoid the contradiction was to eliminate weight as a determinant factor for acceleration in free fall. And that was what Galileo did. Historians of science continue to discuss whether Galileo actually conducted the famous experiment from the leaning tower of Pisa, or whether it is simply a myth. In any event, Galileo's experimentalism did not involve a large random sample of trials of objects falling from a wide range of randomly selected heights under varying wind conditions, and so on, as would be demanded by the thinking of the early Campbell and Giddens. Rather, it was a matter of a single experiment, that is, a case study, if any experiment was conducted at all.

Galileo's view continued to be subjected to doubt, however, and the Aristotelian view was not finally rejected until half a century later, with the invention of the air pump. The air pump made it possible to conduct the ultimate experiment, known by every pupil, whereby a coin or a piece of lead inside a vacuum tube falls with the same speed as a feather. After this experiment, Aristotle's view could be maintained no longer. What is especially worth noting in our discussion, however, is that the matter was settled by an individual case due to the clever choice of the extremes of metal and feather. One might call it a critical case: for if

Galileo's thesis held for these materials, it could be expected to be valid for all or a large range of materials.

Random and large samples were at no time part of the picture. Most creative scientists simply do not work this way with this type of problem. Carefully chosen experiments, cases and experience were also critical to the development of the physics of Newton, Einstein and Bohr, just as the case study occupied a central place in the works of Darwin, Marx and Freud. In social science, too, the strategic choice of case may greatly add to the generalizability of a case study.

In their classic study of the 'affluent worker', John Goldthorpe et al. (1968–9) deliberately looked for a case that was as favourable as possible to the thesis that the working class, having reached middle-class status, was dissolving into a society without class identity and related conflict. If the thesis could be proved false in the favourable case, then it would most likely be false for intermediate cases. Luton, a prosperous industrial centre with companies known for high wages and social stability – fertile ground for middleclass identity – was selected as a case, and through intensive fieldwork the researchers discovered that even here an autonomous workingclass culture prevailed, lending general credence to the thesis of the persistence of class identity. As suggested, discuss more systematically this type of strategic sampling. As regards the relationship between case studies, large samples and discoveries, W.I.B. Beveridge observed immediately prior to the breakthrough of the quantitative revolution in the social sciences: '[M]ore discoveries have arisen from intense observation than from statistics applied to large groups.'

This does not mean that the case study is always appropriate or relevant as a research method, or that large random samples are without value. The choice of method should clearly depend on the problem under study and its circumstances.

Finally, it should be that formal generalization, be it on the basis of large samples or single cases, is considerably overrated as the main source of scientific progress. Economist Mark Blaug (1980) – a self-declared adherent to the hypothetico-deductive model of science – has demonstrated that while economists typically pay lip service to the hypothetico-deductive model and to generalization, they rarely practise what they preach in actual research.

More generally, Thomas Kuhn has shown that the most important precondition for science is that researchers possess a wide range of practical skills for carrying out scientific work. Generalization is just one of these.

In Germanic languages, the term 'science' (*Wissenschaft*) means literally 'to gain knowledge'. And formal generalization is only one of many ways by which people gain and accumulate knowledge. That knowledge cannot be formally generalized does not mean that it cannot enter into the collective process of knowledge accumulation in a given field or in a society. A purely descriptive, phenomenological case study without any attempt to generalize can certainly be of value in this process and has often helped cut a path towards scientific innovation. This is not to criticize attempts at formal generalization, for such attempts are essential and effective means of scientific development. It is only to emphasize the limitations, which follows when formal generalization becomes the only legitimate method of scientific inquiry.

The balanced view of the role of the case study in attempting to generalize by testing hypotheses has been formulated by Eckstein: [C]omparative and case studies are alternative means to the end of testing theories, choices between which must be largely governed by arbitrary or practical, *rather than logical, considerations.* ... [I]t is impossible to take seriously the position that case study is suspect because problem-prone and comparative study deserving of benefit of doubt because problem-free. Eckstein here uses the term 'theory' in its 'hard' sense, that is, comprising explanation and prediction. This makes Eckstein's dismissal of the view that case studies cannot be used for testing theories or for generalization stronger than our own view, which is here restricted to the testing of 'theory' in the 'soft' sense, that is, testing propositions or hypotheses. Eckstein shows that if predictive theories existed in social science, then the case study could be used to test these theories just as well as other methods.

More recently, John Walton (1992: 129) has similarly observed that 'case studies are likely to produce the best theory'. Eckstein observes, however, the striking lack of genuine theories within his own field, political science, but apparently fails to see why this is so: Aiming at the disciplined application of theories to cases forces one to state theories more rigorously than might otherwise be done – provided that the application is truly 'disciplined,' i.e., designed to show that valid theory compels a particular case interpretation and rules out others.

As already stated, this, unfortunately, is rare (if it occurs at all) in political study. One reason is the lack of compelling theories. The case study is ideal for generalizing using the type of test that Karl Popper called 'falsification', which in social science forms part of critical reflexivity. Falsification is one of the most rigorous tests to which a scientific proposition can be subjected: if just one observation does not fit with the proposition, it is considered not valid generally and must therefore be either revised or rejected. Popper himself used the now famous example of 'All swans are white', and proposed that just one observation of a single black swan would falsify this proposition and in this way have general significance and stimulate further investigations and theory-building.

The case study is well suited for identifying 'black swans' because of its in-depth approach: what appears to be 'white' often turns out on closer examination to be 'black'. Finding black swans was an experience with which we became thoroughly familiar when we did our first in-depth case study, of urban politics and planning in the city of Aalborg, Denmark. For instance, at university we had been trained in the neoclassical model of 'economic man', competition and free markets. As we dug into what happened behind closed doors in Aalborg, we found that economic man does not live here.

The local business community were power-mongers who were busy negotiating illicit deals with politicians and administrators on how to block competition and the free market and create special privileges for themselves. The neoclassical model was effectively falsified by what we saw in Aalborg. Similarly, the model of representative democracy, which on the surface of things appears to apply, and by law is supposed to apply in Aalborg and Denmark, was strangely absent in the deep detail of the case.

Here we found a highly undemocratic, semi-institutionalized way of making decisions, where leaders of the business community and of the city government had formed a secret council, which in actual fact replaced the democratically elected city council as the place where important decisions on urban politics and planning were made.Colleagues in third-world nations, who appear to hold fewer illusions about markets and democracy than academics in the first world, get a good laugh when we tell our Aalborg stories. They see that, after all, we in the North are not so different; we are thirdworld in some ways too. We shall return to falsification in discussing the fourth misunderstanding of the case study. For the present, however, we can correct the second misunderstanding – that one cannot generalize on the basis of a single case and that the case study cannot contribute to scientific development – so that it now reads: One can often generalize on the basis of a single case, and the case study may be central to scientific development via generalization as supplement or alternative to other methods. But formal generalization is overvalued as a source of scientific development, whereas 'the force of example' is underestimated.

STRATEGIES FOR CASE SELECTION

The third misunderstanding about the case study is that the case method is claimed to be most useful for generating hypotheses in the first steps of a total research process, while hypothesistesting and theory-building is best carried out by other methods later in the process. This misunderstanding derives from the previous misunderstanding that one cannot generalize on the basis of individual cases.

And since this misunderstanding has been revised, we can now correct the third misunderstanding as follows: The case study is useful for both generating and testing of hypotheses but is not limited to these research activities alone. Eckstein – contravening the conventional wisdom in this area – goes so far as to argue that case studies are better for testing hypotheses than for producing them. Case studies, Eckstein asserts, 'are valuable at all stages of the theory-building process, but most valuable at that stage of theory-building where least value is generally attached to them: the stage at which candidate theories are tested'.

Testing of hypotheses relates directly to the question of 'generalizability', and this in turn relates to the question of case selection. Here generalizability of case studies can be increased by the strategic selection of cases. When the objective is to achieve the greatest possible amount of information on a given problem or phenomenon, a representative case or a random sample may not be the most appropriate strategy.

This is because the typical or average case is often not the richest in information. Atypical or extreme cases often reveal more information because they activate more actors and more basic mechanisms in the situation studied. In addition, from both an understanding-oriented and an action-oriented perspective, it is often more important to clarify the deeper causes behind a given problem and its consequences than to describe the symptoms of the problem and how frequently they occur. Random samples emphasizing representativeness will seldom be able to produce this kind of insight; it is more appropriate to select some few cases chosen for their validity. Table summarizes various forms of sampling.

The *extreme case* can be well suited for getting a point across in an especially dramatic way, which often occurs for well-known case studies such as Freud's 'Wolf-Man' and Foucault's 'Panopticon'. In contrast, a *critical case* can be defined as having strategic importance in relation to the general problem. For example, an occupational medicine clinic wanted to investigate whether people working with organic solvents suffered brain damage.

Instead of choosing a representative sample among all those enterprises in the clinic's area that used organic solvents, the clinic strategically located a single workplace where all safety regulations on cleanliness, air quality and the like had been fulfilled. This model enterprise became a critical case: if brain damage related to organic solvents could be found at this particular facility, then it was likely that the same problem would exist at other enterprises that were less careful with safety regulations for organic solvents. Via this type of strategic choice, one can save both time and money in researching a given problem.

Another example of critical case selection is the strategic selection of lead and feather for the test of whether different objects fall with equal velocity. The selection of materials provided the possibility to formulate a generalization characteristic of critical cases, a generalization of the sort, 'If it is valid for this case, it is valid for all (or many) cases'. In its negative form, the generalization would be, 'If it is not valid for this case, then it is not valid for any (or only few) cases'.

How does one identify critical cases? This question is more difficult to answer than the question of what constitutes a critical case. Locating a critical case requires experience, and no universal methodological principles exist by which one can with certainty identify a critical case. The only general advice that can be given is that when looking for critical cases, it is a good idea to look for either 'most likely' or 'least likely' cases, that is, cases that are likely to either clearly confirm or irrefutably falsify propositions and hypotheses.

Eventually we realised that this logic was flawed, because our research of local relations of power showed that one of the most influential 'faces of power' in Aalborg, the Chamber of Industry and Commerce, was substantially stronger than their equivalents elsewhere. This had not been clear at the outset because much less research existed on local power relations than research on local planning. Therefore, instead of a critical case, unwittingly we ended up with an extreme case in the sense that both rationality and power were unusually strong in Aalborg, and our case study became a study of what happens when strong rationality meets strong power in the arena of urban politics and planning.

But this selection of Aalborg as an extreme case happened to me, we did not deliberately choose it. It was a frustrating experience when it happened, especially during those several months from when we realised we did not have a critical case until it became clear that all was not lost because we had something else.

As a Type of selection purpose A. Random selection To avoid systematic biases in the sample.The sample's size is decisive for generalization. 1 Random sample To achieve a representative sample that allows for generalization for the entire population. 2 Stratified sample To generalize for specially selected sub-groups within the population. B. Information-oriented selection To maximize the utility of information from small samples and single cases.

Cases are selected on the basis of expectations about their information content:

- Extreme/deviant cases To obtain information on unusual cases, which can be especially problematic or especially good in a more closely defined sense.
- Maximum variation cases To obtain information about the significance of various circumstances for case process and outcome, e.g. three to four cases that are very different on one dimension: size, form of organization, location, budget, etc.
- Critical cases To achieve information that permits logical deductions of the type, 'if this is (not) valid for this case, then it applies to all (no) cases'.
- Paradigmatic cases To develop a metaphor or establish a school for the domain that the case concerns. case researcher charting new terrain one must be prepared for such incidents, we believe. A model example of a 'least likely' case is Robert Michels's (1962) classical study of oligarchy in organizations. By choosing a horizontally structured grass-roots organization with strong democratic

ideals – that is, a type of organization with an especially low probability of being oligarchical – Michels could test the universality of the oligarchy thesis, that is, 'If this organization is oligarchic, so are most others'. A corresponding model example of a 'most likely' case is W.F. Whyte's (1943) study of a Boston slum neighbourhood, which according to existing theory should have exhibited social disorganization, but in fact showed quite the opposite.

Cases of the 'most likely' type are especially well suited to falsification of propositions, while 'least likely' cases are most appropriate to tests of verification. It should be remarked that a most likely case for one proposition is the least likely for its negation.

For example, Whyte's slum neighbourhood could be seen as a least likely case for a hypothesis concerning the universality of social organization. Hence, the identification of a case as most or least likely is linked to the design of the study, as well as to the specific properties of the actual case. A final strategy for the selection of cases is choice of the *paradigmatic case.*

Thomas Kuhn has shown that the basic skills, or background practices, of natural scientists are organized in terms of 'exemplars', the role of which can be studied by historians of science. Similarly, scholars like Clifford Geertz and Michel Foucault have often organized their research around specific cultural paradigms: a paradigm for Geertz lay for instance in the 'deep play' of the Balinese cockfight, while for Foucault, European prisons and the 'Panopticon' are examples. Both instances are examples of paradigmatic cases, that is, cases that highlight more general characteristics of the societies in question.

Kuhn has shown that scientific paradigms cannot be expressed as rules or theories. There exists no predictive theory for how predictive theory comes about. A scientific activity is acknowledged or rejected as good science by how close it is to one or more exemplars, that is, practical prototypes of good scientific work. A paradigmatic case of how scientists do science is precisely such a prototype. It operates as a reference point and may function as a focus for the founding of schools of thought. As with the critical case, we may ask, 'How does one identify a paradigmatic case?'

How does one determine whether a given case has metaphorical and prototypical value? These questions are even more difficult to answer than for the critical case, precisely because the paradigmatic case transcends any sort of rule-based criteria. No standard exists for the paradigmatic case because it sets the standard. Hubert and Stuart Dreyfus see paradigmatic cases and case studies as central to human learning. In an interview with Hubert Dreyfus (author's files), we, therefore asked what constitutes a paradigmatic case and how it can be identified. Dreyfus replied: Heidegger says, you recognize a paradigm case because it shines, but I'm afraid that is not much help. You just have to be intuitive. We all can tell what is a better or worse case – of a Cézanne painting, for instance.

But we can't think there could be any rules for deciding what makes Cézannne a paradigmatic modern painter. … [I]t is a big problem in a democratic society where people are supposed to justify what their intuitions are. In fact, nobody really can justify what their intuition is. So you have to make up reasons, but it won't be the real reasons. One may agree with Dreyfus that intuition is central to identifying paradigmatic cases, but one may disagree that it is a problem to have to justify one's intuitions. Ethnomethodological studies of scientific practice have demonstrated that all variety of such practice relies on takenfor- granted procedures that feel largely intuitive.

However, those intuitive decisions are accountable, in the sense of being sensible to other practitioners or often explicable if not immediately sensible. That would frequently seem to be the case with the selection of paradigmatic cases. We may select such cases on the basis of takenfor- granted, intuitive procedures but are often called upon to account for that selection. That account must be sensible to other members of the scholarly communities of which we are part. This may even be argued to be a general characteristic of scholarship, scientific or otherwise, and not unique to the selection of paradigmatic social scientific case studies.

For instance, it is usually insufficient to justify an application for research funds by stating that one's intuition says that a particular research should be carried out. A research council ideally operates as society's test of whether the researcher can account, in collectively acceptable ways, for his or her intuitive choice, even though intuition may be the real, or most important, reason why the researcher wants to execute the project. It is not possible consistently, or even frequently, to determine in advance whether or not a given case – Geertz's cockfights in Bali, for instance – is paradigmatic. Besides the strategic choice of case, the execution of the case study will certainly play a role, as will the reactions to the study by the research community, the group studied and, possibly, a broader public. The value of the case study will depend on the validity claims that researchers can place on their study, and the status these claims obtain in dialogue with other validity claims in the discourse to which the study is a contribution.

Like other good craftsmen, all that researchers can do is use their experience and intuition to assess whether they believe a given case is interesting in a paradigmatic context, and whether they can provide collectively acceptable reasons for the choice of case. Finally, concerning considerations of strategy in the choice of cases, it should be that the various strategies of selection are not necessarily mutually exclusive. For example, a case can be simultaneously extreme, critical and paradigmatic. The interpretation of such a case can provide a unique wealth of information, because one obtains various perspectives and ceases on the case according to whether it is viewed and interpreted as one or another type of case.

DO CASE STUDIES CONTAIN A SUBJECTIVE BIAS?

The fourth of the five misunderstandings about case-study

research is that the method maintains a bias towards verification, understood as a tendency to confirm the researcher's preconceived notions, so that the study therefore becomes of doubtful scientific value. Diamond (1996: 6), for example, holds this view.

He observes that the case study suffers from what he calls a 'crippling drawback', because it does not apply 'scientific methods', by which Diamond understands methods useful for 'curbing one's tendencies to stamp one's pre-existing interpretations on data as they accumulate'. Francis Bacon (1853: xlvi) saw this bias towards verification not simply as a phenomenon related to the case study in particular, but as a fundamental human characteristic. Bacon expressed it like this: The human understanding from its peculiar nature, easily supposes a greater degree of order and equality in things than it really finds. When any proposition has been laid down, the human understanding forces everything else to add fresh support and confirmation.

It is the peculiar and perpetual error of the human understanding to be more moved and excited by affirmatives than negatives. Bacon certainly touches upon a fundamental problem here, a problem that all researchers must deal with in some way. Charles Darwin (1958: 123), in his autobiography, describes the method he developed in order to avoid the bias towards verification: we had ... during many years followed a golden rule, namely, that whenever a published fact, a new observation or thought came across me, which was opposed to our general results, to make a memorandum of it without fail and at once; for we had found by experience that such facts and thoughts were far more apt to escape from the memory than favourable ones.

Owing to this habit, very few objections were raised against our views, which we had not at least noticed and attempted to answer. The bias towards verification is general, but the alleged deficiency of the case study and other qualitative methods is that they ostensibly allow more room for the researcher's subjective and arbitrary judgement than other methods: they are often seen as less rigorous than are quantitative, hypothetico-deductive methods.

Even if such criticism is useful, because it sensitizes us to an important issue, experienced case researchers cannot help but see the critique as demonstrating a lack of knowledge of what is involved in casestudy research. Donald Campbell and others have shown that the critique is fallacious, because the case study has its own rigour, different to be sure, but no less strict than the rigour of quantitative methods. The advantage of the case study is that it can 'close in' on real-life situations and test views directly in relation to phenomena as they unfold in practice.

Campbell, Ragin, Geertz, Wieviorka, Flyvbjerg and others, researchers who have conducted intensive, in-depth case studies typically report that their preconceived views, assumptions, concepts and hypotheses were wrong and that the case material has compelled them to revise their hypotheses on essential points.

The case study forces upon the researcher the type of falsifications. Ragin (1992: 225) calls this a 'special feature of small-*N* research', and goes on to explain that criticizing single-case studies for being inferior to multiple-case studies is misguided, since even single-case studies 'are multiple in most research efforts because ideas and evidence may be linked in many different ways'. Geertz (1995: 119) says about the fieldwork involved in most in-depth case studies that 'The Field' itself is a 'powerful disciplinary force: assertive, demanding, even coercive'. Like any such force, it can be underestimated, but it cannot be evaded. 'It is too insistent for that', says Geertz.

That he is speaking of a general phenomenon can be seen by simply examining case studies, as Eckstein (1975), Campbell (1975) and Wieviorka (1992) have done. In a case study done by an alert social scientist who has thorough local acquaintance, the theory he uses to explain the focal difference also generates prediction or expectations on dozens of other aspects of the culture, and he does not retain the theory unless most of these are also confirmed. ... Experiences of social scientists confirm this.

Even in a single qualitative case study, the conscientious social scientist often finds no explanation that seems satisfactory. Such an outcome would be impossible if the caricature of the single case study ... were correct – there would instead be a surfeit of subjectively compelling explanations. It is falsification and not verification that characterizes the case study. Moreover, the question of subjectivism and bias towards verification applies to all methods, not just to the case study and other qualitative methods. For example, the element of arbitrary subjectivism will be significant in the choice of categories and variables for a quantitative or structural investigation, such as a structured questionnaire to be used across a large sample of cases.

And the probability is high that:

- This subjectivism survives without being thoroughly corrected during the study and
- That it may affect the results, quite simply because the quantitative/structural researcher does not get as close to those under study as does the case-study researcher and therefore is less likely to be corrected by the study objects 'talking back'.

Ragin: this feature explains why small-*N* qualitative research is most often at the forefront of theoretical development. When *N*'s are large, there are few opportunities for revising a casing [that is, the delimitation of a case]. At the start of the analysis, cases are decomposed into variables, and almost the entire dialogue of ideas and evidence occurs through variables. One implication of this discussion is that to the extent that large-*N* research can be sensitized to the diversity and potential heterogeneity of the cases included in an analysis, large-*N* research may play a more important part in the advancement of social science theory.

Here, too, this difference between large samples and single cases can be understood in terms of the phenomenology for human learning. If one thus assumes that the goal of the researcher's work is to understand and learn about the phenomena being studied, then research is simply a form of learning. If one assumes that research, like other learning processes, can be described by the phenomenology for human learning, it then becomes clear that the most advanced form of understanding is achieved when researchers place themselves within the context being studied.

Only in this way can researchers understand the viewpoints and the behaviour that characterizes social actors. Relevant to this point, Giddens states that valid descriptions of social activities presume that researchers possess those skills necessary to participate in the activities described: 'We have accepted that it is right to say that the condition of generating descriptions of social activity is being able in principle to participate in it.

It involves "mutual knowledge", shared by observer and participants whose action constitutes and reconstitutes the social world'. From this point of view, the proximity to reality that the case study entails, and the learning process that it generates for the researcher, will often constitute a prerequisite for advanced understanding.

In this context, one begins to understand Beveridge's cease that there are more discoveries stemming from the type of intense observation made possible by the case study than from statistics applied to large groups. With the point of departure in the learning process, we understand why the researcher who conducts a case study often ends up by casting off preconceived notions and theories. Such activity is quite simply a central element in learning and in the achievement of new insight.

More simple forms of understanding must yield to more complex ones as one moves from beginner to expert. On this basis, the fourth misunderstanding – that the case study supposedly contains a bias towards verification, understood as a tendency to confirm the researcher's preconceived ideas – is revised as follows: The case study contains no greater bias towards verification of the researcher's preconceived notions than other methods of inquiry.

On the contrary, experience indicates that the case study contains a greater bias towards falsification of preconceived notions than towards verification.

IRREDUCIBLE QUALITY OF GOOD CASE NARRATIVES

Case studies often contain a substantial element of narrative. Good narratives typically approach the complexities and contradictions of real life. Such narratives may be difficult or impossible to summarize into neat scientific formulae, general propositions, and theories.

This tends to be seen by critics of the case study as a drawback. To the case-study researcher, however, a particularly 'thick' and hard-to-summarize narrative is not a problem. Rather, it is often a sign that the study has uncovered a particularly rich problematic. The question, therefore, is whether the summarizing and generalization, which the critics see as an ideal, is always desirable. Nietzsche is clear in his answer to this question. 'He says about doing science, 'one should not wish to divest existence of its *rich ambiguity*' (emphasis in original). In doing the Aalborg study, we tried to capture the rich ambiguity of politics and planning in a modern democracy.

We did this by focusing in depth on the particular events that made up the case and on the minutiae that made up the events. Working with minutiae is time-consuming, and we must concede that during the several years when we was toiling in the archives, doing interviews, making observations, talking with our informants, writing, and getting feedback, a nagging question kept resurfacing in our mind. This is a question bound to haunt many carrying out indepth, dense case studies: 'Who will want to learn about a case like this, and in this kind of *detail*?'

We wanted the Aalborg case study to be particularly dense because we wished to test the thesis that the most interesting phenomena in politics and planning, and those of most general import, would be found in the most minute and most concrete of details. Or to put the matter differently, we wanted to see whether the dualisms general–specific and abstract–concrete would metamorphose and vanish if we went into sufficiently deep detail. Richard Rorty has perceptively observed that the way to re-enchant the world is to stick to the concrete. Nietzsche similarly advocates a focus on 'little things'. Both Rorty and Nietzsche seem right to me. We saw the Aalborg case as being made up of the type of concrete, little things they talk about. Indeed, we saw the case itself as such a thing, what Nietzsche calls a discreet and apparently insignificant truth, which, when closely examined, would reveal itself to be pregnant with paradigms, metaphors and general significance. That was our thesis, but theses can be wrong and case studies may fail. We was genuinely relieved when, eventually, the strategy of focusing on minutiae proved to be worth the effort. Lisa Peattie explicitly warns against summarizing dense case studies: 'It is simply that the very value of the case study, the contextual and interpenetrating nature of forces, is lost when one tries to sum up in large and mutually exclusive concepts.'

The dense case study is more useful for the practitioner and more interesting for social theory than either factual 'findings' or the highlevel generalizations of theory. The opposite of summing up and 'closing' a case study is to keep it open. Here We have found the following two strategies to work particularly well in ensuring such openness. First, when writing up a case study, we demur from the role of omniscient narrator and summarizer. Instead, we tell the story in its diversity, allowing the story to unfold from the many-sided, complex and sometimes conflicting stories that the actors in the case have told me.

Second, we avoid linking the case with the theories of any one academic specialization. Instead we relate the case to broader philosophical positions that cut across specializations. In this way we try to leave scope for readers of different backgrounds to make different interpretations and draw diverse ceases regarding the question of what the case is a case of. The goal is not to make the case study be all things to all people.

The goal is to allow the study to be different things to different people. We try to achieve this by describing the case with so many facets – like life itself – that different readers may be attracted, or repelled, by different things in the case.

Readers are not pointed down any one theoretical path or given the impression that truth might lie at the end of such a path.

Readers will have to discover their own path and truth inside the case. Thus, in addition to the interpretations of case actors and case narrators, readers are invited to decide the meaning of the case and to interrogate actors' and narrators' interpretations in order to answer that categorical question of any case study:'What is this case a case of ?' Case stories written like this can neither be briefly recounted nor summarized in a few main results.

The case story is itself the result. It is a 'virtual reality', so to speak. For the reader willing to enter this reality and explore it inside and out, the payback is meant to be a sensitivity to the issues at hand that cannot be obtained from theory. Students can safely be let loose in this kind of reality, which provides a useful training ground with insights into real-life practices that academic teaching often does not provide. If we return briefly to the phenomenology for human learning, we may understand why summarizing case studies is not always useful and may sometimes be counterproductive. Knowledge at the beginner's level consists precisely in the reduced formulas that characterize theories, while true expertise is based on intimate experience with thousands of individual cases and on the ability to discriminate between situations, with all their nuances of difference, without distilling them into formulas or standard cases.

The problem is analogous to the inability of heuristic, computer-based expert systems to approach the level of virtuoso human experts, even when the systems are compared with the experts who have conceived the rules upon which these systems operate.

This is because the experts do not use rules but operate on the basis of detailed case experience. This is *real* expertise. The rules for expert systems are formulated only because the systems require it; rules are characteristic of expert *systems,* but not of real human *experts*. In the same way, one might say that the rule formulation that takes place when researchers summarize their work into theories is characteristic of the culture of research, of researchers, and of theoretical activity, but such rules are not necessarily part of the studied reality constituted by Bourdieu's 'virtuoso social actors'. Something essential may be lost by this summarizing – namely the possibility to understand virtuoso social acting, which, as Bourdieu has shown, cannot be distilled into theoretical formulas – and it is precisely their fear of losing this 'something', that makes case researchers cautious about summarizing their studies. Case researchers thus tend to be sceptical about erasing phenomenological detail in favour of conceptual closure. Ludwig Wittgenstein shared this scepticism.

Gasking and Jackson, Wittgenstein used the following metaphor when he described his use of the case-study approach in philosophy: In teaching you philosophy I'm like a guide showing you how to find your way round London. We have to take you through the city from north to south, from east to west, from Euston to the Embankment and from Piccadilly to the Marble Arch.

After We have taken you many journeys through the city, in all sorts of directions, we shall have passed through any given street a number of times – each time traversing the street as part of a different journey.

At the end of this you will know London; you will be able to find your way about like a born Londoner.Of course, a good guide will take you through the more important streets more often than he takes you down side streets; a bad guide will do the opposite.

In philosophy I'm a rather bad guide. This approach implies exploring phenomena first-hand instead of reading maps of them. Actual practices are studied before their rules, and one is not satisfied by learning only about those parts of practices that are open to public scrutiny; what Erving Goffman (1963) calls the 'backstage' of social phenomena must be investigated, too, like the side streets that Wittgenstein talks about. With respect to intervention in social and political affairs, Abbott has rightly observed that a social science expressed in terms of typical case narratives would provide 'far better access for policy intervention than the present social science of variables'. MacIntyre similarly says, 'I can only answer the question "If we can answer the prior question "Of what story or stories do we find myself a part?"' Several observers have noted that narrative is an ancient method and perhaps our most fundamental form for making sense of experience It must again be emphasized that, despite the difficulty or undesirability of summarizing case studies, the case-study method in general can certainly contribute to the cumulative development of knowledge; for example, in using the principles to test propositions under the second and third misunderstandings. Today, when students and colleagues present me with the conventional wisdom about case-study research – for instance, that one cannot generalize on the basis of a single case or that case studies are arbitrary and subjective.

By and large, the conventional wisdom is wrong or misleading. For the reasons, the case study is a necessary and sufficient method for certain important research tasks in the social sciences, and it is a method that holds up well when compared to other methods in the gamut of social science research methodology. Let me reiterate, however, that this cease, and the revision of the five misunderstandings should not be interpreted as a rejection of research that focuses on large random samples or entire populations; for example, questionnaire surveys with related quantitative analysis.

Index